05113901

301.431 STI
STICKLAND
74/1165

KT-583-269

B.C.H.E. – LIBRARY

00106142

THE VOICES
OF CHILDREN

THE VOICES
OF CHILDREN

1700 — 1914

———

Compiled by
IRINA STICKLAND

OXFORD · BASIL BLACKWELL

© 1973 Basil Blackwell

All Rights Reserved. No part of this publication may
be reproduced, stored in a retrieval system, or transmitted, in any form or by any means, electronic,
mechanical, photocopying, recording or otherwise,
without the prior permission of Basil Blackwell &
Mott Limited.

ISBN 0 631 11780 6

TO MY CHILDREN

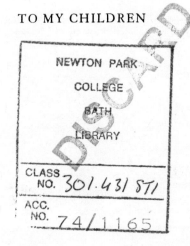

NEWTON PARK
COLLEGE
BATH
LIBRARY

CLASS
NO. 301.431 STI

ACC.
NO. 74/1165

DISCARD

Printed in Great Britain by
Western Printing Services Ltd, Bristol

CONTENTS

LIST OF PLATES

(Between pp. 116 and 117)

1. The Robinson Family: 'Tommy' and his Siblings.
   Portrait at Newby Hall, by Phillippe Mercier, of 'The Children of the 1st Lord Grantham', by permission of Major Edward Compton.

2. (a) Nanny's Picture.
   Newby Hall Papers, Leeds City Archives.
   (b) A Midwife.
   The Oxford Sausage, 1815, Longman, Hurst, Rees, Orme & Brown.

3. Street Sellers: 'Fine Thread Laces'.
   Cryes of the City of London. Printed and sold by P. Tempest over-against Somerset House in the Strand.

4. The Departure.
   Poems of Goldsmith and Parnell, 1804, W. Bulmer & Co. (by Bewick).

5. Rule Brittania.
   Jonas Hanway: *An Account of the Marine Society*, 1759.

6. Reading Aloud.
   Mrs. Radcliffe: *The Mysteries of Udolpho*, 1823.

7. Straw Hat Maker.
   The Book of English Trades, J. G. & F. Rivington (S.P.C.K.), 1835.

8. Cast Out.
   T. P. Prest: *Ela the Outcast: or the Gipsy of Rosemary Dell*, 1838, E. Lloyd.

9. Brick Makers.
   The Boy's Book of Trades, N.D., George Routledge & Sons.

10. Street Acrobats.
    Gavarni in London, 1849, David Bogue.

PREFACE

This book consists of extracts from various sources including unpublished letters and diaries. The extracts are arranged chronologically.

A brief background of life in the eighteenth and early nineteenth centuries has been given from contemporary sources. The differentiation between the child's world and that of the adults was relatively uncommon during this period, particularly among the poor.

There was no sharp line of demarcation between the first decade of the eighteenth century and the last of the seventeenth. Certain attitudes were about to disappear. Queen Anne was the last monarch to 'touch for the Evill'. But Comenius' *Orbis Sensualium Pictus* (an innovation in 1659) retained its influence for many subsequent decades.

It has not been possible to deal equally with all classes of society. The majority of poor children left no personal records for at least half of the period under consideration. The Newby Hall papers show that the lives of rich children changed remarkably little. The greatest change occurred in the lives of poor children. Child labour was no new phenomenon in 1700, when children were employed in agriculture and the domestic industries. Arthur Young saw them working in copper works in 1767. Later there was a period of economic distress during the Napoleonic wars. Simultaneously there was an increase in the population and a growth of industrialization. These factors, plus the exhortations of a dynamic evangelist, combined to extend child labour on a massive scale. Medical men (including Shaftesbury) perceived both its immediate and its long-term disadvantages. Finally, the emergence of a new industrialized society necessitated a literate labour force. This made it essential to educate children, and for their parents to work for their support.

The changing comments in successive decades show the impress of the main events which affected the lives of children and young people. The agricultural revolution, the industrial revolution, and finally the growth of education were the most directly influential.

ACKNOWLEDGEMENTS

Primarily the author's thanks are due to Professor Asa Briggs for his invaluable inspiration, encouragement, and advice.

The author also thanks Dr. B. S. Page, Mr. D. Cox, and Mr. D. I. Masson of the Brotherton Library, University of Leeds; Mr. F. Beckwith and Mrs. M. J. Pearce of the Leeds Library; and Mr. J. Mitchell, Curator of the City Museum, Leeds.

In particular the author is grateful to Mr. J. M. Collinson, Leeds City Archivist, for his indispensable assistance.

The author is also indebted to all those who have contributed unpublished manuscripts; and especially to Major Edward Compton for permission to use the Newby Hall papers.

The following have very kindly given permission for copyright material to appear in the book:

Jonathan Cape, extracts from *Kilvert's Diary;* Cassell and Company Ltd, an extract from *The Early Years of Alec Waugh;* Rupert Crew, extracts from *The Glass of Fashion* by Cecil Beaton; Granada Publishing Ltd, extracts from *The Rainbow Comes and Goes* by Lady Diana Cooper; Mrs S. C. Harris, extracts from *The Journal of J. G. Stedman;* Alfred Knopf Inc., The Oxford University Press, extracts from *The History of the Foundling Hospital* by R. H. Nicholls and F. Wray; and *The Diary of a Country Parson* by James Woodforde.

Thanks are also due to the Leverhulme Trust for their generous award in respect of the research for the book.

CHAPTER I
1700–1729

1. INTRODUCTION

In his *Journey through England* John Macky describes early eighteenth-century England with enthusiasm. He begins, 'We have often admired ... why *Englishmen* should be so fond of seeing other countries ... How often have we reflected ... that a Nation, which has made the greatest Figure in Europe during our Time, should be so little known in the World!' Apart from a few adverse comments Macky and Defoe present a largely favourable view of the English countryside. Macky writes: 'Twittenham, a Village remarkable for abundance of curious Seats.' Also, 'Gardens ... delightful, pleasant and Stately, adorned with exquisite Water works, as 1. Neptune with his Sea-Nymphs, 2. a Pond where Sea-Horses continually Rowl ..., a Cascade ... and several Statues of Gladiators.' These, and many other marvels besides, were to be found at Chatsworth.

Epsom was 'a Village ... deliciously situated ... between the finest Downs in the World on one side ... and certain clay hills on the other side, which are variously chequered with woods ..., the intoxicating Yew, the florid White-Beam ... and the correcting Birch are not wanting ... numberless Copses ... agreeably diversify all this Country. Nor that for the most part, they are amorously clasp'd in the twining Embraces of Ivy and Honey Suckles. The Downs are said to be finer than Persian Carpets, and perfumed with Thyme and Juniper. There are well-wooded Parks stocked with Deer.'

Many country markets and fairs provided agreeable diversions. 'You would think yourself in some enchanted Camp, to see Peasants ride to every House with the choicest Fruits, Herbs, Roots, and Flowers ... thus to see the fresh and artless Damsels of the Plain, either accompany'd by their amorous Swains or aged Parents, striking their bargain with the nice Court and City Ladies who, like Queens in a Tragedy, display all their Finery on Benches before their doors ...'

Watering-places were particularly delightful. '. . . at Bath . . . Every Thing looks gay and serene ... It's plentiful and cheap ...

there is a little Theatre ... and a fine Ball Room and pleasant Gardens.'

We are given very little information about other cities than London. Macky notes that 'Bristol is a large, opulent and fine City ... here is nothing but Hurry, Carts or Sledges driving along with Merchandize, and People running about with Cloudy Looks and busy Faces.' 'The Town of Birmingham ... so famous for all manner of Iorn-Work, and its incredible Number of People maintained by those Iorn- and Bath-Metal Works, and the great Perfection they have brought 'em to; furnishing all Europe with their Toys, as Sword-Hilts, Buckles, and innumerable other Works,' Defoe describes Coventry as 'a large and populous City, and drives a very great Trade; the Manufacture of the Tanneries is their chief Employ, and next to that, weaving of Ribbons. The Buildings are very old, and in some Places much decay'd. The Timber-built Houses project forwards, till in the narrow Streets they are ready to touch one another at the Top; a Method of Building formerly much practised in London.'

Defoe writes, on London, that it is 'a Prodigy of Buildings that nothing in the World does, or ever did, surpass it, except old Rome in Trajan's Time ... London, as to its Figure must be own'd to be very irregular, as it is stretched out in Buildings, just at the Pleasures of every Undertaker of Buildings and as the Convenience of the People directs, whether for Trade, or otherwise. This has given it a very confused Face, and made it uncompact and unequal.'

In the words of the *Spectator*, 'The Cries of London may be divided into the Vocal and Instrumental. As for the latter, they are at present under a very great disorder. A Freeman of London has the Privilege of disturbing a whole Street for an Hour together, with the Twanking of a brass Kettle or a Frying Pan. The Watchman's Thump at Midnight startles us in our Beds ... Milk is generally sold in a Note above Elah, and in sounds so exceedingly shrill that it often sets our Teeth on edge; the Chimney-Sweeper is confined to no certain Pitch, he sometimes utters himself in the deepest Base, and sometimes in the sharpest Treble, ... The same Observation might be made on the Retailers of Small-coal, not to mention broken Glass or Brick-dust ...'

De Mandeville describes the bustle. 'There are, I believe, few People in London of those that are at any time forc'd to go afoot, but what could do with the Streets of it much cleaner than they generally are . . . For if we mind the Materials of all Sorts that must supply such an infinite number of Trades and Handicrafts, as are always going forward, the vast Quantity of Victuals, Drink and Fewel that are daily consum'd in it, the Waste and Superfluities that must be produced from them, the multitudes of Horses and other Cattle that are always daubing the Streets, the Carts, Coaches, and more heavy Carriages that are perpetually wearing and breaking the Pavement . . ., and above all the numberless Swarms of People that are continually harrassing and trampling through every part of them . . .'

Londoners frequented many different places of recreation. Eventually Vauxhall became the most celebrated one. It was visited by all but the poorest classes. There were many taverns, with or without gardens. There were equestrian displays, fireworks, evening concerts, and masquerades to attend.

By the early eighteenth century the gardens at Vauxhall were called 'a kind of Mahometan Paradise'. A mid-century account includes the following superlatives: 'Fox-hall is laid out in so grand a taste that they are frequented in the summer months by most of the nobility and gentry . . . and are often honoured with some of the royal family, who are here entertained with the sweet song of nightingales, in concert with the best band of music in England. Here are fine pavilions, shady groves, and most delightful walks, illuminated by 1,000 lamps, so disposed that they all take fire together . . .' The company wore bright, decorative clothes, and varied in mood from sober satisfaction to gaiety and enthusiasm.

News sheets published in the early eighteenth century included *The Post Man*, *The Flying Post*, *The Post Boy*, etc. Often a whole page was given up to miscellaneous notices. Missing people were described, such as 'A Melancholy Person in a sad-coloured stuff Gown . . .' Announcements of missing animals were more common. 'A young Sutty dun gray-hound dog', for instance, and 'Lost, a small green Parrot with a white Bill flew away last Sunday'. Plenty of remedies for ailments were offered, such as 'Pepticon', and 'Anti-Hectic Lozenges'. 'A Physician with 20 Years Practice announces that he can cure (with God's Blessing) Melancholy and Hypochondriacal Distempers, which variously affect the Mind, with strange Fears and dismal Apprehension, great Oppressions and Sinkings of the Spirits . . .'

Also common nuisances: 'Whereas many People in and about the

Cities of London and Westminster are troubled with that stinking Vermin call'd Bugs: This is to give Notice that the Author of this Advertisement will undertake *Perfectly to Destroy them* in any House ...' 'Evans Hummums in Brouton Street, where Persons of both Sexes may be privately Sweated, Bathed and Cupt' might have been useful to such householders prior to disinfection.

Many articles were offered for sale. The items included 'a small part of the Right Usquebagh, 12/0 per gallon', and 'The Royal Lutestring Company will expose to sale by inch of Candle ... a parcel of English Allamodes ...' In 1702, Mrs. *Frances Purcel*, widow of Mr. *Henry Purcel*, wishes to dispose of some music. 'Also for sale, a good walnut-tree Harpsichord.'

The patriotic enthusiasm of early eighteenth-century writers continued to echo the elated passages in the music of the late Mr. Henry Purcel. But the solemn reverberations of his funeral music for Queen Mary II (in 1694) might well have served as an obsequy for the passing century. In 1700, a bereaved mother, Princess Anne (soon to be Queen) mourned the untimely end of the only one of her children to survive infancy. Eventually this sad occasion brought the Stuart dynasty to a close. Lady Gardiner writes: '... I am glad I am not the messenger of that dismal nues of the Death of the Duck of Gloster, who is sadly lamented; tis belived by all that he overheated his blod, in dancing on his birthday, which nevar was kept with so great Joy as now; & I am told there never was so great a body of the Clargy as that day with him, & that hee took great notis of them & of all as came to him, & behaved himselfe as a man, to the admiration of all; so tis now said hee filld the subjects' harts with A high expectation of their futur Comforts in him. So tis lookt upon as A great punishment to have him taken from us. The Jacobits confes hee is a bitter loss to us, but sayes it is a Just Judgment on us. The Princess's affliction is very great ...'

'They say the Duck is to be buryed privatly so is brought to St. Jamsis, wher the princess is come to. Tis believed the King will have him strictly morned for, and in long morning, which time will show.'

2. NEWSSHEETS

The following extracts are taken from a large quantity of early-eighteenth-century newssheets. References to children are scant, and become negligible in later numbers. The first extract is characteristic of the tone of the *Post Angel* for 1701.

Superstition is decried, but both natural and supernatural (or in-credible) events are presented with equal impartiality. No doubt the 'cabbin boy' mentioned in the account of the shipwreck had cause to remember the first month of the new century.

(a) SHIPWRECK

Lemington. Jan. 25, 1701. One Richard Hutton, Master of the Michael of *London*, bound for *Lisbon*, sailes out of the *Downs*, the 4th instant, and on the 6th ditto about two in the morning, in a violent storm, struck upon the *Caskets*, and staved to pieces imme-diately. The *master* and six men were drowned, and nine saved; They did not save any Bread or other Provisions, but lived Fourteen days upon the Ships Dog, which they did eat raw, and on Limpots and weeds that grew on the Rocks; About the Eighteenth or Nine-teenth one Taskard's Son, dream'd he was taking up several men about the *Caskets*, and told it to his Father, who took no notice of it; but on the 20th instant set sail in his Bark, and when he came in view of the *Caskets*, the boy said there was men on them; his Father contradicted him, but the Boy insisting on it, the old Man, took his glass and lookt on the Rocks, and espied one, waving his Cap; upon which he steered with the Rock and came to an anchor on the Leeward on't, it being a great Sea. He took 'em all into his Little Boat, and carried them on board, and the 21st ditto brought them safe to Hampton. *Stephen Hutchins*, second Mate, hartened them all the time, viz., Thomas Meade, chief Mate, Stephen Hutchins, second Mate, John More, John Baldock, John Boulter, Ambrose Rawlinson, Nath. Freeman, and Isaac Leader, Cabbin Boy.

THE POST ANGEL, Jan 25, 1701

(b) GOD'S DISPLEASURE

Sir, The Gentlewoman told me, that in going to correct her Child, her Child struck at her again; which a CAT perceiving, flew at the Child, and was with great difficulty pull'd off. —Sir, This being a Remarkable Instance of God's Displeasure against Dis-obedient Children.

THE POST ANGEL, October 1701, p. 203

(c)

Sir, One HUET a Poor Woman had Children every Year; . . .
Soon after she was deliver'd [again], one of the Neighbours (a
Rich Woman) takes the Child in her Arms, and looking upon it
cries, *Ay! Here's a Mouth, but where's the Meat to feed it?* Not long
after, this Rich Woman was herself deliver'd of *a Child which had
no Mouth*, which brought to her Mind what she had said concerning the *Poor Woman's Child* and was accounted a *just Judgment
of God* upon her.

THE POST ANGEL, 1701, p. 215

(d) DEFECTS OF NATURE

Mr *Charles Leane*, at the *Woolpack* in *Cannon-street*, hath Nine
Children, whereof Four were born both Deaf and Dumb. One is a
Son, of about 16 Years of Age, who writes an excellent Hand;
his Father is a Wool-Merchant, and this young Man knows the
Goodness of each several sort of Wool, and its Price: And so can
his Sister also; She Writes, Dresses, and Dances very well; and is
a very pretty and accomplished Gentlewoman.

THE POST ANGEL, 1701, p. 412

(e)

The Relation is this—On *Thursday Nov.* 20 there was seen in *the
Royal Exchange*, a seeming Country-Wench. Under her Arm she
held a Hand-Basket, in which appear'd two Turkeys Heads and
Necks. Her Strange Deportment was not a little taken notice of, but
more particularly by two young Men; her unusual Gesture raised
at once in them Thoughts of making their Advantage on that
Innocent Simplicity which is not uncommon in Country Strangers,
. . . and the Hopes of deceiving her of her two Turkeys; with this
Design, they chuse to walk and stand by her, by which, She chose
the Opportunity to ask them, in her artificial Country Dialect;
what fine Place that was? And the like impertinent Queries. At last
one of them proffer'd to shew her what was chiefly rare in it, upon
the Condition of the other's Promise to guard her Basket, and secure
her Turkeys. She accepted to go with him in the Interim, the other
making the best use of this Opportunity to drop the Wench, and
hurry'd to the afore-designed place, designing to sup there with some

others of their Acquaintance. But upon ripping open the Basket, they found the Event as Surprizing, as the Prize before was satisfying; when to their no small Wonder, they found only a lovely Male-Child, and two Necks of Turkey fasten'd at each Corner. This put them into an unaccountable Consternation; upon so sudden a palling of their Hopes of so delicious a Supper. In fine, they gave Security for the Child, and both of 'em joined in its Maintenance; it being now at Nurse, and is, in Appearance, likely to do well.

The Observator. What more Bastards still? In my last I had one sent in a Band-box, and here's one in a Hand-basket, and perhaps next (pretty Innocence) we hear of, may be handed about in an Oister-Barrel.

THE POST ANGEL, Dec., 1701, p. 422

3. FORCIBLY TAKEN AWAY

The abduction of heiresses was not uncommon, and usually excited a great deal of interest. The ceremony of marriage could be performed in a notoriously easy manner at this time. Justice Powel says in the summing-up of the following trial, to Svendsen, 'Your Offence is of a very high Nature, and I am glad that you have had such a solemn Trial, in that all People may know how great a Crime this of Fortune-stealing is (which is Death by the Law) and may take Warning by you'. Eventually Svendsen was executed, but Sarah Baynton was reprieved.

The Trial of HAAGEN SVENDSEN, at the Queens-Bench for forceably taken away and Marrying Mrs. PLEASANT RAWLINGS, Nov. 25. 1702. Mich. 1 Ann.

Cler. of Arr. Haagen Svendsen hold up thy Hand. Which he did.

Cler. of Arr. Gentlemen of the Jury look upon the Prisoner at the Bar. *He stands indicted by the name of* Haagen Svendsen; *for that on the Sixth of* November 1702, *one* Pleasant Rawlins, *Gentlewoman, and a Virgin, and unmarried, Grand-daughter and Heir of* William Rawlins, *Sen. then deceased, and Daughter and Heir of* William Rawlins, *Jun. before then also deceased, was above the Age of Sixteen, and under the Age of Eighteen, and then had Substance and Estate in Moveables and in Lands and Tenements, viz. in Money, Goods and Chattels, to the Value of* 2000 *l. and in Lands and Tenements to the Value of* 20 *l. per Ann. to her and the Heirs of her Body.*

And that the several Persons . . . with Force and Arms . . . for the

Lucre of such Estate . . . did unlawfully, feloniously, violently, and
against the Will of the said Pleasant Rawlins, *take, carry, and lead*
away, with Intent to cause and procure the said Pleasant Rawlins,
against her Will, in Matrimony to the said Haagen Svendsen *to*
be joined . . .

Sol. Gen. Give an Account to his Lordship after what manner
you were Arrested, and carried from Tavern to Tavern.

Mrs. *Rawlins.* My Lord, I was Arrested with Madam Busby, and
carried to the *Star* and *Garter* Tavern in *Drury-Lane* . . . Then they
took me thence to the *Vine* Tavern in *Holbourn*, where I was an
Hour or two before I heard any Thing of marrying or any such
Thing.

Coun. What did they do with you all that Time?

Mrs. *Rawlins.* They got a Dinner ready, and after we had dined,
she begged of me to have her Brother, and said, that if I did not
marry him, I should be ruined. I desired my Friends to be sent for,
but they would not admit it. She looked on my Ring on my Finger,
and said, let me see your Ring from your Finger, I said, No, you
shall not. She said, I will force it off. I said, I'll try that: But she
forced it from me.

Prisoner. Remember you are upon Oath.

Mrs. *Rawlins.* I know I am. When she took my Ring away, I
asked her what she would do with it? she said, we should go and
get a Wedding Ring made by it. I told her I would not marry
without the Advice of my Friends. Away she went and bought a
Ring, and came up again, and said to her Brother, she had a Ring;
well said I, give me my Ring and do what you will with the other;
she said, If I did not marry her Brother I should be ruined for
ever.

There was a Minister in the House, whom they said had been
there about a Quarter of an Hour, but I supposed longer; they
brought him, with the Clerk, up Stairs; he asked no Questions, but
told me, if I did not marry this Gentleman, I should be sent to
Newgate and ruined for ever.

Coun. Give me an Account of what was after the buying of the
Ring.

Mrs. *Rawlins.* When they brought the Ring, they said to me, will
you be married or no? I answered, I will not, I will not marry without the Consent of my Friends; They said, If I did not I should be
ruined for ever. So with many Threats and Persuasions, they at last

prevail'd with me to marry. I was forced to marry him out of Fear, not of going to Newgate, but of being murdered.

L.C.J. Holt. Was there any Force or Threats us'd?

Mrs. *Rawlins.* Yes, there was, my Lord.

L.C.J. Holt. Give an Account of it.

Mrs *Rawlings.* They thrust me up Stairs, and ordered to have a Bed sheeted. Mrs. *Baynton* said to me, Undress and go to Bed. I said I would not. She said, she would pluck my Cloathes off my Back and make me go to Bed.

Coun. What did she do with you?

Mrs. *Rawlins.* She put me to Bed.

Coun. Did she use any Violence with you?

Mrs. *Rawlins.* Such Violence that made me go to Bed.

L. C. J. Holt. How came you to be released?

Mrs. *Rawlins.* It was Saturday Morning before I was released; there was some of my Friends came to the Place where I was.

A COLLECTION OF TRIALS of Persons for HIGH-TREA-SON etc., Vol. I, p. 311

4. A GRANDFATHER'S ADVICE

It is evident (by its survival) that George Norton's letter to his Grand-daughter was appreciated. It is interesting for the good advice it contains, and also for its reference to suitable books for her to read. In 1703 children's reading matter was limited. Caxton printed Aesop's *Fables* in 1484, and Mallory's *King Arthur and the Knights of the Round Table* appeared in 1485. This was probably intended for family reading.

Apart from these works there were the chap books, which were included amongst other items of use to isolated householders. They are mentioned in 1597, with such titles as *Tom Thumb, Valentine and Orson, The Children in the Wood, Jack the Giant-Killer,* and *Dick Whittington.* Other stories, of a coarse nature, intended for adults, may have been read by children as well. The Puritans had their own genre. Whilst girls were supposed to read fairy tales, boys enjoyed the more robust Adventures of *Don Bellianis of Greece, Guy of Warwick,* and *The Seven Champions of Christendom.*

The Whole Duty of Man (first published in 1640) would probably not have interested Mary (or Mally) Norton overmuch; neither would Quarles' *Enchiridion.* Probably she would have been far more attracted by Quarles' *Emblem* book and *The School of the Heart.* Seventeenth and eighteenth-century copies exist with children's writing on the fly leaves.

ffor
Mrs. Mary Norton att her
ffathers house in
Rippon.
Disforth, June yᵉ 12th. 1703

My Deare Mally Norton

You are now goeing abroad in yʳ blossoming & promiseing
years betwixt 11 & 12 which may lay you open to many & seuerall
temptations to vice & vanitie in this fickle Age; & you haue noe
Mother to giue you advice in what manner to avoid & beare upp
against them: And yʳ ffather tho' tender enough of yʳ wellfaire &
prudent enough to direct you, yet has he much varjety of businesse
to attend & many inducements to carry him abroad, & soe cannot
always haue his Jndulging Eye upon you to observe that you treade
true measures.

Therefore Deare Childe giue me your most affectjonate & aged
Grandffather leaue now in the eighty fourth yeare of my Age to
manifest my tender affectjon for you in these few lines for the better
improvement of yʳ time when now left to yr.selfe.

Itt will bee expected now that yʳ growing yeares should capacitate
your towardly Nature, to bring yʳ promising blossoms to that per-
fectjon of Maturity & ripenesse, as may render you a Phoenixe of
your Age, & an Exemplary pattern for your Effeminjne Assocjates
to Jmitate & coppy after.

And now (My Deare Mally) In yᵉ first place, lett me advise you to
continue yʳ Deuotjon & Prayers to Almighty God both morning
& euening to guide & direct you that day in all your actjons, & to
protect & defend you att your Laying down and at yʳ riseing upp:
To which end lett the often reading ouer that Excellent booke
(The Whole Duty of Man) bee a President & a continuall Guide to
direct you: And by all meanes continue your perseuerance in thee
Protestant Religion. And if for morrall precepts you looke sometimes
into Quarles his Enchiridjon (and others that you haue) itt may not
goe amisse for your Diuertjon.

You will meete wᵗʰ seuerall acquaintance in yʳ Educatjon who
may endeauour to endeare you & render themselues capable of being
a pritty companion & perhapps a bosome ffrjende too; but Deare
Childe the old rule is ffirst trye & then trust, & lett not ffaire pretences
circumvent you & delude you: yet bee respectiue & civill to all, but
ffamiljar wᵗʰ ffew; too much ffamiljarity brings contempt on yᵉ one

hand, as Morositye & sullennesse Disdaine on ye other: Jmitate the best, & by noe meannes adhere to loose or gadding Company; Modesty, much better becomes a Vertuous Lady, then a tatling Tongue can doe an opinjonated Mistresse: You will finde varjety of humours, & perhapps some to sett upp for witts, who when well tryed betrayes their Jngenuitjes, & render themselues guilty of many negligences, & as greate Jgnorances.

J could enlardge much more but J feare (Deare Childe) J haue been too toedjous & too impertinent wth you, & yet to conclude, giue me leaue to tell you, that as you come to a little more Maturitye, you may haue many Eyes upon you, & your Deameanour & well qualifyed Deportments bee the subject of many discourses; but J hope in God your Deare ffather will liue to take care, you bee well & comfortably setled, wheneuer you betake y^rselfe to another conditjon of life. And Deare Mally, lett me in the last place reminde you that you are the only care & comfort that both your ffather & J haue, & y^r health, wellfaire & welldoeing the greatest blessing that both or either of us can enjoy in this world, and J hope in God, you will timely and truely consider itt; such is, & euer will bee, the noe lesse hearty prayer, then earnest request, of,

My Deare Hearte,

Y^r entirely & trulye affectjonate old

Grandfather

George Norton.

NEWBY HALL PAPERS

5. NEWSSHEETS: ADVERTISEMENTS AND ANNOUNCEMENTS (CONT.)

The announcements that follow are taken from a variety of news sheets such as *The Daily Courant, The Post Man, The Post Boy, The Flying Post,* etc. References to children and young people are relatively infrequent.

(a)

A Negro Maid aged about 16 Years, named Bess, having a stript stuff wastcoat and peticoat, is much pitted with the small pox, and hath lost a piece of her Left Ear, speaks English well, ran away from her Master, Captain Benj. Quelch, on Tuesday the 8th December. If any persons secure the said Negro, and delivereth her to Mr Lloyd, at his Coffee House in Lombard Street, shall receive a Guinea Reward and reasonable charges.

POST MAN, no. 1069. Sat. Jan. 2, 1703

(b)

John Dod, a Negro, about 18 years of Age, in a light Grey Cloath Suit, edg'd with Blue, flat Pewter Buttons, & a Hat with Silver Edging; is run away from his Master Edmund Dummer, Esq., living in Coleman Street. Whoever can find & secure him to his said Master shall have a Guinea reward for the same.

POST MAN, 1705

(c)

On Thursday Morning Sir Stephen Fox and his Lady was brought to Bed of a Boy & a Girl.

POST MAN, no. 1437, 1705

(d)

Whereas on Tuesday the 31st of July last, Thomas Dolbe about 8 years old, reddish Hair with a dark Drugget Coat, blue waistcoat, and white Cloth Breeches, went away from his Friends with Isaac Barrant, a Barber Surgeons Apprentice, a Lad of about 17 years of Age, on his left hand being a stump with but 3 small fingers on it, having a Leather Cap, and light coloured Waistcoat, and took with them a large Spaniel Dog, with liver coloured Spots, which Boys have not since been heard of & are supposed to have strayed towards some of the Sea Ports. Any persons who can give any account of them, or secure 'em, are earnestly desired by their distressed Friends to send word to Mr Edward's at the Cock in St. James Market & they shall be gratefully rewarded.

POST MAN, no. 1437, 1705

(e)

A Boy, about 18 years old, dark lank short brown Hair, full faced, fresh colour'd, in a Grey Cloath Straight Coat, & a dark colour'd Waistcoat, wooden Buttons in both, a pair of old Leather Breeches, goes by the Name of W. Starling, rid away on Monday morning

the 29th of October last, from his Master's House Mr Tho. Oksover
of Tilney St. Lawrence Marshland, Norfolk, with a black Mare,
14 hands and a half high, 5 years old, a good Star, the off Foot
behind white, she is a little long back'd, a long tail never dockt, shod
only before. Whoever discovers the Mare or Boy, that his Masters
may have them again, shall have reasonable Charges & Satisfaction
for them. He took away a little Hunting Saddle, the Seat cover'd
with Velvett, almost worn out.

   POST MAN, no. 1553, 1705

6. 'THE KING OF THE BEGGARS'

   The Rev. Mr. Carew had several other children, sons and
daughters, besides Bamfylde. At twelve years of age [in 1705]
Bamfylde was sent to Tiverton school, where he contracted an
intimate acquaintance with young gentlemen of the first rank in
Somersetshire, Devonshire, Cornwall, and Dorsetshire.
   The Tiverton scholars had at this time the command of a fine cry
of hounds. It happened that a farmer, who used to hunt with the
Tiverton scholars, acquainted them of a fine deer which he had
seen, with a collar about its neck, in the fields about his farm, which
he supposed to be the favourite deer of some gentleman not far off:
this was very agreeable news to the Tiverton scholars, who went in
a great body to hunt it; this happened a short time before the harvest;
the chase was very hot, and they ran the deer many miles, which did
great damage, the corn being almost ripe. Upon the death of the deer,
and examination of the collar, it was found to belong to Colonel
Nutcombe. Those farmers and gentlemen, that sustained great
damage, complained very heavily to Mr. Rayner, the school-master,
of the havock made in their fields, which occasioned strict inquiry
to be made concerning the ringleaders, who proved to be our hero
and his companions, who on being severely threatened, absented
themselves from school, and the next evening fell into company
with a society of gipsies, who were feasting and carousing at the
Brick-house near Tiverton.

   ANON., *The King of the Beggars*, p. 3.

7. FAMILY LETTERS

   The Verney family experienced a reverse of fortune resulting from the
friendship of Sir Edmund Verney with King Charles I. Claydon was

sequestrated in 1643. Little John Verney, the heir, ran wild in the
empty house between three and eight years of age. Later he helped to
restore the family fortunes; married three times, and became the first
Viscount Fermanagh.

(a) From the Diary of Daniel Baker (Lady Fermanagh's brother)

March, 1705

I had a very fiery bay guelding and as I was all alone riding of him
in the Common, away he did runn and none were able to catch him;
by God's great mercy I have not been killed, and my wife was this
very time in the straw, and then lay in of her fifteenth child, and
what sad news it must have been for her to have heard of my being
killed.

MARGARET MARIA VERNEY (ed.), *Verney Letters of the Eighteenth Century*, vol. ii, p. 153

8. NEWSSHEETS: ANNOUNCEMENTS (CONT.)

(a)

Perrolla & Izadora, a Tragedy written by Mr Cibber

A Play-Book for Children, to allure them to read as soon as they
can speak plain, composed on purpose not to tire Children, &
printed with a fair & pleasant Letter. The Matter & Method plainer
than any yet extant. Sold by H. Rhodes at the Star the Corner of
Bride-Lane, Fleet street. Price four Pence. Those that take a dozen
may have an Allowance.

THE FLYING POST or the POST-MASTER, no. 1672, 1706

(b)

John Townsend, alias John Tausin, aged about 15 years, of small
Stature, dark brown Complexion, straight brown Hair, lame of his
left Leg, as also Samuel Groley, a short Lad, Short brown curled
Hair, about the aforesaid Age, both Sea Boys, left their Master
George Beach the 15th day of May last at Portsmouth. If any Person
can give Notice of either of the Boys to Mr George Akers, an
Anchor-Smith; in Shad-Thames Southwark, or to Mr Francis
Chiffant, at the Green-Man and Still at Charing Cross, shall be well
rewarded.

LONDON GAZETTE, 1706

(c)

A Black Indian Boy, 12 Years of age, fit to wait on a Gentleman, to be disposed of at Denis's Coffee-house in Finch Lane near the Royal Exchange.

THE TATLER, no. 132, Feb. 9–11, 1709

9. WENTWORTH LETTERS

The family of Wentworth was known before the Norman conquest. Sir William Wentworth's son, who became Earl of Strafford, was executed by Act of Attainder in 1641. The following letters chiefly concern the children of Thomas Wentworth, baptized in 1672. After a period as Ambassador, Lord Raby, as he became, settled in Yorkshire and was created Earl of Strafford.

(a)

February, 1709

Dearest Brother,

I give you a grate many thanks for the siszers you sent me by Mr. Shokman. I gave him sixpencs for fear tha should cute love one your side: but for mine 'tis to well gronded to fear ather siszers ar knifs cuting of it. I am vary glad to hear folly is well: it would be grate nonsenc for me to send nuws when you have it from so many better hands: but I am sure nobody wishes more for your health and happyness, tho tha may writ you longer and finer letters then your most

Aficsionat sister
ELIZ: WENTWORTH

JAMES J. CARTWRIGHT (ed.), *The Wentworth Papers*, 1705–1739, p. 76

(b) From a letter from Lady Wentworth to Lord Raby

London, January 4, 1709

... My ink has been fros, and tho I writ with it as it comes boiling from the fire, it's white. If I might tell you all the stories are daily brought in of accidents accationed by the great frost I might fill sheets, as children drown upon the Thames, post-boys being brought in by their horses to stages frose to their horses stone dead, and we are obliged to the horses for having our letters regular.

> JAMES J. CARTWRIGHT (ed.), *The Wentworth Papers,* 1705–1739, p. 68

The widespread mania for buying tickets in the State lotteries frequently caused great distress. This often resulted in the abandonment of children in a state of utter destitution. However, the Wentworth family apparently had no moral objections to this ubiquitous form of gambling. In 1710 Lady Wentworth tells of 'a commecall story'–'ticketts for a six-pany Lottery' were offered to her dog, 'whoe took one and I markt it with JP for Jinney Pug, and she has got a prise, a silver needlecase and silver thimble'.

(c) 'THE RAENING PASSION'

Letter from Elizabeth ('Betty') Wentworth to her brother.

[July] 1710

Dear Brother,

I seldome trouble you with my impertinent Letters, so I hope you will not refewes me this favour, it being the first I have beged of you senc you went over, it is to give me ten pd for a tickit which is the leest sum I can put in. My dearest Brother maye ashure himself if I win a prize I shall be very grateful to you. I have spent all the mony I have saved out of my alowanc in littel jewels, I have bought a dioment Buckle and lettil string for my neck, and I gave you the honour as to tell every body you sent me twenty ginneys towards it: this is ye last favour I will ask tell I am going to be married, and then you will be as good as your word, to give me wedding cloaths, but pray be not frighted, for I believe it will be a long time first if ever, except I win ye thousand p^d a year, for mony now adays is the raening passion. I hope my dearest Brother will excuse this trouble from her who is sincearly

Your most dutyfull
and afectionat sister
Eliz. Wentworth.

> JAMES J. CARTWRIGHT (ed.), *The Wentworth Papers,* 1705–1739, p. 126

10. NEWSSHEETS: ADVERTISEMENTS AND
ANNOUNCEMENTS

(a)

At the 2 Golden Pens next Door to St. Paul's School in St. Paul's Churchyard, Writing, Arithmetick, and Merchants Accounts are carefully taught by T. Cooke; he also (at the desire of several persons) teaches to Write the Greek and Hebrew characters, having been educated at St. Paul's School.

POST MAN, no. 1839. Jan 3–5, 1710

(b)

A Child of about 6 Years Old being led away by a Fat Squat Wench, on Monday at 5 of the Clock in the Evening, from Brook-street, being robbed of a Gold Chain marked A.H., and a Silver Thimble and Purse. Whoever can discover the Wench, so as taken shall have a Guinea Reward, or if Pawned or Sold their Money again, at Tho. Townsends at the Jamaica Coffee-house in Cornhill.

POST MAN, no. 1848. Feb. 10, 1710

(c)

This is to certify, that 2 Children of mine, whose Lives were despaired of by the violent Breeding of their Teeth, were both immediately relieved, and gradually cut all their Teeth with the greatest Ease and Safety imaginable, only by rubbing their Gums with a Remedy I had from Mr Perroner, Surgeon in Dyot Street, Bloomsbury.

POST MAN, Feb. 14–16, 1710

(d)

Dropt in a Handbasket at the Upper End of Foster Lane in the Parish of St. Vedast Alais Foster the 18th instant about 11 of the clock at Night, a Female Child, having upon it—a red and white Callimancoe stripe coat, with a white Frock over it, and a double Lace Cap on its Head, with several other Childs Linnen very ordinary, supposed to be about 4 or 5 Month Old. Whoever discovers who the Parents of the Child are, so that the Parish may be discharged thereof, shall receive of the Church Wardens of the Parish aforesaid 40s. Reward.

POST MAN, no. 1880. March 21, 1710

On the 24th of Jan., there was a Male Child dropt at the West-end of the said Church, about 3 Weeks old, in very old Blankets with a piece of an old Curtain.

DAILY COURANT, no. 2582. 1710

11. SAMUEL JOHNSON

In the *Life of Samuel Johnson, LL.D.*, Boswell not only gives the facts of his hero's life, but also endeavours to probe the enigmatic depths of his personality.

Samuel's childhood seems to have been happy enough. His remarkably active mind perhaps compensated him for his extreme short-sightedness, which was attributed to 'the scrophula or King's-evil'.

(a) SPIRITED INDEPENDENCE

'When Dr. Sacheverel was at Litchfield, Johnson was not quite three years old. Mr. Hammond asked Mr. Johnson how he could think of bringing such an infant to church. He answered, because it was impossible to keep him at home; for, young as he was, he believed he had caught the publick spirit and zeal for Sacheverel, and would have staid for ever in the church, satisfied with beholding him.'

Nor can I omit a little instance of that jealous independence of spirit, and impetuosity of temper, which never forsook him. One day, when the servant who used to be sent to school to conduct him home, had not come in time, he set out by himself, though he was then so near-sighted, that he was obliged to stoop down on his hands and knees to take a view of the kennel, before he ventured to step over it. His school-mistress, afraid that he might miss his way, or fall into the kennel, or be run over by a cart, followed him at some distance. He happened to turn about and perceive her. Feeling her careful attention as an insult to his manliness, he ran back to her in a rage, and beat her, as well as his strength would permit.

JAMES BOSWELL, *The Life of Samuel Johnson, Ll.D.*, Vol. I, p. 11

(b)

It has been said, that he contracted this grievous malady ['scrophula'] from his nurse. His mother, yielding to the superstitious notion, as to the virtue of the regal touch . . . carried him to London, where he was actually touched by Queen Anne. Johnson used to talk of this frankly. Being asked if he could remember Queen Anne,—'He had (he said) a confused, but somehow a sort of solemn recollection of a lady in diamonds, and a long black hood.' This touch, however, was without any effect.

JAMES BOSWELL, The Life of Samuel Johnson, Ll.D., Vol. I, p. 15

12. THE VERNEY FAMILY

Colonel John Lovett married Mary Verney in 1703, while conducting negotiations for the erection of the 'Edistoune Lighthouse'. Their children were Verney, Elizabeth (Bess), and John (Jack). Colonel Lovett's message: 'Tell Deare Bess her Pearle Necklas is come' was sent to his daughter when she was four years old. In the summer he sent her a parcel containing 'a pair of Buckles for my Dr. Little Bess's shoes, who I heare my Lady has made very fine, and all Silver'. Two days later he wrote, 'My Deare Little Bessis's watch is new don, as well as it was Afirst; if she will lett me have it to make a figure in Devonshire & Cornwall, I will bring it to her on my return to London'.

(a) 'THE EVILL'

'Bess' had a swollen neck when she was nine. Her mother was concerned about it, and not much reassured to be informed that it was the 'Evill'.

May, 1714

. . . I showed my poor Girl to a famous Surgeon, one Blundell, who assures me it is the Evill; he sayd shes young and will outgrow it, but he would by no means have me give her any more Physick; she must intirely leave off malt drink and wine, and he bid me get her toucht . . .

As to the child, . . . If she is toucht nothing must be done for her after it, and I have great hopes the Queen will touch her. Lady Denbigh has been so kind to speak for me to the Queen, and there is Intrest making for another young lady to be toucht, so we hope they will both be done together . . . Here is some that I know in town, who the Queen toucht last year that had severall sores on them, but are now as well as I am. Pray God grant the same on my poor Bess.

MARGARET MARIA LADY VERNEY (ed.), *Verney Letters of the Eighteenth Century*, Vol. I, p. 356

'Bess' was probably 'toucht' by Queen Anne; it may have been the last of such occasions, as the Queen died not long after. Patients were given a gold 'Touch-piece' called an 'Angel' on which St. George and the Dragon were depicted. The medallion hung from a white ribbon placed round the patient's neck.

(b)   Letter from Mary Lovett to Lord Fermenagh

29 May, 1714

I this morning set forward Dear little Bess for Claydon where I hope she is safe arrived before this, and I pray God the means that has been used for her may prove effectuall. She must take care of her Gold and wear it about her neck both night and day, and rub the place that swell'd with it every morning . . .

MARGARET MARIA LADY VERNEY (ed.), *Verney Letters of the Eighteenth Century*, Vol. I, p. 358

(c)   LEADING STRINGS

'The honorable John', eldest and favourite son of Catherine and Ralph Verney, was four years old when his mother wrote:

3 Jan., 1715

. . . Pray desire Cousen Peg to buy me a pair of leading strings for Jak, ther is stuf made on purpose that is very strong for he is so heavy I dare not venture him with a common ribin.

22 Apr., 1715

. . . The woman has been hear to see Jak and has given me some streinthen things to give him and hopes he will soon be well . . .

The woman was here agane with Jak, I never let him be a moment out of my sight, so I have never been out since but he has been with me at Church and scolds every day for his Pape to come home.

MARGARET MARIA LADY VERNEY (ed.), *Verney Letters of the Eighteenth Century*, Vol. II, p. 131

13. THE VIRTUES OF IGNORANCE AND POVERTY

Bernard de Mandeville was born in Holland in 1670. After attending Leyden University and taking a medical degree, he came to England, but did not make much use of his training. In the 1729 edition of *The Fable of the Bees* he gives lively descriptions of London and Amsterdam. He also gives some delightful vignettes of children and puts forward an ingenious theory of education. He inveighs against the institution of Charity-Schools and argues that education for the poorer classes is not only unnecessary but also positively harmful. Nearly two centuries were to pass before the climate of public opinion finally turned against his views on this subject.

(a)

An enquiry into the origin of Moral Virtue

Children and Fools will swallow personal Praise ... I thought on the Tricks made use of by the Women that would teach Children to be mannerly. When an awkward Girl, before she can either Speak or Go, begins after many Entreaties to make the first rude Essays of Curt'sying, the Nurse falls into an Ecstasy of Praise; *There's a delicate Curt'sey. O fine Miss! There's a pretty Lady Mama! Miss can make a better Curt'sey than her Sister Molly!* The same is eccho'd over by the Maids, whilst Mama almost hugs the Child to Pieces, only Miss *Molly*, who being four Years Older knows how to make a very handsome Curt'sey, wonders at the Perverseness of their Judgment, and swelling with Indignation, is ready to cry at the Injustice that is done her, till, being whispered in the Ear that it is only to please the Baby, and that she is a Woman, she grows Proud at being let into the Secret, and rejoycing at the Superiority of her Understanding repeats what has been said with large Additions, and Insults over the Weakness of her Sister, whom all this while she fancies to be the only Bubble amongst them.

BERNARD DE MANDEVILLE, *The Fable of the Bees*, p. 22

'Tis the same with Boys, whom they'll strive to persuade, that all fine Gentlemen do as they are bid, and that none but Beggar Boys are rude, or dirty their Cloaths, nay, as soon as the wild Brat with his untaught Fist begins to fumble for his Hat, the Mother, to make him pull it off, tells him before he is two Years old, that he is a Man; and if he repeats that Action when she desires him, he's

c

presently a Captain, a Lord Mayor, a King, or something higher if she can think of it, till egg'd on by the Force of Praise, the little Urchin endeavours to imitate Man as well as he can, and strains all his Faculties to appear what his shallow Noddle imagines he is believ'd to be.

BERNARD DE MANDEVILLE, *The Fable of the Bees*, p. 24

(b)

A Girl, who is modestly educated, may before she is two Years old, begin to observe how careful the Women, she converses with, are of covering themselves before Men; and the same Caution being inculcated to her by Precept, as well as Example, it is very probable that at Six she'll be ashamed of showing her Leg, without knowing any Reason why such an Act is blameable, or what the Tendency of it is . . . Miss is scarce three Years old, but she is spoke to every Day to hide her Leg, and rebuk'd in good Earnest if she shows it; whilst *little Master* at the same Age is bid to take up his Coats, and piss like a Man.

BERNARD DE MANDEVILLE, *The Fable of the Bees*, p. 38

(c)

An Essay on Charity and Charity Schools

If we mind the Passtimes and Recreations of young Children, we shall observe nothing more general in them than that all who are suffer'd to do it, take Delight in playing with Kittens and little Puppy Dogs. What makes them always lugging and pulling the poor Creatures about the House proceeds from nothing else but that they can do with them as they please, and put them into what Posture and Shape they list, and the Pleasure they receive from this is originally owing to the Love of Dominion and that usurping Temper all Mankind are born with.

BERNARD DE MANDEVILLE, *The Fable of the Bees*, pp. 218–23

(d)

. . . in the sight of Charity Children; there is a natural Beauty in Uniformity which most People delight in. It is diverting to the Eye to see Children well match'd, either Boys or Girls, march two and two in good order, and to have them all whole and tight in the same Cloaths and Trimming must add to the Comeliness of the Sight, and what makes it still more generally entertaining is the imaginery share which even Servants and the meanest in the Parish have in it, to whom it costs nothing: Our Parish Church, Our Charity Children.

BERNARD DE MANDEVILLE, *The Fable of the Bees*, p 229

(e)

From what has been said it is manifest that in a free Nation where Slaves are not allow'd of, the surest Wealth consists in a Multitude of Laborious Poor; for besides that they are the never-failing Nursery of Fleets and Armies, without them there could be no Enjoyment, and no Product of any Country could be valuable. To make the Society happy and People easie under the meanest Circumstances, it is requisite that great Numbers of them should *be Ignorant as well as Poor*.

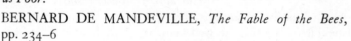

BERNARD DE MANDEVILLE, *The Fable of the Bees*, pp. 234–6

(f)

There are many Examples of Women that have excelled in Learning, and even in War, but this is no reason we should bring 'em all up to *Latin* and *Greek*, or else Military Discipline, instead of Needle-work and Housewifry...

Abundance of hard and dirty Labour is to be done, Coarse Living is to be complied with: Where shall we find a better Nursery for these Necessities than the Children of the Poor?

BERNARD DE MANDEVILLE, *The Fable of the Bees*, p. 256

(g)

Hor: ... why must a Lady have more Pride than a Gentleman?

Cleo: Because the Lady is in the greatest Danger of straying from it: She has a Passion within, that may begin to affect her at twelve or thirteen, and perhaps sooner, and she has all the Temptations of the Men to withstand besides; a Seducer of uncommon Address and resistless Charms may court her to what Nature prompts and solicits her to do: he may add great Promises, actual Bribes; this may be done in the Dark, and when no Body is by to dissuade her.

Gentlemen very seldom have occasion to show their Courage before they are sixteen or seventeen Years of Age.

> BERNARD DE MANDEVILLE, *The Fable of the Bees*, Part II, p. 91.

14. DOLLS

In referring to a 'jointed baby' Pope presumably meant a doll. Until later in the eighteenth century they were described as 'a girl's toy baby' or 'a child's baby'. Fortunate children had a 'Baby House' as well. Queen Anne gave one to her god-child Ann Sharp in the early 1700s, and thus helped to start a new fashion in England.

The custom for children to work samplers as examples of their skill in embroidery was already prevalent by the middle of the sixteenth century.

Letter from Alexander Pope to Edw. Blount, Esq.

Rentcomb in Gloucestershire, Oct. 3, 1721

Your kind letter has overtaken me here ... I am well pleas'd to date this from a place so well known to Mrs. Blount, where I write as if I were dictated to by her ancestors, whose faces are all upon me. I look'd upon the mansion, walls, and terraces; the plantations, and slopes, which nature has made to command a variety of valleys and rising woods; with a veneration mix'd with a pleasure, that represented her to me in those puerile amusements, which engaged her so many years ago in this place. I fancied I saw her sober over a sampler, or gay over a jointed baby. I dare say she did one thing more, even in those early times; 'remembered her Creator in the days of her youth.'

> ALEXANDER POPE, *The Works of Alexander Pope, Esq.* (1751), Vol. VIII, p. 21.

15. FAMILY LETTERS (CONT.)

(a) SCHOOLBOY'S LETTERS

Letter from the Hon. John Verney to Lord Fermanagh

18 Nov., 1723

Dear Papa,—George brought me some Gingerbread which you was so kind as to send me, as also a couple of Handkerchiefs. I beg the favour of you, if it will not be troublesome, that you will

desire my Dear Mama to send me a little Tea & Sugar, as also a
pair of Battledores & Shittlecock.—I remain, Dear Papa, your most
dutiful Son,

John Verney.

MARGARET MARIA LADY VERNEY (ed.), *Verney Letters
of the Eighteenth Century*, Vol. II, p. 134.

(b)

30 September, 1724

...I desire you would send me my Sord a Thursday morning,
because if any of us go to Chelsey I cannot for want of it; and when
you send my Sord if you will send my Phoedrus I shall be obliged
to you.

22 October, 1724

Dear Papa,—I am very glad that you are well and hope my dear
Mama and both my sisters are in the same good health as I am in.
The picture* Mr. Vaslet thinks a Master-Piece, as does everyone else,
and he sends you a thousand thanks for it, and says that though it is
a present that he vallues to the highest degree, yet it cant add anything to the Love he had for me before. I can assure you I strive to
fulfill the design you put me here for...

MARGARET MARIA LADY VERNEY (ed.), *Verney Letters
of the Eighteenth Century*, Vol. II, p. 135.

16. TEACHING OF MATHEMATICS

The Rector of Cotesbach's treatise on mathematics is very clear. He
also appears to be a shrewd observer of human nature. He writes: 'However, because it is not impossible, but some Young Gentlemen may be so
Brisk and Airy, as to think that knowing how to cast ACCOMPT is
requisite only for Underlings, but unnecessary and below Persons of
plentiful Estates. . .' He then cites the case of a young gentleman who
had considerable 'Estate seiz'd upon for Debt', who attributed his misfortune 'to his inability to keep his Accompts'. The Rector implies that
a proper study of his book will assure that, in later years, 'his ESTATE
DO'S NOT RUN FROM HIM through the Knavery of others; consequently, that no Gentleman ought to think Arithmetic below Him,
that do's not think an Estate below him!'

* Lord Fermanagh seems to have sent a portrait of his cherished boy to his
school at Fulham.

(a)

The General PREFACE

As it is an Happiness of *Men* above *Brutes*, that they are *endued with Reason*; so it is an Happiness of *Gentlemen* above the meaner Part of Mankind, that, being free'd from the Common and Bodily Employments of Life, they have Leisure to *exercise their Reason* in more noble Studies: Among which may justly be reckon'd the Study of *Mathematicks*.

For as it is one Branch of the Transcendent Excellency of GOD, that *He is the infinitely Wise* Creator of all Things; so it is one Branch of the Excellency of *Man*, that *he is able to contemplate and apprehend the infinite Wisdom* of his Creator, manifested in the Works of the Creation: Whereunto Nothing conduces more than the Knowledge of Mathematicks. For we are assured by the wisest of Men, that *GOD has order'd all Things in Measure, Number, and Weight*, that is, according to the Rules of Mathematicks.

And, since GOD sends no One into the World, to be idle, or only to take his Pastime therein; but the more He has free'd *Gentlemen* from *bodily* Labour, the more He expects they should exercise the Faculties of their *Minds*, in order to His greater Glory, by raising their Minds to more clear and sublime Apprehensions of his Divine Perfections; and since the Mathematical Sciences are so necessary to the Attainment of such Apprehensions of the Divine Excellency: On these Considerations it may not unjustly be look'd on, as one Part of the Gentleman's Calling, to apply a due or considerable Portion of his Time to the Study of Mathematicks.

As for those, who are not to be influenc'd by Motives of a *Spiritual* Nature, or drawn from their Duty to GOD, consider'd either as their common Creator, or special Benefactor, there are not wanting many sensible Motives, or such as may be drawn from their temporal Interest, to encourage them to the Study of the Mathematical Sciences.

It remains only to observe, that another general Encouragement to *Young Gentlemen* for the Study of the Mathematicks, and that no inconsiderable One, is the Method observ'd in drawing up these Treatises; wherein are selected only such *Elements* as are *most useful* and *easy* to be known. By which Means they may attain to a competent Knowledge of the Mathematicks, with much less Labour, and in much less Time, in going through this Course of Mathematicks, than in going through Others, wherein the more and less useful, the easy and difficult Elements are contained promiscuously together.

> EDWARD WELLS, D.D., *The Young Gentleman's Arithmetic, and Geometry*, (2nd ed., 1723) Preface.

(b)

Example VI. Three Companies of Soldiers passing by, the First takes away from a Shepherd Half of his whole Flock, and Half a single Sheep over. The Second takes away Half of the Remainder of the Flock, and also Half a Sheep over. The third likewise takes away Half the Flock remaining, and Half a Sheep over. All which was done without killing any Sheep, and there remain'd at last twenty Sheep to the Shepherd. How many Sheep therefore had he in his Flock at the First? *Ans.* 167.

> EDWARD WELLS, D.D., *The Young Gentleman's Arithmetic*, p. 151

(c)

Example V. A. Cistern is supply'd with Water by two Pipes, whereof one will fill the Cistern in 20 Hours, the other in 30 Hours. In what Time will both Pipes together fill the Cistern? *Answer*, In 12 Hours.

(d)

Example II. A Man ask'd the Age of his four Sons; made Answer, that the Second was four Years younger than the Eldest, and the Third was four Years younger than the Second, and the Fourth was four Years younger than the Third, and withal just Half the Age of the Eldest. What then was the Age of each Son?

Let a denote the Age of the Elder. Therefore, $a - 4$ will denote the Age of the Second; $a - 8$ the Age of the Third; and $a - 12$ the Age of the Fourth. But now, according to the State of the Question, the Age of the Fourth, was also Half the Age of the Eldest, that is, $a - 12 = \frac{1}{2} a$. Whence it is obvious enough without any more ado, that $a = 24$, or that the Age of the Eldest is 24 . . .

Having thus found the Age of the eldest Son to be 24, the Age

of the Second will be 20, of the Third 16, of the Fourth 12, and
equal to Half the Age of the Eldest.

> EDWARD WELLS, D.D., *The Young Gentleman's Arith-
> metic*, p. 146.

17. A REASONABLE SCHEME

The following letter from Lord Bathurst to Swift reflects the interest
aroused by Swift's *A Model Proposal for Preventing the Children of
Poor People in Ireland from being a Burden to their Parents or Country,
and for making them Beneficial to the Country.*

LETTER CCLXXI

Lord B———— to Dr. Swift

Febr. 12, 1729–30

DEAR DEAN,

Now you must imagine that a man, who has nine children to feed,
can't long afford *alienos pascere nummos*; but I have four or five,
that are very fit for the table. I only wait for the lord mayor's day
to dispose of the largest; and I shall be sure of getting off the
youngest, whenever a certain great man makes another entertainment at *Chelsea*. Now you see, though I am your debtor, I am not
without my proper ways and means to raise a supply answerable to
your demand. I must own to you, that I should not have thought
of this method of raising money; but that you seemed to point it
out to me. For just at the time that scheme came out, you gave me
a hint that you wished I might provide for my numerous family.
I did immediately propose it to Lady *Bathurst* as your advice, particularly for her last boy, which was born the plumpest, finest
thing, that could be seen; but she fell in a passion, and bid me send
you word, that she would not follow your direction, but that she
would breed him up to be a parson, and he should live upon the fat
of the land; or a lawyer, and then, instead of being eat himself, he
should devour others. You know women in passion never mind
what they say; but, as she is a very reasonable woman, I have almost brought her over to your opinion; and having convinced her,
that as matters stood, we could not possibly maintain all the nine,
she does not begin to think it reasonable the youngest should raise
fortunes for the eldest. And upon that foot a man may perform
family duty with more courage and zeal. Or if, by any accident,

whilst his wife lies-in with one child, he should get a second upon the body of another woman, he might dispose of the fattest of the two, and that would help to breed up the other. The more I think upon this scheme, the more reasonable it appears to me; . . . Well, Adieu.

> JOHN HAWKESWORTH, Ll.D., *Letters Written by Jonathan Swift, D.D.*, Vol. II, p. 297

18. CHILDISH LOYALTY

Horace Walpole, born in 1717, was the youngest child of Sir Robert's first wife. He remembered it said, 'That child cannot possibly live'. His parents treated him with special attention, consequently, when he expressed a vehement wish to 'see the king', his mother asked the Duchess of Kendal to obtain 'the honour of kissing his Majesty's hand'. He was then ten years old.

Accordingly, my mother carried me at ten at night to the apartment of the Countess of Walsingham.

Notice being given that the King was come down to supper, Lady Walsingham took me alone into the Duchess's ante-room, where we found alone the King and her. I knelt down, and kissed his hand. He said a few words to me, and my conductress led me back to my mother.

The person of the King is as perfect in my memory as if I saw him but yesterday. It was that of an elderly man, rather pale, and exactly like his pictures and coins; not tall; of an aspect rather good than august; with a dark tie-wig, a plain coat, waistcoat, and breeches of snuff-coloured cloth, with stockings of the same colour, and a blue riband over all.

My childish loyalty, and the condescension in gratifying it, were, I suppose, causes that contributed, very soon afterwards, to make me shed a flood of tears for that sovereign's death, when, with the other scholars at Eton College, I walked in procession to the proclamation of the successor; . . .

> PETER CUNNINGHAM (ed.), *The Letters of Horace Walpole*, Vol. I, p. xcix

CHAPTER 2
1730–1759

1. MACKY'S JOURNAL

(a) Eaton

This Place is join'd to *Windsor* by a wooden Bridge . . . There are fine Gardens belonging to the College . . . The College has a settled Revenue of about 5000 *l. per annum,* for the maintenance of a Provost, seven Fellows, of whom one is Vice-Provost, seventy King's Scholars, two School-masters, eight Ushers, ten Choristers, a Register and twelve Servants; who have all . . . a good maintenance in the College, which consists of an Apartment for the Provost and Fellows, a large Hall, Chappel, Library, and School-House. The School is divided into Upper and Lower, and each into three Classes. Each School has one Master, and each Master four Assistants or Ushers. None are received into the Upper School till they can make *Latin* Verse, and have a tolerable knowledge of the *Greek*. In the Lower School the children are received very young, and are initiated into all School-Learning. Besides the seventy Scholars on the Foundation, there's always abundance of Children, generally speaking of the best Families, who are boarded in the Houses of the Masters, and within the College.

JOHN MACKY, *A Journey through England,* Vol. I, p. 54

2. EARLY INDUSTRIALIZATION

John Lombe, a good mechanic and draughtsman, went out to Italy . . . On his arrival in England he determined to fix upon Derby . . . in the year 1717 agreed with the Corporation . . . for an island or swamp in the river Derwent, at a rent of £8 p.a. . . . he erected [the mill] which is still existing, at an expense of 30,000 *l.*

William Hutton . . . went to the Lombe Mill in 1730, when about 7 years of age. One of the Clerks remarked to the person who took him there, that the offer was needless, I was too young. However, the offer was made; and as hands were wanted in the infant state of this work I was accepted. It was found, upon trial, that

nature had not given me length enough to reach the engine; for, out
of three hundred persons employed at the mill I was by far the
youngest. The superintendent wisely thought that if they lengthened
one end it would affect both. A pair of high *pattens* were therefore
fabricated and tied fast about my feet, to make them steady companions. They were clumsy companions, which I dragged about one
year, and with pleasure delivered up.

THE PENNY MAGAZINE, April 1843, p. 163

3. NEW INFLUENCES

John Wesley's theories on the education and upbringing of children
had a far-reaching practical application. He was born in 1703, of parents
with very differing temperaments. The children were brought up with
unvarying strictness. Wesley's missionary zeal brought him more than
once to the verge of martyrdom. He persisted so effectively in dissemin-
ating his ideas that he founded the sect of Methodism. Before his death
in 1791 he had profoundly stirred the emotions of an important section
of the community—the hard-working and thrifty poor. His influence on
them and their children helped to further the industrial revolution.
Wesley believed that 'Satan finds some work for idle hands to do'. He
was of the opinion that a child needed no other education than a knowledge of the catechism and the Bible. These theories helped to stifle
endeavours to establish primary education, which had been in force in
the early years of the century. It was just at this point in the development of industry that the demand for child labour began to rise. This
produced a conjunction of theory and practice which rejoiced the hearts
of thrifty, devout parents and ambitious industrialists alike. The long
hours and low wages paid to child-workers in the next few decades un-
doubtedly contributed to the vast fortunes made by manufacturers,
whose ingenuity and determination enabled England to become the
premier industrial nation of the world.

(a) Susanna Wesley and her eldest Child

Samuel Wesley was the first-born. He did not attempt to speak
until he was five years old, and it was feared he never would. To
their surprise he began at once. He had a cat, of which he was
very fond, and he would carry it about with him and play with it
by the hour. One day 'Sammy' was missing, Mrs. Wesley was
greatly alarmed, and went through the house loudly calling him
by name. At last she heard a voice from under the table, saying,
'Here am I, mother'. She looked under, and saw with surprise

Sammy and his cat. From that time he spoke clearly and without
hesitation.

> THE REV. J. B. WAKELEY, *Anecdotes of the Wesleys*, p. 59

(b) Susanna Wesley and the Education of her Children

Mrs. Wesley was the instructress of the children in their earlier years.
The old parsonage was, in fact, a theological seminary. She took each
child by itself and gave instructions adapted to its capacity.

'On Monday I talked with Molly, on Tuesday with Hetty,
Wednesday with Nancy, Thursday with Jacky, Friday with Patty,
Saturday with Charles, and with Emilia and Sukey together on
Sunday.'

> THE REV. J. B. WAKELEY, *Anecdotes of the Wesleys*, p. 60

4. CHILDREN'S LETTERS

(a)

December, 1730

Dear Papa,
Master Wallpole came to me last night wee playd at Quadarill and
I won 10 pence at a penny a fish. I hope I shall see you sone in
London. My cosin Lee has sent me the dor-mice. We have had very
good weather hear—I hope you have had the same: this Letter is of
my one Spilling: I am, &c.

> JAMES J. CARTWRIGHT (ed.), *The Wentworth Papers*,
> 1705–1739, p. 462

(b)

December 12, 1730

Dear Papa,
I have no news to tell you but Mr Southwell is dead. Monswer I
beleve is gone to France for he sent for his Trink to the kings arms
and was ready in a hackney coach and toke in in to him and bid
them drif a way to jerin crose.* This Letter is of my one spilling. I'
am Dear Papa

Your most affectionate
and most dutifull son
Wentworth.

> JAMES J. CARTWRIGHT (ed.), *The Wentworth Papers*,
> 1705–1739, p. 462

* Charing Cross?

(c)

London, December 26, 1730

Dear Papa,

Master Wallpole was to see me yesterday. My cousen Lee has sent me the Dor-mous But it is dead. The old Dor-mous is very well and in perfect good health. Lord Delorain and Mrs. Whitworth are both dead of a fit of an Appoplex: I have tired you long enough with my silly scroll. I am, &c.

JAMES J. CARTWRIGHT (ed.), *The Wentworth Papers*, 1705-1739, p. 462

(d)

London, January 3, 1734

Dear Papa,

. . . I went yesterday with my uncle to see the great man, I never saw such a monster, he is eight foot and three inches high, he was dress'd like the Algerinains embassadors, his wastcoat was yellow with gold loops and a robe of scarlet velvet or damask laced round with gold and a turband on his head.

JAMES J. CARTWRIGHT (ed.), *The Wentworth Papers*, 1705-1739, p. 498

(f)

London, May 27, 1735

Dear Papa,

We had a very good dinner, for we had at the first course three macerell, then after that we had beans and bacon and boyl'd chikens, and then we had four little plates pidgeons one rabbits. in an other goosberry tart and sparrow grase and no desart. I think I have told you all the news I know, so I will tire you no longer with stupid letter.

JAMES J. CARTWRIGHT (ed.), *The Wentworth Papers*, 1705-1739, p. 518

(g) From Lady Lucy Wentworth

London, January 8, 1737

Dear Papa,

. . . My mamma has been so good as to give me leave to goe to the Opera to night with Lady Anne. 'Tis to be a new one call'd

Meropy, but the foolish Buffo's are to be left out which I am very glad of. The Opera is to be heard but once for he says 'tis the worst that was ever composed. We were very sorry the Queen wou'd not keep Twelf night, I believe nobody regretted more than I, except the Groom Porter, who I hear is much disturb'd about it, tho to comfort us both her majesty says when the King comes she'll make a Twelf night, which I don't credit much. We were at court last night, . . . the whole study of my life will be in every respect how to please your Lordship and to prove how sincerely I am as I ought to be Dear Papa

Your most affectionate and most dutifull daughter,
L. Wentworth.

Lady Hariot beggs her duty to your Lordship.

JAMES J. CARTWRIGHT (ed.), *The Wentworth Papers,* 1705–1739, p. 528

5. NATURE DISPLAY'D

It is doubtful that the Duke of Cumberland remembered any precepts from the *Spectacle de le Nature* on the battlefield of Culloden. The most interesting feature of the book is the reference to the experiments of Leeuwenhoek, which demonstrated that spontaneous generation of life does not take place. However, his findings were not to be widely believed till over a century later.

(a)

Dedication

To His Royal Highness the Duke of Cumberland.

Sir,

The universal Approbation which the several *French* Editions of this Volume have received, furnished me with an Inducement to lay the following Translation at Your Royal Highnesses Feet.

As the Mind of Your Royal Highness has been watered with the purest Streams that Learning could dispense, and as you have long been habituated to those Institutions which render a young Prince the Darling of those who have the Honour to approach him, there is sufficient Reason to believe, that any generous Attempt to promote useful Knowledge, and inspire the Sons of Men with Gratitude to their great Creator, will obtain a favourable Reception from Your

Royal Highness, whose Cabinet has ever been inaccessible to the low Singularities of Infidels and Sceptics.

SAMUEL HUMPHREYS, *Le Spectacle de la Nature: or, Nature Display'd*, (dedication)

(b)

Prior. If Chance does not any way interpose in placing the Eggs of Insects, it has still less to do in forming them.

Count. Nothing happens here by Chance. The Motions of minute Animals seem indeed accidental and capricious, but they as really tend to a certain Point as those of the largest Beings. No Insect abandons her Eggs to Chance, and the Parent is never deceiv'd in the Choice of a proper Situation for them. But you will never meet with this Creature, either in a Plant, or Wood, of even in putrified Meat. On the contrary, 'tis in this last, that the Fly deposits her Eggs. What Interest attracts her there? Would not her Eggs be better lodg'd in a fine *China* Vase, which she might always use as she pleased?—Experience will convince you better what it is that regulates her Choice.

Take a Slice of Beef newly killed,* and put it into an open Pot; put likewise another Slice into a Pot that's very clean, and cover it immediately with a Piece of Silk, so that the Air may transpire, and the Flies be prevented from sliding their Eggs into the Vessel. The first Slice will undergo the common Consequence; because the Flies have their full Liberty to lay their Eggs. The other Piece will change and decay by the Admission of the Air; and at last be reduced to Powder by Evaporation; but neither Eggs, Worms, nor Flies will be found there: The most that can happen will be this, the Flies allured by the exhaling Odour, will settle in Swarms upon the Cover, and endeavour to enter; but at last will leave their Eggs upon the Silk, being unable to penetrate any farther.

SAMUEL HUMPHREYS, *Nature Displayed*, p. 14

6. APPRENTICES

The apprenticeship system has existed for about seven hundred years. At its worst it led to exploitation; at its best it was an excellent method

* See the Experiments of *Redi*, *Arezzo* and *Leuwenhoek*'s Anat. & Contempl. Arcan. Nat. Tom. I.

of transmitting crafts and skills. The original records of 'the Mistery of
Goldsmiths of the City of London' show a fascinating diversity of
signatures in the eighteenth century. James Smith's father Nehemiah
was 'late of the Parish of St. Botolph without Aldersgate, Woolwich.'
James de Saûmarez came from Guernsey. A few were illiterate; Thomas
White's mark was a scrawled M. There were a surprising number of
girl apprentices. Among them were Ann Tow (illiterate), Tabitha
Greene, Sabina Edwards, Margaret Wyersdale, Dorothy Scrotton and
Ann Bostock.

1737
6   Be it Rembred that I Mary Seeley Daughter of Robert Seeley
    late of the Liberty of St. Martin's Le Grand London Cord-
    wainer deced Do put my self Apprentice to Cristable Bullman
    Citizen & Goldsmith of London for the term of Seven Years
    from this day there being paid to my sd. Mistress the sum of
    Thirty Pounds

                                                          Mary Seeley

6: Be it Rembred that I William Lewis Son of Charles Lewis late
    Citizen & Girdler of London Do put my self Apprentice to
    Gabriel Fleming Citizen Goldsmith of London for the term of
    seven years from this day there being paid to my sd. Mar: the
    Sum of Ten Pounds being the Charity of Christ's Hospital
    London

                                                          Willm Lewis

From the MS. Apprenticeship Book of the Goldsmiths'
Company

7. JOHN WESLEY
From John Wesley's diary.

   Fri. Feb. 9 1739   A note was given me at Wapping, in (nearly)
these words:—
    'SIR,
'Your prayers are desired for a child that is a lunatic, and sore
vexed, that our Lord would be pleased to heal him.'
    Tues. 13.   I received the following note:—
    'SIR,
'I return hearty thanks for your prayers on Friday for my tortured
son. He grows worse and worse: I beg your prayers still to our

Redeemer, which will cure him, or give us patience to bear the rod, hoping it is dipped in the blood of the Lamb.

'Sir, he is taken with grievous weeping, his heart beating, as if it would burst, he swells ready to burst, sweats great drops, runs about beating and tearing himself. He bites and pinches me, he lays his hands on the fire, and sticks pins in his flesh. Thus he has been these five years. He is in his eleventh year, a wonder of affliction: I hope, of mercy also, and that I shall yet praise Him, who is my Redeemer and my God.'

THE JOURNAL OF THE REV. JOHN WESLEY A.M., Vol. I, p. 17

8. FAMILY LETTERS

The main part of the Newby Hall papers used in this work concerns the Robinson family and their relatives. Thomas Robinson, a distinguished diplomat, married Frances, daughter of Sir Thomas Worsley of Yorkshire. The heir, Thomas (Tommy), was born in Vienna, 1738, Frances (Fanny) in 1758. The birth dates of the other girls are not recorded. They were Anne (the second), called Nanny, Mary (Molly) and Therese or Teresa.

The letters show a remarkably lively interest in the children's welfare, from birth onwards. Thomas Robinson and Frances were the most devoted of parents, and their initial joy is well expressed in the following letter.

(a) A BIRTH

Vienna Dec. 3rd N.S. 1738

Dearest Sister—Your Fanny is at last a Mother. All safe, all happy. She could not be brought to bed on Thursday the 16th of last month old stile, as she had promised on her father's birth day. On the Sunday morning; at six of the clock things began to be serious. At half an hour after eleven at night, her forces were almost exhausted, but she gave one effort more, and that effort gave me the finest boy imaginable. This is the third day & she & her Tommy are as well as can be expected . . .

Fanny was a Heroine, oh she is the loveliest creature alive!

Your most affectionate of Brothers   T. Robinson

NEWBY HALL PAPERS, 2824/38

D

(b) SMALL-POX

Small-pox was endemic throughout the eighteenth century.

Hovingham. Jan^{ry} ye 16 1738

My Dearest Dear Sister ... My Father is so afraid of ye little girl that because of ye small pox is in York he dare not let us go, which reason will hold good this twenty year for to be shure it is never out.

NEWBY HALL PAPERS, 2825/2

(c) FIRST STEPS

March 25 1739 N.S.

Your letter ... gave me more pleasure than you can imagine: besides, how should I know any thing of that sweet little Nanny if you did not tell me. a Dear little Creature: I see her walk like Mrs Wombal with her frock all gathered to gether I have thought much of her ever since I got your letter. does she walk without strings yet? What does she eat? Pray, tell me every thing.

NEWBY HALL PAPERS, 2825/22

(d)

April 3rd

O that I could but be with my Dearest sister this summer to take care of her Chickins & sit with her when Hubby goes out, Little Anna runs quite alone, she has A string at her back tho sum times she wont totch it, she has more conciet then you can imagine any thing of her age, I was laid down yesterday upon her bed against she come up & pretend'd to be asleep, so she comes by her own self looks at me A while then kiss's me but I w:d not wake so then kiss's again & fell A stroking & said in her way poor Sissy, poor Sissy for an hour together—was not this pretty—perhaps I may tell you sum pretty storry of Mahomet for we are going to the Turkish History now, but where ever we go or whatever I do I allways am My Dearest Sister's sincerely   EW.

NEWBY HALL PAPERS, 2825/27

(e) MAY DAY

... to day being ye first of May Nurse has drest Nanny in flowers from head to foot in imatation of your Picture, & put her on A

corenit of flowers & call her the Queen of May, you never saw any
thing look so pretty; kiss my little Newphy for his Aunt Ellsebeth . . .

NEWBY HALL PAPERS, 2825/31

(f) TEETHING

Beverley June yᵉ 15 [1739]

. . . I am very glad to hear my Little Nephew is so well. it is not att
all worse for him that he has got no teeth yet for he will have more
strength to go through with it, in case he shou'd cut e'm with any
difficulty. you must expect some disorder when ever it happens so
I hope you won't make yʳ self uneasy if one can prevent fits one has
not much to fear, & if ye Child be strong & healthy I think there is
no sort of Danger of them, I wou'd advise you to give him very
Gentle openers if you find he wants them which most Children
does at that time. I don't mean by way of Physick but some innocent thing to drink a Little of sometimes that will keep him cooll &
free from any feaverish disorder.

NEWBY HALL PAPERS, 2825/41

(g) FEVER

Quinine, 'the bark' or cinchona, was introduced to Europe by the
Jesuits in the sixteenth century, and its use popularized by Sydenham,
1624–89, who specialized in the study and cure of fevers, which included typhoid and malaria.

Nov: yᵉ 15ᵗʰ [1739]

My Dear Lady Fanny it is very near the Birth Day of yr little
Cupid, . . . Poor little Nanny has had two terrible fits of intermitting, was in a high feavour for about twelve hours each time,
she has took Decoctions of yᵉ Bark & a Solution of yᵉ Extract since
Saturday, & missd her fit Yesterday, it was every third Day which is
worse then every other Day, poor thing she is to take her febrifuge
three times a Day sometime longer, tis a terrible affair for she Crys
every time she expects it, and only gets it swallowd from fearing
she shall be whipd. what can she think of us to see us all in a
Combination either to let her be ill, or Poyson her or Whip her
three things she has never been usd. to, but yᵉ piece of treachery
yᵗ hurt me the most was waking her in the Night with kisses and
good words, & then having yᵉ Cup & Rod appear from behind the

Curtain, she has 17 or 18 teeth, & two or three more a cutting which helpt to make her worse, but now all is better. Adieu. I love you A.W.

NEWBY HALL PAPERS, 2825/70

(h)

Nanny said yesterday not to beat her and when she would not be drest, but if she would but come again she would stand still, what would I give y^r you did but see this dear Little Creature, she is a Comical Monkey, . . .

NEWBY HALL PAPERS, 2825/76

9. NEWBY HALL LETTERS

As children's names were duplicated in the various branches of the Worsley and Robinson families, it is not always possible to be certain which children are being referred to in the subsequent letters. However, it would appear that Molly and Tommy Robinson paid a visit to the Worsleys at Hovingham in the 1740s.

(a) RICKETS

1740

Dukky continue's being A fine boy, very senceable & strong, Molly is fine Red & White, Tommy like Molly only A largeer face & head, had A bad Nurse that suckel'd him but did not excersize him enough so that he is rather Recetty, he understands every thing one bids him but wont attempt to speak one word, Rose is A fine fat flubby black eye'd Girl with A great deal of spirit . . .

NEWBY HALL PAPERS, 2826/4

(b)

Little Nanny was at church last Sunday for the first time, call'd out that ye Parson was in his shift, tell Nurse . . .

(c) WHIPPING

6 July, 1740

I receiv'd my Dear Sisters to day, which rejoyc'd me much to find that Tommy was well for about ten days ago M. Robinson writes A most frightful letter that he wd. not go to bed but cry'd sadly & that you & he was greatly alarm'd; but glad I am that whipping him, & Polly's tears was A cure.

NEWBY HALL PAPERS, 2826/6

(d) FAMILY NEWS

October ye 12 [1740]

To
  Mrs Robinson
        at
            Vienna

ye 7 Sep^b:^{r}

I went to Beverley last week for one night to bring Molly & Tommy home with me she is A very fine girl with a great spirrit but so troublesumly fond of me that I cant stir out of the room without her, If you was to come into the dining room at Six A clock till Seven you wd: think it Bedlam for that hour we dedicate to the Children their Sets the Old Grandfather Looking on with as much pleasure as you can imagine . . .

NEWBY HALL PAPERS, 2826/16

(e)

ye 21 of De^b:^{r}

Miss Constable had been very ill all night in A fevor up I got & found her with every Symptom of the Small pox, then Miss Nanny began & tho she was not one half as ill yet my Father fancy'd she wd: dye of A mortifycation in her bowels, such chemiras we have at our house, all the Children in the Country has been in the same way, but I must tell you that it is only girls so you may be easy about your little Tommy. I wipt Tom twice this Morning for saying he wd: not do what I bid him & yet he loves me better than any thing & wd: never be out of my arms so you may imagine I humour him sum-times, he is vastly improve'd since he came hear.

E Worsley

NEWBY HALL PAPERS, 2826/22

10. THE FOUNDLING HOSPITAL

(a) Thomas Coram

Thomas Coram was born at Lyme Regis in 1668. After a venturesome career as the captain of a vessel trading to the colonies he retired. It is said that he was so moved by the sight of foundlings abandoned in London that he determined to open a Foundling Hospital. In spite of his lack of influence and limited means, his persistence, and warm-hearted sincerity finally enabled him to achieve his object. A royal Charter for the incorporation of the Hospital was granted in 1739. Coram continued to take a personal interest in the foundlings to the end of his life. In his old age his income was completely depleted by his benevolence, and he lived on a 'subscription' of about £100 a year. His greatest pleasure at the close of his life was to sit out of doors in fine weather and give little comfits to the foundlings.

First Publication for Admittance in 1741

'The Governors and Guardians of the Hospital for the maintenance and education of exposed and deserted young children, do hereby give notice.

That on   next, the   of   at   at night, and from that time until the house is full, their house over against the charity-school in *Hatton-Garden*, will be opened for the reception of children, under the following regulations:

That no child exceeding the age of two months is to be taken in.

Nor any such as have the French-Pox, Evil, Leprosy, or disease of the like nature, whereby the health of other children may be endangered.

When *notice* shall be affixed over the door, That the House is full, all persons having children not received, are to return with them, without dropping any by the way.

If any particular marks, writing, or other thing, shall be left with a child, great care will be taken for the preservation thereof: and each child will be baptized according to the rites of the church of England, and by a minister of that church, if it does not appear to his satisfaction, that such child has been before baptized.'

Form of a Receipt for a Child and the Clothes

Received of the Governors and Guardians of exposed and deserted young children, a   child, named   together with

	l.	s.	d.
2 cheque linen cloths to pin before, at 6d. each	0	1	0
3 caps, at 6d. each	0	1	6
3 shirts, at 9d. each	0	2	3
1 linsey coat	0	2	2

Which clothes I promise to deliver to the said Governors and Guardians, or allow the value of such of them as shall be lost, out of my wages, at the prices above-mentioned; and that the said child shall be maintained by me at the rate of   a week, so long as the said Governors and Guardians shall think proper, in the parish of   in the county of   .

JONAS HANWAY, *Letters on the Importance of the Rising Generation*, p. 152

(b)

Publication in regard to the ragged naked Condition in which some Children were brought.

'Whereas many children, who have been brought to this Hospital, were almost naked, and have appeared to have violent colds, and other distempers, supposed to have been contracted for want of proper clothing; and it being suspected, that such children have been stripped of their clothing by the persons who have been instructed to bring them to the Hospital: *This is to give notice,* That any person who shall be detected in stripping any such child or children of their clothing, or any part thereof, shall be prosecuted at the expense of this *Corporation* with the utmost severity.'

Signed by the SECRETARY.

JONAS HANWAY, *Letters on the Importance of the Rising Generation*, pp. 161 and 163.

(c)

. . . one of the earliest regulations of the Hospital, that persons leaving children should 'affix on them some particular writing, or other distinguishing mark or token.'

Very early notes are:

'A female child, aged about six weeks, with a blue figured ribbon, and purple and white printed linen sleeves, turned up with red and white.'

'A male child, about a fortnight old, very neatly dressed; a fine holland cap, with a cambric border, edged biggin and forehead-cloth, diaper bib, striped and flowered dimity mantle and another holland one; India dimity sleeves, turned up with stitched holland, damask waistcoat, holland ruffled shirt.'

The recording clerk was laconic at times. Of one of the children he merely says:

A paper on the breast—
Clout on the head.

R. H. NICHOLS and F. A. WRAY, *The History of the Foundling Hospital*, pp. 119 and 121

11. JOHN WESLEY (CONT.)

Tues. 8 [March, 1743] In the afternoon I preached on a smooth part of the fell, near Chowden. I found we were got into the very Kingswood of the North. Twenty or thirty wild children ran round us, as soon as we came, staring as in amaze. They could not properly be said to be either clothed or naked. One of the largest, (a girl about fifteen,) had a piece of a ragged, dirty blanket, some way hung about her, and a cap on her head, of the same colour. My heart was exceedingly enlarged towards them.

THE JOURNAL OF THE REV. JOHN WESLEY, A. M., Vol. I, p. 416

12. SIR HORACE WALPOLE

Letters from Sir Horace Walpole to Sir Horace Mann

(a)

Arlington Street, April 25, 1743

. . . I must tell you an odd thing that happened yesterday at Leicester-House. The Prince's children were in the circle: Lady Agatha heard somebody call Sir Robert Rich by his name. She concluded there was but one Sir Robert in the world, and taking him for Lord Orford, the child went staring up to him, and said, 'Pray, where is your blue string? and pray what has become of your fat belly?' Did one ever hear of a more royal education, than to have rung this mob cant in the child's ears till it had made this impression on her!

PETER CUNNINGHAM (ed.), *The Letters of Horace Walpole*, p. 407

(b)

Arlington Street, Nov. 29, 1745

. . . A ridiculous thing happened when the Princess saw com-

pany: the new-born babe was shown in a mighty pretty cradle, designed by Kent, under a canopy in the great drawing-room. Sir
William Stanhope went to look at it; Mrs. Herbert, the governess,
advanced to unmantle it: he said, 'In wax, I suppose.'—'Sir!'—
'In wax, Madam?'—'The young Prince, Sir.'—'Yes, in wax, I
suppose.' This is his odd humour: when he went to see this Duke
at his birth, he said, 'Lord: it sees!'

> PETER CUNNINGHAM (ed.), *The Letters of Horace Wal-*
> *pole*, p. 407.

13. NEWBY HALL (CONT.)

All the Robinson children are now together with their mother Frances
(Fanny) on the continent. The following letters to their father give a
vivid impression of their experiences and hopes to be reunited with him.

(a) THE '45'

Letter from E. Worsley to Lady Robinson at Vienna

write I must to my Dear Sister to let
her see we are in the Land of the liveing, tho what Account to give
of us I hardly know, by today's Post the Duke is in full pursuit of
them [the rebels] & we in great hopes of his comeing up with them
not fearing A good Account if they do but stand A Battle, if the
get back to Scotland their is so manny more rose in their interest
since they Left it, that it will be A very Long Affair, they commit
terrible outrages now, besides raising great sum's of Monny. My
Sis: Constable can think nor write of nothing else, as an Instance
of it her Eldest is in the Small Pox which she has wrote me word
of to day after writeing down tow sides of Papper about the Rebells
she says in a Poscript that Dukky is Quit well again, & that she
expects every day that rest of the Children will fall ill for they are
in the room all day; Mrs Aisalbie is hear drove from York with
the Panick that seize'd all People upon hearing the Rebells was in
full March for Leeds,
God bless you all great & small, belive I love you
& am Sincerely yours
E. Worsley

Hov: Decbr: ye 15.

NEWBY HALL PAPERS, 2830/18

(b)

Dear Papa,
Yesterday Princess Trautsohn's Secretary came here with a box
& said that the Archdutchess Marianne sent it us, & we opened it &
we found some flowers, & under the flowers three Purses, the one
marked Tomy, which I opened & found a China Snuf Box, & in
this Box a piece of Paper which I thought of no Consequence, but
when I opened it, I was astonished to find a Diamont Ring. Fanny
found another Purse marked Fany, she opened it & found a golden
Snufbox, Nanny found a Purse, with a Patch box composed of
two Shells & a King with Diamonds. & afterwards we went to the
Opera Boufon Orazio. I put on my Ring, & gave imaginary snuf
to several people. Having nothing more to say I am
  Dear Papa,

> Your most obedient
> & dutiful Son,
> T. Robinson

NEWBY HALL PAPERS, 2833/39

(c)

Dear Papa
As I arrived at Würtzbourg I saw the Bishops Palace, Prince
Eugenes House at Vienna is a Hen House to this, I saw in a room
there a Cabinet of Amber, a tree of Coral, & a Statue of Abraham
of one piece of Ivory, & the Chair in which late Bishop Schönburn
died, his bed & the bed where the Empress lay in going to Francfort.
I overtook my Sisters, who will be here to day. I hope Dear Papa I
will soon have the pleasure of seeing you, in the mean while I am
                    Dear Papa,

> Your most obedient
> & most dutiful Son
> T. Robinson

NEWBY HALL PAPERS, 2833/60

Fanny writes to her husband on the journey back to England. The
eventual arrival of the whole family is described in the letters which
follow. The intense devotion of the parents to one another, as well as
to their children, is touchingly recorded in no. 2834/9. Subsequently the
letters present a record of the vicissitudes of the Robinson family in
England.

(d) TRAVELLING

my Dear Soul I am just got to Lints we are all sadly tierd but very well the Children dont like seting so long in the Coach, tho I make them get out some times and walk, I dread the roads from here. God preserve the my life and bring thy Fanny soon and safe to thee

Dear Papa I am not so tired but can let you know that I am glad I am glad be so much nearer you   T.R.

and so am I too my Dear Papa   A.R.

NEWBY HALL PAPERS, 2833/52

(e)

A letter from T. Robinson to his sister-in-law

Aix, Jan. 7, 1749 NS

Dearest Sister—I have to return to England & shall have a seat at the board of trade & in St. Stephen's Chappel. I was so desirous of quitting my foreign employments, that the smallest of my children set out to morrow morning for Calais, & your Fanny with me & the two eldest follow them on Saturday next . . .

NEWBY HALL PAPERS, 2834/2

(f) SAFE LANDING

From a letter from Frederick Frankland to T.R.

. . . a messenger's arrival in the afternoon & telling me you was attach't and ordered to Antwerp, & y^t the five younger children all landed safely the Night before . . . I hope to send you word next post of your Little Cargoe being safely Housed & well . . .

NEWBY HALL PAPERS, 2834/4

(g)

Letter from F.F. to T.R.

It is with great pleasure I can tell you & my Niece y^t the dear Little Cargoe arrived safe yesterday noon at their Hotel in Convent Garden. To morrow I am to have the pleasure of giving them Small Soup, Pudding & Chicken, in Spring Garden . . . I hear they are quite well this morning & y^t Miss Therese's cold does not encrease & is only a little running at the nose.

NEWBY HALL PAPERS, 2834/5

(h) From a letter from F.F. to T.R.

Jan. 16, 1748 O.S.

As no letters have come . . . I am a little at a loss where to find you . . . but y^t I saw all the Babbys this morning full of play & very brisk, tho every one has a slight cold, & running at ye nose . . .

NEWBY HALL PAPERS, 2834/6

(i)

Spencer the Messenger brought me this morning the agreeable news of your safe arrival at Calais . . . I was this morning in Convent Garden & found the four eldest all alert & merry, their colds much better, their appetites good. Little Betty's Cold is not so well, & she is about Teeth which makes her rather fevorish, but I see nothing in her that at all alarms me . . .

NEWBY HALL PAPERS, 2834/8

(j) Letter from Thomas Robinson to his son-in-law

We landed your dear Fanny the two eldest and myself the Day before yesterday . . . in the afternoon after a passage of five hours, and some danger in passing out of the ship into a boat which was to carry her a shore. Fanny said to the sailor who lifted her out, take no care of me, but there are two children behind, only take care of them. Fanny & I agreed not to be drowned but with one another.

Ever y^rs   T.R.

NEWBY HALL PAPERS, 2834/9

(k) SCHOOLING

Abingdon Mar. 1 1748 O.S.

Sr

Taking this place in my way homeward I pay a short visit to y^r son—you will not expect many remarkable occurrences in ye history of two or three days: yet his setting out in this new scene of life, considering ye circumstances of his Education is somewhat singular. He at once plung'd into ye midst of matters, with an uncommon spirit, pursuing his new diversions & studies with equal alacrity—

wild among his Playfellows, yet in school observing a strict decorum; he is placed with those who read Cornelius Nepos &ᶜ in yᵉ school;

I am yʳ oblig'd humble friend

John Burton.

NEWBY HALL PAPERS, 2834/21

(l)

Abingdon 6ᵐᵉ Mars 1748 O.S.-9

Monsieur mon très cher Pere &
Madame ma tres chere Mere,

Cette lettre est pour vous convaincre combien Je fais d'attention à l'Ordre que vous me fites de vous ecrire toutes les Semaines. J'ai le plaisir de vous assurer que je suis parfaitement content de ma situation, & que la campagne m'agrée que les brouillards de Londres. Je sais deja jouer au Criquet & a Bandy mais parmi mes plaisirs je ne doit pas oublier ce qui vous fera plus de plaisir. J'ai l'honneur de vous apprendre que Mʳ woods me fait la Grace de me louer & dit que je n'ai besoin ni de bride ni d'eperons & m'a mis presque à la tete de la seconde Claisse qui aulieu d'etre la plus proche des plus petits enfans est las plus proche meilleurs ecoliers. Je vous prie d'avoir la bonté de donner mille & mille baiser à toute la petite famille. J'ai l'honneur d'etre de

Monsieur mon trés cher Pere &
Madame ma tres chere Mere

Le tres respectueux &
tres obeissant Fils.

Thomas Robinson

NEWBY HALL PAPERS, 2834/24

(m) From a letter from Thomas Woods (schoolmaster)

Abingdon Sept. 21ˢᵗ 1749

I esteem myself greatly honoured by being favoured with the Care of Master Robinson's Education . . . Tis a pleasure to me, to find in Master so strict a regard to Honour & Veracity, & a Sense of his Duty to God & Man rarely to be found with in a Gentleman of his age . . .

NEWBY HALL PAPERS, 2834/36

(n)

Monsieur mon très cher Pere

Comme j'ai voiagé 47 miles d'Angleterre à cheval il est bien juste que je vous dise quelques choses de mes Voiages. Par votre permission je suis allé à maple Durham ou je restai 4 ou 5 jours. aprés je suis revenu de Maple Durham ou je me suis tant diverti, à Abingdon ou je demandai permission d'aller á Oxford qui est une magnifique Ville.

comme j'y suis arrivé j'ai d'abord vu Magdalene College qui est un assez beau Batiment mais Queens College est bien plus beau il y a des arcades en front, il y a tant de belles choses qu'il faut les remettre à un autre fois en attendant je suis

Monsieur Trés honoré Pere

Votre trés humble
& tres obeissant Serviteur
T. Robinson

NEWBY HALL PAPERS, 2834/28

(o) Letter from T. Woods

I was much pleas'd to hear . . . that you intended to take the Opportunity of sending Mr. to wait on his Relations in Yorkshire . . . When Mr Walker Masters Chum was sent for to Town to see the Fireworks (which tho I did not approve of, yet could not prevent) I put Master into a more commodious Room. His Bedfellow is Lord Traceys Son, & the other two Chums the two Seniors of the school, All of them very good and studiously inclined, whose examples will excite him to Diligence & direct his Conduct.

NEWBY HALL PAPERS, 2834/43

(p)

London, the 16 Decembre. 1749

Hond. Madam,

I hope that you will excuse the Liberty I take in writing this letter to you, for I thought it proper, to let you know, I was come to Town. I was last night at the latin Play at Westminster & am to night to go to that at Covent Garden. Mama says I shall go to no more, till I am inoculated, & that you all think I am afraid of it, but I assure you I am not, & wish I was inoculated for I am pretty sure that it is very useful as well to my Sisters as to me & Fritz.

Pray be so kind as to pay my Respects to my Grandpapa, to all my Aunts & Uncles. I have nothing more to say to you at present. But I am.

Hon^d Madam

Your most obedient &
most dutiful Grandson.
Thomas Robinson.

NEWBY HALL PAPERS, 2834/104

(q) INOCULATION

Letter from Ann Worsley

Jan: ye 13th 1749–50

We fancyd the dear Children had been inoculated this week & y^t you would not let us know, surely delivering children from a lasting fear, and from having their Eyes health & faces spoilt, besides saveing perhaps their lives, is ye greatest kindness one can do em. . . God bless Dear Fanny and all the Pocky babes, how shall we all be for em this Day fortnight I hope.

NEWBY HALL PAPERS, 2835/7

(r)

January 10 1749–50

I take pen in hand quite jaded in the house of commons quite alone in my own for the little ones left me last week & Fanny yesterday. I sent her & the three eldest all blooded together the day before yesterday.   T.R.

NEWBY HALL PAPERS, 2835/8

(s)

London   J. 23 1749 [O.S.]

As the critical moments come on apace I shall let you know by every post how things proceed in Albemarle Street. They were inoculated on the 17th Inst. and they are not to go down stairs any more to their Mama. It was thought last night that Therese was beginning but I suppose two or three of them will begin tomorrow.

Fanny has given the least proof as yet that the inoculation has taken
place.   T.R.

> NEWBY HALL PAPERS, 2835/11

(t)

By what I can gather from my Wife's letter Tommy & Molly must
have the distemper. She says *Tommy is in a very good way, sleeps a
great deal—Molly also—Nanny is beginning and is gone to bed.*
                                                                         J: 25.

> NEWBY HALL PAPERS, 2835/13

(u)

It is with difficulty that I find this moment to tell you that Tommy
has a good many out & of a fine large sort. Fanny is in bed, but it is
not sure that hers will take place. Nanny has a good many out;
Molly's are expected to be out this evening. Therese too has some out,
but Fritz is in Molly's case as yet.

> NEWBY HALL PAPERS, 2835/15

(v)

L. Feb 3ᵈ 1749 O.S. ... now I can only add that the 5
children are as well as they ever were in their lives & are to be
physicked to morrow for the first time. Fanny has been inoculated
again; if it does not take, she will at least have double reason to
flatter herself she will never have it at all.

                                                                  yʳ T.R.

> NEWBY HALL PAPERS, 2835/7

(w)

                                                                         Feb 6

... My two boys & the three youngest girls are so well that they
will dine to day below stairs with their Mama. As to Fanny, she has
been reinoculated, ..
PS. I can only add that all are prefectly well in Albemarle Street
& that fanny will probably go thither tonight in order to lye in.
Little Fanny lye in. Oh Comical!

                                                          Ever yʳˢ   TR

> NEWBY HALL PAPERS, 2835/19

(x)

F. 8

Tommy only of those that took the distemper remains something weak, but this they say is common & will be rectifyed by fresh air.

Ever & Ever y^{rs}

Fanny may still have it, but they will not *pronounce* before Sunday. Tommy too is better.

NEWBY HALL PAPERS, 2835/20

(y)

F 17

. . . poor Nanny is at last out of danger. My little ones are gone to day to Kinsington.

NEWBY HALL PAPERS, 2835/21

(z)

Febry 13

Fanny Jemmy & I, we had our first rendezvous in the Park. My little Fanny is yet persuaded she shall never have the small-pox: all the others we persuaded they have had it.

NEWBY HALL PAPERS, 2835/27

(aa)

April 10

Tommy's meazles go off as churlishly as they came on, his cough abates but slowly; the eldest girl ill at Kensington. Adieu, pity us, for we are terribly alarmed. . .

NEWBY HALL PAPERS, 2835/41

(bb) TEETH

[1750]

Nothing is so terrible as Nanny's accident. . . At Paris they would pull them all out if there was a danger of the others, but the false ones are never white and of little use in eating. If you ever think of a false one, the stump must be left to fix it upon. The great business is to take as great & as early care as possible of the rest and that is not to be done by tampering with powder & brushes. The best method is to keep the mouth constantly cool by washing it every morning and after every meal & in going to bed, with luke warm water & especially to clean them gently every morning the moment one wakes with a soft dimaty cloth or a piece of cotton dipt in water, from the root downwards in the upper jaw, and from the root upwards in the under jaw . . . but what is no less important is the keeping the tongue & the gums equally fresh, which is done, the first by scraping it the moment one wakes with a thin piece of whalebone, the other by wrenching them often with as cold water as one can bear.

PS.   Fritz says he is a child of God & an inheritor of the Kingdom of Heaven.

NEWBY HALL PAPERS, 2835/42

(cc) ILLNESSES

Ap. 21.   1750

. . . Tommy not recovered of the effects of the meazels, & at Kensington in a separate lodging that he may not impart his cough, which has been deemed a chincough to the others. Fanny is just recovered of the Meazles of a more favourable sort. Nanny Therese & Fred all in bed, but of a favourable sort too: while we tremble for little Molly not knowing whether it would be best or worst for her to take them.

NEWBY HALL PAPERS, 2835/43

(dd)

Kensington   April 17

We are all here together, tho the young man is in a separate lodging at the next door, & must get rid of what is called his Hooping cough before he sees his Sister & Fritz. But poor Molly does not want this additional tryal of her strength. We cannot say she is better for this fine air. Perhaps she will go with her Mamma to Tunbridge.

NEWBY HALL PAPERS, 2835/47

14. NEWBY HALL (CONT.)

In spite of an apparent improvement in her health, and a visit to salubrious Tunbridge Wells, Fanny died. Thomas Robinson writes of his loss with moving resignation. Further demands on his fortitude were made by another tragedy which took place almost immediately afterwards.

(a) DEATH

1750

My dearest sister—I should have answered your kind offers of the
12th about my little ones... In the mean while they make a little
school together, & live as if they were in a boarding house. God bless
them. *I have dedicated myself to their service.*

NEWBY HALL PAPERS, 2835/100

(b) MOURNING

London November 23. 1750

Dear Sir

I received last night your favour of the 20 Ins^t. It was and
I said it in my first letter to my sister, impossible for me to write to
you upon the subject you touch upon. We have nothing left but to
mix our tears, you for such a daughter I for such a Wife as never
fell to the lot of any men. My sole care now turns upon the Babes,
and no care shall they want. Poor Molly will I believe go to
Mr Hawkin's at Kensington for the present, and if all goes tolerably
with her till spring, she shall accept of your kind offer.
truly and more tenderly than I am

Dear sir

Your most obedient

& most faithfull affectionate servant

T. Robinson

NEWBY HALL PAPERS, 2835/101

(c)

December 10 1750

Molly has been very ill, but is now something better at Kensington.
We all think she cannot hold, so that we are forewarned—

January 5. 1751 [N.S.]

My dearest dear sister. Must not I wish you a happy New Year.
The last was a terrible one—but let its own Veil cover it. Adieu
Ever & Ever y^{rs}   T.R.

NEWBY HALL PAPERS, 2835/104

(d)

Whitehall. January 15. 1751

My dearest sister   My wound is opening again with the opening of
the vault at Chiswick for my poor Molly! The dear Child *went out*
Yesterday, & it seems only to have been reserved some days to
blacken the account of *this* year too.   Ever y^{rs} T.R.

NEWBY HALL PAPERS, 2835/105

(e) SURVIVAL

February 19 [1751]

Tommy does very well at School, and the rest are the best little
babes in the World. Fritz grows surprisingly clever. They are now
with their dancing master, afterwards they step into the Park, & at
noon have their writing master.

My Tommy is still at home & been bled thrice & has always a
blister on his back; but the Doctor flatters me he will do well . . .

NEWBY HALL PAPERS, 2835/113 and 119

After the death of Molly the bereaved father encouraged his remaining children to develop forward-looking attitudes, and the many letters
which they wrote to him subsequently are natural, lively and even gay.
Only the following betrays anxiety at parental disapproval.

(f)

Stanmer   Decbr. 6th. 1758

My Dear Papa

Mrs Pelham received a letter from my Uncle
to day wherin he mentions your being uneasy at my having won so
much money at Kidbrook . . . I cannot help writing to excuse myself
as I should never have thought of playing if Mr Pelham had not
gone my halves as it was only at penny Loo altho' it chanced to run
so very high & Mrs Pelham thought we could not well avoid it.
Mrs Pelham went Thereses halves & she won to her share two
Guineas & I won ten, Therese & I shall certainly not play on any
account as I would much rather forego any amusement especially so

trifling a one than run the least risque of displeasing you which I
hope you will always belive of

Dear Papa
your most affectionate
& Dutifull Daughter
Ann Robinson

NEWBY HALL PAPERS, 2836/27

15. IMPROVEMENT OF THE MIND

Isaac Watts was born in 1674 and died in 1748. His interesting *Discourse on the Education of Children and Youth* was published posthumously. His parents were Nonconformist; he became an eminent preacher at Mark Lane chapel in London. He wrote both doctrinal and educational treatises and wrote more than five hundred hymns, some of which remain popular to this day.

(a)

A Guard against Evil Influences from Persons and Things.

Let not nurses or servants be suffered to fill their minds with silly
tales and with senseless rhimes, many of which are so absurd and
ridiculous that they will not bear to be represented in a grave
discourse.

Let not any persons that are near them terrify their tender minds
with dismal stories of witches and ghosts, of devils and evil spirits,
of fairies and bugbears in the dark.

Nor let their little hearts be frighted at three or four years old
with shocking and bloody histories, with massacres and martyrdoms,
with cuttings and burnings, with the images of horrible and barbarous murders, with racks and red hot pincers, with engines of
torment and cruelty, with mangled limbs, and carcases drenched in
gore. It is time enough, when their spirits are grown a little firmer,
to acquaint them with these madnesses and miseries of human
nature.

Let their ears be ever kept all immodest stories and from wanton
songs: from riddles and puns with double meanings and four intentions: Let them not be suffered to read wanton jests or amorous
romances: Nor let their eyes be entertained with lewd and unclean

pictures, and images of things or actions that are not fit to be exposed...

ISAAC WATTS, *The Improvement of the Mind*, p. 151

(b)

On proper degrees of liberty and restraint in the education of daughters.

Sometimes a too rigid confinement will have the contrary effect, and make the impatience of youth break out beyond all bounds, as soon as ever they get the first relish of freedom.

ISAAC WATTS, *The Improvement of the Mind*, p. 204

16.   EFFECTS OF OPIUM

The use of opium was widespread in Europe during the eighteenth century. It was used to cure or alleviate a variety of conditions in adults, children and infants. Opium administered to a mother in the last stages of childbirth can be dangerous to the newly born infant. They are very susceptible to the toxic effects of morphine during the first two or three weeks of life, and after this period the dose would have to be calculated with great care to avoid fatal results.

(a)

Some children are crammed every day by their fond mothers with a variety of sweet-meats, and perserves. To those, when their digestion is quite spoiled, we often add many stomachic draughts; and all this betwixt their meals, at which they are never stinted. A constant looseness is the usual effect: in which case, if the mother conceals the confects and restoratives from the knowledge of the doctor, he will be too apt to prescribe *diascordium* or *laudanum*, when chalk and water, with a spare diet, would be much more proper.

GEORGE YOUNG, M.D., A Treatise on Opium, p. 38

(b) *Of the effects of opium in the* diarrhoea, *attending the weaning-illness of children.*

The weaning-illness of infants is often attended with a *diarrhoea*, which is probably owing to their change of diet from breast-milk to spoon-meat: the best way of preventing it is, to accustom the children, for some months before their weaning, to such diet as differs least from breast-milk, and to wean them gradually. But if notwithstanding a looseness comes on, four or five drops of liquid *laudanum*, with the absorbent powders, given every night in any convenient form, will seldom fail, unless after eating too much; for an opiate always disagrees with a plentiful meal.

GEORGE YOUNG, M.D., *A Treatise on Opium*, p. 40

(c)

Of the effects of opium in the milk-fever.

Altho' the grinding-pains after delivery require opium, yet the milk-fever, which comes about the third day, will not admit of the continued use of it.

GEORGE YOUNG, M.D., *A Treatise on Opium*, p. 65

(d)

Of the effects of opium in the rickets and scrophula.

I have seen many scrophulous and rickety children, who, after weaning, and rarely before, became weak, pale, and chill; and they commonly had a violent *diarrhoea* at the time of breeding their teeth: but tho' there was a variety in their cases, their ages, and regimen, yet from experience I was convinced, that four or five drops of *liquid laudanum*, or more, given every night, was of great service to them; especially if they had pains in the belly with looseness, as is often the case.

In order to keep weakly children in tolerable health, steel and Peruvian bark are useful, and their diet and regimen must be carefully attended to; it should consist in part of flesh-meat, and the drink should be chalk and water mixed with wine.

GEORGE YOUNG, M.D., *A Treatise on Opium*, p. 117

(e)

Of the effects of opium in the measles.

... there is one symptom in the measles, which is as inseparable as the eruption itself, (I mean the dry tickling cough) for which opium is an excellent medicine, though only a palliative; indeed a palliative is all that can be required, because this symptom is not to be cured 'till the measles are gone.

GEORGE YOUNG, M.D., *A Treatise on Opium*, p. 155

17. THE MARINE SOCIETY

Jonas Hanway

Jonas Hanway was a model philanthropist. He was born at Portsmouth in 1712 and died in 1786. He began a prosperous mercantile career at the age of 17 in Lisbon. He then went to Russia and Persia. While he was living at St. Petersburg a legacy, combined with his own ample means, enabled him to return to England. The rest of his life was spent in ameliorating the lot of the unfortunate. The Marine Society proved to be an enduringly successful venture. Its purpose was to find recruits for the navy, and equip them for their arduous career. The Foundling Hospital also interested him. The founding of the Magdalen Hospital also engaged his attention. Hanway also concerned himself with the welfare of the 'Infant parish poor', and travelled to France and Holland to learn the best methods of dealing with the problem. The publication of his findings resulted in the improvement of many workhouses. He was instrumental in obtaining two Acts relating to the keeping of records of admission and mortality among the infant poor in workhouses; the last was known among the poor as 'the Act for keeping children alive'. It is thought that his efforts resulted in the saving of many hundreds of lives.

(a)

XX   OF THE BOUNTY OF CLOTHING TO BOYS

The *quality*, *quantity*, and *kind*, have continued nearly the same ever since the first establishment of the SOCIETY.

G.

1 Felt-hat, with a cockade, and quality-binding.
2 Worster caps.
1 Blue kersey-jacket, with blue horn-buttons.
1 Waistcoat of blue half-thick, *ditto*.
1 Pair of drawers, *ditto*.
1 Pair of canvas-trousers.
1 Pair of yarn-hose.

2 Pair of shoes.

2 Handkerchiefs.

3 Check-shirts.

1 Ticken mattress.   1 *Ditto* pillow.   1 Blanket.   1 Coverlet.

1 Paper, containing 7 needles, 5 Balls of worsted, 2 Ounces of thread.

1 New testament.

1 Seaman's monitor,   1 *Dr. Synge's* christian knowledge, bound together.

1 Knife.   1 Pair of buckles.   1 Pair of buttons.   1 Haver-sack.

All the boys are clothed at the SOCIETY'S warehouse, over the *Royal Exchange*; . . .

No boy is clothed, without being seen, and examined by the SOCIETY. or their *secretary*, as to his *age, stature, health, parentage,* and if he is an *apprentice*, &c.

Such boys as are newly come in, and found to be in health, not having been *washed* and *cleansed* before they came to the *office, over the Royal Exchange*, are there made clean with *water* and towels prepared for that purpose, before they are clothed.

N.B. *The cast-off clothings are immediately disposed of as rags at the* SOCIETY'S *warehouse over the Royal Exchange.*

JONAS HANWAY, An Account of the Marine Society, p. 95

(b)

XXII.   OF THE INSTRUCTIONS TO THE OFFICERS, &c.

The instructions to the several *officers* of the SOCIETY; the letters addressed to the *captains*, requesting their *kindness* to, and *protection* of the boys; the *advice* to the *men*, and *instructions* to the boys, are the subjects next in course. And here it is necessary to observe, that several circumstances are mentioned relating to these regulations, which are not mentioned in any other place, as seeming most proper in the duty *required* of the *several officers*.

I.

Instructions to the SECRETARY, *and his duty.*

5. Some parents will also be desirous to send their *children to sea,* before they are of a *proper age, others* will endevor to prevent their

children's going to sea, when they have an inclination, and it is *fitting* for them to go. And, notwithstanding all possible care, it will sometimes happen, that a boy will *elude the vigilance of the* SOCIETY, by persisting that his parents do *consent* he should go to sea, when they do not; or that he is *no apprentice*, though he really is one.—— In these, and all other cases, you are to hear people with attention, and give them *friendly answers*, and inform the *committee* upon every difficult case; that all foundation for complaint may be removed. Above all things, you are to be careful, for the *honor* of the SOCIETY, not to violate the *rights* of any *parent* or *master*.

JONAS HANWAY, *An Account of the Marine Society*, p. 99

(c)

L.

Instructions to the PROVEDITOR of the boys, and his duty.

As you engage to take charge of such *lads* and *boys* as are *sent*, or *come* to you by means of the SOCIETY; you are to accommodate all such as apply to you, being under the description hereafter mentioned, till such time as the SOCIETY can conveniently send them to their respective ships.

1. You are to treat these boys *well*, particularly in the following instances. The rooms which they occupy must be kept *clean;* and you will also see that they use such *beddings* and *clothings* as the SOCIETY will furnish.

4. If any boy appears to be defective in *sight, lame, dwarfish*, or *labouring* under any *chronical* distemper, you are to give notice to one of our *secretaries*.

5. You are to put all *boys* who have the *itch*, into a *separate* apartment, the same of boys with *fevers*, or other curable distemper, and call in our *apothecary*, who will attend your house for such purposes.

6. Boys who have *foul bushy hair*, which only serves to disfigure them, or to harbour filth, you are desired to see it cut off, and wash their heads with *brandy*; proper care being taken, they can receive no harm; and you are to recommend to all the boys to *cut their hair off*, and they will be supplied with caps.

JONAS HANWAY, *An Account of the Marine Society*, p. 109

(d)

P.

The Fifer's credentials to his Admiral, or Captain, are as follows:

SIR,

Being informed that musicians are wanted in His Majesty's ships, and that they are of great service on board the fleet, the [Marine] SOCIETY intends that a certain number of boys shall be taught to play on the fife. It is presumed, this will be an introduction to their knowledge of other instruments, and answer other good purposes, at a moderate charge.

JONAS HANWAY, *An Account of the Marine Society*, p. 122

(e)

Advice of the *noblemen, gentlemen,* and *others,* called the MARINE SOCIETY, printed in a book presented, together with clothing to *landsmen* volunteers, when they enter in *London* for the *sea-service.*

My good lads,

As some of you are going into a way of life to which you have not been accustomed, and in which you may probably be exposed to some *temptations,* permit me to give you a few hints.

...9. In the mean while, remember that a DRUNKARD is worse than a beast; that he disables himself for every duty; and if he is overtaken in his drink, tho' he should not become a prey to his *enemy,* which often happens, yet he will certainly be punished by his *friends.*

10. The LIAR must be a villain; for he is an enemy even to his friends, and to all mankind as well as to himself: he endevors to deceive every one; and *every one* will be glad to see him severely punished for it.

11. THIEVING, you know, is punishable with great severity, even to death, and it is *more easily discovered in a ship, than on shore.* Besides, for men who engage in so noble a cause as the *fighting for their country,* to become *thieves* is shameful indeed, and they seldom pass without their just reward.

12. SWEARING, which some well-meaning men are subject to, is however abominably foolish and wicked.

13. WHORING is certainly forbidden by the christian law, and is punishable as a damnable sin, if *unrepented of*: and it certainly brings on *pain* and *diseases*. If you do not shun *bad women*, you must be sensible that you will *die in misery*; ...

JONAS HANWAY, *An Account of the Marine Society*, p. 135

18. THE FOUNDLING HOSPITAL

(a)

An Account of several Parts of this Kingdom, which have been found to be the least, and others the most fortunate in the Preservation of Infants, sent to nurse by the Hospital.

LETTER LI

Upon a critical inspection, I find the following places have proved the most mortal to the children of the Hospital; ... In regard to the following nurseries, being all of children of the same ages received and sent out in the course of about 5 years, by the Hospital, the facts stand thus:

County	Nursery	Number of children sent	Number dead	Dead per cent.
Kent	Charlton	108	73	67
Middlesex	Edmonton	157	136	86
	Kensington	72	58	80
	Knightsbridge	30	25	83
	Stoke Newington	24	18	75
	Bow	150	130	86
	Finchly	77	59	76
Surry	Camberwell	74	60	81
		692	559	80

The next greatest mortality is in capital towns, or in the neighbourhood of them, tho' far short of the villages about London, viz.

Nurseries in towns	Number of children sent	Dead	Per cent
Newbury	308	179	58
Reading	147	87	59
St. Albans	105	55	52
Barnet	204	104	51
Dorking	493	315	64
Farnham	325	177	54
	1582	917	58

The places where the *least* mortality of the hospital children has prevailed is in small villages about 40 miles round London, where the average number dead was 41 per cent.

JONAS HANWAY, *Letters on the Importance of the Rising Generation*, p. 211

(b)

5312.   Admitted August 2, 1757.

Sir

Here I am brought without a name
Im' sent to hide my mother's shame,
I hope you'll say, Im' not to Blame,
Itt, seems my mothers' twenty five,
and mattrymonys Laid a side
Why, what is to be Done
poor woman thatt Can nere say none
to men that make and Break the Law
'twas by that Law I Came
Increas and multiply was heavens command
and thats a Text my mother understands
I am a son, you are my Brother—
itt tis, no matter whos my mother,
in mattremony she was born—
tho now itt seems, tis held in scorn
Unless she has a mony^{d} purse
to give for better, or for worse
I am, but young, and cannot chew
Who shall be Chancellor, or I rew?

if I could speak, i^de tell you who
I^de Chuse for King and Country to
make me a man and I will fight
both for my King, and Country's Right
Which every Inglish man should do
for his own Rights and Countrys to
Blame not the woman that is week
When monarks are afraid to speak
their minds in truth, and so we find
that all mankind is of one mind.

Yours

Born 1st August 1757

R. H. NICHOLS and F. A. WRAY, *The History of the Foundling Hospital*, p. 121

CHAPTER 3
1760–1799

1. CHILDREN'S WORK AND WAGES

Arthur Young, the indefatigable traveller, noted that the *White-Lyon* inn at Bristol was 'good, but very dear'. He also recommends a visit to 'Mr. Champion's copper-works'.

(a)

They display the whole process; from the melting of the ore, to making it into pins, pans, etc. The wires are cut into them [pins] and compleated here, employing a great numbers of girls, who with little machines, worked by their feet, point and head them with great expedition; and will do a pound and a half in a day.

ARTHUR YOUNG, *A Six Weeks Tour through the Southern Counties of England and Wales*, p. 150

At Rotherham Young paused to note that no boys of under fourteen were employed at the 'foundery' there. Those of fourteen and over earned from 3*s*. to 4*s*. a week. Boys of nine and ten years old earned 2*s*. and 2*s*. 6*d*. a week at the pottery. The road from Rotherham to Sheffield was 'execrably bad, very stony, and excessively full of holes'.

(b)

In the plated work some hundreds of hands are employed; Girls earn 4*s*. 6*d*. and 5*s*. a week; some even to 9*s*. No men are employed that earn less than 9*s*. Their day's work including the hours of cessation, is thirteen . . .

Here is likewise a silk mill, which employs 152 hands, chiefly women and children; the women earn 5 or 6*s*. a week by the pound; girls at first are paid but 1*s*. or 1*s*. 2*d*. a week.

ARTHUR YOUNG, *A Six Months Tour through the North of England*, pp. 132 and 134

Young was primarily an observer of the agricultural scene. He mentions that the wages of a 'Lad of 13 or 14 years old' are 4*d*. a day, 'Boy of 10 or 12 years old' to 6*d*. per day. Upon coming to *Salisbury* he noticed the farms 'were in general extremely large'. Many farms kept from 300 to 3000 sheep and 50 horses. They kept about 20 men and boys in employment all the year. He then quotes the following figures:

(c)

DAY-LABOUR

In winter, and quite to harvest,	10*d*. a day
In harvest,	1*s*. 8*d*.
Reaping wheat,	5*s*. 0*d*. an acre
Mowing corn,	10*d*.
A boy of seven or eight years old,	2*d*.

IMPLEMENTS

A new waggon,	20 *l*.
A plough,	18*s*.

PROVISIONS

	d.
Bread,	2 *per lb*.
Butter,	7
Beef,	4
Cheese,	3

ARTHUR YOUNG, *A Six Weeks Tour through the Southern Counties of England and Wales*, p. 157

2.   EARN THEIR OWN BREAD

For many centuries, the woollen industry was second only to agriculture. The different processes had originally been carried out in the home, later on the premises of employers, and eventually in factories. From the earliest times the onus of providing clothing for the family had been the responsibility of the housewife, assisted by children, young people, and elderly dependants. The family linen was often woven from home-grown flax. But later in the eighteenth century wool was more readily available and it was easier to spin and weave than flax.

In the early part of the eighteenth century Defoe observes that:

(a)

We came to *Taunton* . . . One of the chief Manufacturers here told us, that they had eleven hundred Looms going for the weaving of Sagathies, Duroys, and such kind of Stuffs; He added, That there was not a Child in the Town, or in the Villages round it, of above five Years old, but, if it was not neglected by its Parents, and untaught, could earn its own Bread.

> DANIEL DEFOE, *A Tour thro' the Island of Great Britain*, Vol. II, p. 18

In 1767 Arthur Young visited Sudbury, 'an exceeding dirty, but a great Manufacturing town'. He was informed that the inhabitants

(b)

. . . possess a great number of hands, who earn their livelihood by working up the wool to the weaving it into says and burying-crape . . .; a stout girl of fifteen or sixteen, not being able to earn above 6*d.* a day; [for spinning] besides these articles they weave ship-flags, which employ the women, and girls of seven or eight years of age, yielding the latter about 2*s.* 6*d.* or 3*s.* a week.

He proceeds to Bocking and Braintree.

I found that they [the weavers] earned on an average about 9*s.* a week; stout girls, fifteen or sixteen years old, four-pence or five-pence a day at spinning; and girls of seven or eight 1*s.* a week for rolling the weavers' quills. They further informed me that in summer they did whatever husbandry-work they were able, such as hoeing turnips and wheat, making hay, and harvesting. That the prices of necessaries are as follows: bread 2*d. per* lb., mutton 5*d.*,

> ARTHUR YOUNG, *A Six Weeks Tour through the Southern Counties of England and Wales*, pp. 58 and 65

3. DISHONESTY

Tuesday 21 December [1762]. This evening I was passing by Whitehall when a little boy came and told a girl who sold ginger-bread nuts that he had just given her sixpence instead of a farthing. She denied this. Upon which the poor boy cried most bitterly. I thought myself bound to interfere. The boy affirmed the charge with the open keen look of conscious innocence, while the young jade denied it with the bitterness of expression that betrayed guilt. But what could be done? There was no proof. At last I put it to this test: 'Will you say, Devil take you, if you got his sixpence?' This

imprecation the little gipsy roared out twice most fervently. Therefore she got off. The boy was in very great distress. I asked him if
the sixpence was his own. He said it was his mother's 'There, Sir,'
said I, 'is the sixpence to you. Go home and be easy.' I then walked
on much satisfied with myself.

> FREDERICK A. POTTLE, *Boswell's London Journal* 1762–
> 1763, p. 99

4. THE MAGDALEN-CHARITY

Jonas Hanway was instrumental in establishing the Magdalen-Charity.
It was primarily a 'House of repentance' for women 'generally between
sixteen and twenty-one years of age.'
The Officers of the Magdalen-House consisted of a Secretary, Chap-
lain, Physician, and honorary Surgeons. There were apothecaries to
dispense medicines costing sixty pounds per annum. There was a Matron
and her assistants, a Steward, and Messengers. 'They are not to bring
any letter, verbal or written message into the house, or carry out any
letter, verbal or written message, without the knowledge and inspection
of the Matron.'

(a)

PREFACE

1. It is with great satisfaction we now publish these *Rules and
Regulations* of the *Magdalen-Charity*.
2. To conceive a just idea of this Establishment, it should be
remembered that there is a peculiar disadvantage under which it
labours, arising not from the difficulty of repentance, but from the
nature of the Charity itself. The women who prove worthy of it,
do for that very reason conceal themselves from public view; and
those who are profligate, and repugnant to the mercy which is
offered to them, revel in the dreadful scenes of licentiousness, and
publish their shame without remorse.
3. To succour the wretched who are plunged, perhaps, by the
most insidious arts, into the labyrinth of misfortunes is a task reserved for this Charity. Here the Pious and Humaine, may enjoy
the exalted pleasure of snatching from an early grave, many young
women, who would otherwise be devoted to destruction, under the
direction of wretches who traffic in sin and misery . . .
10. The women who are admitted being generally between sixteen and twenty-one years of age, cannot be supposed very old in

sin; nor ought it to be imagined that all the objects who offer them-selves for admittance, have arrived to the height of vice.

11. Such are the happy effects of this Charity, that not only num-bers of subjects are preserved, but several of the women discharged, have been married to sober and industrious persons, and are now joyful mothers of children.

14. To give a true description of the infernal arts which are em-ployed by mercenary Panders to seduce unwary females, would be too shocking to humanity: it is only a good education, and the fear of God, which can be effectual preservatives against such tempta-tions . . .

ANON. *The Rules and Regulations of the Magdalen-Charity,* (Preface).

(b)

XVII *Of* ADMISSION

1. The Committee sit to admit objects on the first *Thursday* in every month, at five o'clock in the afternoon.

2. The method of admission is by Petition, presented to the Com-mittee in the form prescribed (No. II) the blanks in which Petition are filled up by the Steward from the report of the Petitioner.

7. Every Petitioner who is judged proper, is examined as to the state of her health by the Nurse attending for that purpose; and, if necessary, by the Surgeon also. If she is infected with the foul disease, she is not admitted; but upon her obtaining her cure, may be reconsidered by the Committee, and if then found proper is ad-mitted.

ANON. *The Rules and Regulations of the Magdalen-Charity,* p. 17

(c)

XVIII *Of the* WARDS *and* PRECAUTIONS

2. The women are classed in each Ward, and the Assistants to the Matron appointed to preside, are accountable for the conduct and behaviour of their respective Wards.

4. Each woman lies in a separate bed, and has a box for her cloaths and linen under a lock and key, which is kept by herself.

XIX *Sick* WARD

1. In each class and division of the house a room is set apart for the sick.

2. There is a Nurse appointed to attend the sick, and every necessary for their recovery supplied.

XX   *Of the* NAMES

1. If the women are desirous of concealing their true names, they have liberty to assume others.

2. Reproaches for past irregularities are forbidden; no enquiry into family is permitted; but all possible discouragement given to the making any discovery which the parties themselves do not approve.

XXI   *Of their* DRESS

1. If, upon their admission, their apparel is clean, or fit to wash, it is ticketted, and laid by, in order to be returned to them whenever they leave the house.

2. They wear light shalloon gowns; and in their whole dress are plain and neat, and exactly alike.

XXIII   *Of their* EMPLOYMENT

In their work, as in every other circumstance, the utmost propriety and humanity are observed; and all loose or idle discourse, sluttishness, indolence, or neglect of moral or religious duties, are closely attended to; and if these are not in the degree to occasion a discharge, they are at least severely reprehended.

ANON. *The Rules and Regulations of the Magdalen-Charity*, pp. 19–22

5. CHARITY

Children of all but the poorest classes were enjoined to perform acts of charity. This is a recurring theme in innumerable children's books.

To George Montagu, Esq.

Paris, March 21, 1766

T'other day, in the street, I saw a child in a leading-string, whose nurse gave it a farthing for a beggar; the babe delivered its mite with a grace and a twirl of the hand. I don't think your cousin Twitcher's first grandson will be so well-bred.

Select Letters of Horace Walpole, p. 235

6. A HOBBY HORSE

'Fanny' (Frances) Burney was a self-taught enthusiastic 'scribbler' by the time she was ten in 1762. Her step-mother persuaded her to destroy her writings in 1767. Nevertheless, Fanny started her diary in 1768. It records the feelings and observations of an exceptionally lively sensitive girl.

(a)

July 17. [1768]

Such a set of tittle tattle, prittle prattle visitants! Oh dear! I am so sick of the ceremony and fuss of these fall lall people! So much complimentary nonsense—In short—a Country Town is my detestation—all the conversation is scandal, all the attention, dress, and *almost* all the heart, folly, envy, and censoriousness.

We breakfast always at 10, and rise as much before as we please— we dine at 2, drink tea about 6—and sup at 9. I make a kind of rule, never to indulge myself in my two *most* favourite pursuits, reading and writing, in the morning—no, I give that up wholly, accidental occasions and preventions excepted, to needle work.

ANNIE RAINE ELLIS (ed.), *The Early Diary of Frances Burney*, Vol. I, p. 15

(b)

Wednesday—August

We had a large party to the Assembly on Monday, which was *so-so-so*—I danced but one country dance—the room was so hot, 'twas really fatiguing. Don't you laugh to hear a girl of fifteen complain of the *fatigue* of dancing?—My partner was a pretty youth enough—younger than myself—poor dear creature, I really pitied him, for he seemed to *long* for another caper—in vain—I was inexorable.

ANNIE RAINE ELLIS (ed.), *The Early Diary of Frances Burney*, p. 23

(c)

[1769]

O dear! O dear! how melancholy has been to us this last week, the first of this year! The poor Susy [her sister, aged 14], who I told you was disappointed of her Lynn journey by a violent cold, was just put to Bed somewhat better when I wrote to you this day se'night—I soon after went to her, and found her considerably worse.

'My dear Fanny,' cried she, 'I love you dearly—my *dear* sister! —have I any more sisters?'—O how I was terrified—surprised!— 'O yes!' continued she, 'I have a sister Hetty—but I don't wish her to come to me now, because she'll want me to drink my barley water, and I can't—but I will if *you* want me—and where's papa?' For my life I could not speak a word, and almost choak'd myself to prevent my sobbing. 'O dear! I shall die!' 'My dear girl.' 'O but I must though!—But I can't help it—it is not my fault you know!'—She kiss'd me, and again said 'How I love you! my *dear* Fanny!—I love you dearly!' 'My sweet girl!' cried I—'you—you *can't* love me as much as I do you!' 'If I was Charly I should love you—indeed I should—Oh!—I shall die!'—'But not *yet*, my dear love—not *yet*!' 'Oh yes—I shall!—I should like to see my papa first tho'!'

The fever increased—she could not swallow her medicines, and was quite delirious. O what a night she had! We all sat up—She slept perpetually, without being at all refresh'd . . . On Monday however, the Dr. and apothecary thought her *somewhat* better, tho' in great danger. On Tuesday, they ventured to pronounce her out of danger—We made Hetty go to bed, and my aunt and I sat up again—and on Wednesday, we two went to bed, the dear girl continuing to mend, which she has, tho' very slowly, ever since.

ANNIE RAINE ELLIS (ed.), *The Early Diary of Frances Burney*, p. 40

(d)

. . . Mr. Seton and myself declined playing—I never do but at *Pope Joan*, (*Commerce*,) or *My Sow's Pig'd*! We therefore entered into a very comfortable conversation.

ANNIE RAINE ELLIS (ed.), *The Early Diary of Frances Burney*, p. 90

(e)

Lynn Regis.

My Susette and I are very comfortable here . . . We work, read, walk, and play on the harpsichord—these are our employments, and we find them sufficient to fill up all our time without ever being tired.

Friday.

I am just returned from making a visit to 5 sisters. There is with them a child, not 3 years old, they have taught him to speak like a parrot, they make him affect the language of a man, and then boast that *no child ever* talked like him . . .

Then they permit him to amuse himself at pleasure with all insects—flys, butterflys—poor little animals—the torture . . . and one of the last really turned me so sick . . . I could not recover myself the whole . . . Is not humanity disgraced by this barbarity to the dumb creation? The poor child belongs to a sex sufficiently prone to cruelty: is it for *women* thus early to encourage it?

ANNIE RAINE ELLIS (ed.), *The Early Diary of Frances Burney*, p. 100

7. MEDICAL MATTERS

Eighteenth-century medicine became increasingly concerned with paediatrics as the century advanced. Perhaps this influenced the slightly lower mortality rate in London at the beginning of the 1770s. In 1762, 54 per cent died under two years, 69 per cent under five. By 1771, the figures were 48 and 62 per cent respectively. Some of the diseases most frequently discussed and some of the panaceas were as follows:

(1) Small Pox. Chief emphasis was still placed on various methods of inoculation, preceded by purgings etc.

(2) Convulsions. 'Chiefly owing to the brutality and laziness of nurses who are forever pouring *Godfrey's Cordial* down their little throats, which is a strong opiate and in the end as fatal as Arsenic. This they will pretend they do to quiet the child—thus indeed many are *for ever quieted.*'

(3) Rickets. 'The child to be drawn in a little waggon. The clothes to be red and white, a strict fat-free diet to be followed.' Medicines included 'Jesuit's Bark', dry ox-gall, and gilded pills made of the 'Italian Friers Hood'.

(4) 'Thrush' was common, and a mouth wash including ether, white claret, and honey recommended.

(5) Teething, or 'the breeding of the teeth' as it was formerly called, occasioned much conflicting advice.

(6) Swaddling.

The general opinion was that new born infants should be protected by a 'stay to the neck', and flannel wound many times round the body. The infant was 'coated' at one month, with a 'stay' for the waist, but a 'roller' at night. The 'Stay in the Neck is left off after some Months, and the Roller in about a Year'. Stays were stiffened when the child was two. Boys discarded them when they were 'breech'd'. Girls never discarded them.

Finally, a Dr Watson observed 'it is still more dangerous to frighten them suddenly with harsh words, disguised persons, stories of ghosts and goblins.'

Dr George Armstrong's *Essay on the Diseases Most Fatal to Infants* is full of common sense and benevolent interest in the welfare of mothers and children. This charitable attitude culminated in the practical step of organizing a *Dispensary for the Infant Poor*. Stress was laid on the advisability of saving the lives of children of 'the industrious Poor', as 'the preservation of their lives is an essential Benefit to the public'.

(a) RULES TO BE OBSERVED IN THE NURSING OF CHILDEN:

With a particular View to those who are brought up by Hand

I do not advise the dry nursing of infants, when they can be properly suckled, yet I would not have parents to be discouraged from trying it when it becomes requisite.

There are two ways of feeding children who are bred up by the hand; the one is by means of a horn, and the other is with a boat or spoon. The latter is preferable.

The horn made use of for sucking, is a small polished cow's horn, which will hold about a gill and a half. The small end of it is perforated, and has a notch round to which are fastened two small bits of parchment, shaped like the tip of the finger of a glove, and sewed together in such a manner, as that the food poured into the horn can be sucked through between the stitches. The food which the child sucks through this artificial nipple must be thin, in order to pass between the stitches, there requires a larger quantity of it to nourish the child.

While the child is suckled, I think the best food is crumb of bread boiled in soft water, to the consistence of what is commonly called pap, or a thin panada. The bread should not be new baked, and, in general, I think rolls preferable to loaf bread; because the former is commonly baked with yeast only, whereas the latter is said to have allum sometimes mixed with it.

This pap should be sweetened with soft sugar, unless the child is of a lax habit of body, in which case the finest loaf sugar should be used; and in this case too, the pap should be made with biscuit, instead of roll. It should not be made sweeter than new milk; for too much sugar palls the appetite, and grows sour upon their stomach.

Before the child is weaned, the victuals should be made thicker, by which means it will become less fond of the breast, and consequently, as was mentioned above, easier to wean.

If the infant is bred up by hand from the birth, it ought to have new cow's milk mixed with its victuals as often as possible, and now and then some of it alone to drink. Asses milk will be still better, when it can be conveniently had, and the parents can afford it.

About the same age, or rather before, that is, as soon as the child can hold any thing in its hand, the nurse should every morning give it a piece of the upper crust of a loaf, cut in the shape, and about the size of a large Savoy biscuit, one end of it dipped in its food, or a little milk, and put into its mouth, and the other to be held in its hand. The child will lie and divert itself with this, gnaw and swallow it by degrees, which will not only help to nourish it, but bring a greater quantity of saliva into its mouth, whereby the gums will be softened, and at the same time, by the gentle and repeated friction, the cutting of the teeth will be greatly promoted.

Though I would by all means advise the keeping of infants as dry and clean as possible, through the day, yet I think it better not to open them in the night, if it can be avoided, for fear of giving them cold, and disturbing their rest.

Some infants are more wakeful in the night, than in the day, which is hurtful to themselves, and irksome to those about them; and therefore they ought to be broke of it as soon as possible. The safest and most natural way of attaining this end is, by keeping them awake as much as you can throughout the day, and feeding them pretty plentifully at about ten or eleven at night. As to opiates, in this case, I reckon them pernicious, though I am afraid some careless nurses use too much freedom with them, by giving them to children in the day as well as the night, in order to keep them quiet, and prevent them disturbing them in their business.

The first exercise I shall mention proper for infants, is dandling, which is certainly of service to divert them, and keep them awake; but then it should be done very gently for a good while at first, and never with a jerk. Neither should they be hoisted up high in the air between the hands, as some people heedlessly do; for they begin very early to be susceptible of fear, much sooner than persons not accustomed to them would imagine.

But the most useful exercise for very young infants, is rubbing with the hand; which cannot be too often repeated, nor continued too long at a time. They should be well rubbed all over, before the fire, twice a day at least, that is, morning and evening, when they are dressed and undressed . . .

GEORGE ARMSTRONG, M.D., *An Essay on the Diseases Most Fatal to Infants*, (2nd ed., 1771), p. 121 *et seq.*

(b)

PROPOSALS
for administering
ADVICE and MEDICINES
to the
CHILDREN OF THE POOR

The many noble Hospitals and Colleges which have at several Times been erected and endowed in this Nation for the Relief of the Diseased, will be everlasting Monuments of its generous and humane Spirit.

In the mean Time, one main Duty of Humanity is thought by some not to have been sufficiently attended to; I mean the Care of Infants from their Birth to their fourth Year compleated; in which Period, by the London Tables, one Half of all that are born die. If by proper Means, even a moderate Part of this Loss can be prevented, the Object seems important, were we to view it only in a political Light.

Children, till they arrive at Three or Four Years of Age, cannot be received into Hospitals (except in cases of Accidents and the Stone) for several obvious Reasons.

The Situation and Air of *Hampstead*, where I have lived for these Fifteen Years past, being remarkably dry and healthy, and at a small Distance from the most populous City in *Europe*, there is constantly a great Number of Children from *London* bred up there; and as, amongst such Numbers, there must always be some indisposed, I have had more Opportunities of improving myself in treating the various Complaints of Infants, than almost any other Situation in *England* affords.

PROPOSALS

I   That I shall attend to give Advice *gratis* to poor Children Four Days in the Week; viz., on the *Mondays, Wednesdays, Fridays*, and *Saturdays*; and at first, Two Hours on each of those Days.

II   That these Expenses be defrayed by private Subscriptions, on the following Terms: That is to say, that every Person subscribing One Guinea *per* Annum, shall be intitled to have always One Patient at a Time under my Care.

III   That the Parents or Friends of every Patient be obliged to give an Account to me of the Success of the Medicines administered.

London, Feb. 1, 1771.   G. ARMSTRONG

Agreeable to this Plan a House was opened the 24th of April 1769, in *East-Street*, near Red-Lion Square, under the Denomination of the DISPENSARY FOR THE INFANT POOR, where Advice and Medicines were administered *gratis*, to the Children of the Poor, four Times a Week; on the Days mentioned in the Proposals, till about two Months ago, when finding that very few brought their Children on *Saturdays* (most of them being employed in Marketing and cleaning their Houses) I took off that Day for private Practice; and *for this Purpose* do attend *Tuesdays* and *Saturdays*, in *East-Street*, from Twelve till Two o'Clock.

It is now a Year and Ten Months since the Dispensary was first opened, during which Time I have had 1719 poor Children as Patients under my Care, out of which Number I have lost 87. Most of the Complaints have been Fevers of different Kinds, but chiefly remitting or intermitting; many of them are attended with a Cough, some with Convulsions, some with Purgings, and some with Inward Fits, which had reduced several of them to such a low

State, that their Parents, when they first brought them, had little or no Hopes of their Recovery.

The principal Objects of this Charity since its first Institution, have been the Children of the industrious Poor, *viz.* of Journeymen-Artificers, Handicraftsmen, and Labourers, who are commonly brought up by their Parents to some useful Employment; and consequently the Preservation of their Lives is an essential Benefit to the Public.

> GEORGE ARMSTRONG, M.D., *An Essay on the Diseases Most Fatal to Infants*, p. 175 *et seq.*

8. A LIVELY DIARIST

Boswell said of Mrs. Thrale that she was 'a lady of lively talents improved by education'. She was a devoted mother, and found time to record her domestic preoccupations in a spirited, senstive diary.

(a)

Lord Westcote told me once that when George the 3ᵈ & his Broʳ Prince Edward were Children, one ten Years old & the other eleven; as they were playing about the Princess's Apartment; She overheard the youngest say—Brother when I am a Man I think I'll keep a Mistress; Fye Edward says the Lady do you know what that is; Why yes Mama a Mistress is to a Wife what a Pronoun is to a Noun I take it—that it is a Substitute & a Representative.

A Boy who played in a surprising manner upon the Hautboy was called to perform before King George the 3ᵈ and beginning with a slow movement which his Majesty took for Bashfulness don't be afraid my little Fellow says he, don't be afraid I say: Afraid! cries the Lad with a wide Stare, why I have played before the Emperour.

> KATHARINE C. BALDERSTONE (ed.), *Thraliana*, pp. 140–1

(b)

Some foolish People, of no mean Rank—they were the Clegg's of Gat'n my Relations, carried a'visiting with them their only Son six Years old & near a Natural—says Sir Robert Cotton to the Father, Cousin what does this child say? *Lilly Lolly* is it not? Yes replies the Mother, it *says* Lilly Lolly, but it *means* how d'ye do Sʳ Robert Cotton.

A Lady was teaching her little Boy how God made the World how God made the Sun, the Moon, the Trees &c. and pray Mama says the Child after a Pause—Who paid him for his Work?

A good Mother was taking a dirty Ballad out of her Boy's Hand which he had bought in the Street, and bid him not read such Stuff —Why says he don't you read them? no truly replyed She; why then Mama do read them, indeed you would be *merrier* if you did.

KATHARINE C. BALDERSTONE (ed.), *Thraliana*, Vol. I, p. 147

9. A PRODIGY

Dr. BURNEY'S *Account of an Infant Musician.*

'There is now in this city a musical prodigy, which engages the conversation and excites the wonder of every body. A boy, son to a carpenter, of only two years and three quarters old, from hearing his father play upon an organ which he is making, has discovered such musical powers as are scarcely credible. He plays a variety of tunes, and has from memory repeated fragments of several voluntaries which he heard Mr. GARLAND, the organist, play at the cathedral. He has likewise accompanied a person who played upon the flute, not only with a treble, but has formed a base of his own, which to common hearers seemed harmonious. If any person plays false, it throws him into a passion directly; and though his little fingers can only reach a sixth, he often attempts to play chords. He does not seem a remarkable clever child in any other respect; but his whole soul is absorbed in music. Numbers croud daily to hear him, and the musical people are amazed.

PHILOSOPHICAL TRANSACTIONS OF THE ROYAL SOCIETY OF LONDON, Vol. LXIX for the Year 1779, Part I, p. 193

10. MATERNAL ANXIETY

(a)

Bath 19: Nov:1783. Heavens! a new Distress! my Child, my Sophia will dye: arrested by the hand of God—apparently so: She will die without a Disease—Fits, sudden, unaccountable, unprovoked; Apoplectic, lethargic like her Father. Woodward and Dobson are called: they say her Disorder should be termed *Attonitus*.

'tis an instant Cessation of all Nature's Powers at once. I saved her in the first Attack, by a Dram of the fine Old Usquebough given at the proper Moment—it reviv'd her, but She only lives I see to expire with fresh Struggles.

She lives, I have been permitted to save her again; I rubbed her while just expiring, so as to keep the heart in Motion: She knew me instantly, & said you warm *me* but you are killing *yourself*—I actually was in a burning Fever from exertion, & fainted soon as I had saved my Child.

> KATHARINE C. BALDERSTONE (ed.), *Thraliana*, Vol. I, p. 580

(b)

I was saying this was the Time for Women to shine, tis likewise the Shining-Season for Children: Little Bridgetower—a Boy not quite ten Years old plays on the Violin like a 1st rate performer—and as the best proof of his Merit,—is paid like one. Bridgetower is a Mulatto, Son to a Polish Dutchess we are told—and to an African Negro, the handsomest of his Kind & Colour ever seen.

> KATHARINE C. BALDERSTONE (ed.), *Thraliana*, Vol. II, p. 757

11. BEAUTY'S DAUGHTER

Georgina, the Duchess of Devonshire, gave birth to her first child, called after herself, in July 1783.

(a) Letter from the Duchess to Lady Elizabeth Foster

. . . She is very much admir'd and has a number of visiters. Her cradle, robes, baskets, etc., are, I am afraid, foolishly magnificent. They are cover'd with the finest lace. She has a present coming from the Queen of France, but I don't know what it is yet.

> THE EARL OF BESSBOROUGH, P.C., G.C.M.G., *Georgiana*, p. 62

(b) Letters from the Duchess to her mother

Monday night, Chatsworth
1 Sept. 1783

Here we are, I as usual the most nervous of beings. I fancy'd I had hit the child's head against a door, which I certainly did, but she never cried or left off sucking, and is now fast asleep, and we have examin'd her head twice, and rub'd it all over, so that I think I cannot have hurt her, but I shall not take her thro' a double door again in a hurry . . .

8 Sept. 1783

. . . You know I w^d bring the Rocker with me, meaning to keep her while I suckled. She was only rather dirty till last night, when she was quite drunk. My D^r little girl sleeps now in her bed with me after her first sucking, as it is too cold to move her, and the Rocker was to turn her dry and lay her down to sleep. I perceived that she made the bed stink of wine and strong drink whenever she came near it . . . This rather alarm'd me, but this morning I learnt that she had been so drunk as to fall down and vomit . . . I have therefore sent her 10 guineas and told I w^d pay her journey up to town, and that I parted with her because I wanted her no longer . . .

THE EARL OF BESSBOROUGH, P.C., G.C.M.G.,
Georgiana, p. 63

The Duchess' young black boy was born a year after the 14,000 slaves in Britain were set free in 1772. This event was brought about largely by the efforts of Granville Sharp. He was a philanthropist who interested himself in the cause of such people as William Hickey's 'little pet boy Nabob', who was dressed as a Hussar, and others less fortunately placed. Eventually the Lord Chief Justice was forced by Sharp's intervention to free 'Negro Somerset', thus creating an inalienable precedent.

(c) Letter from the Duchess to her mother

March, 1784

Tir'd to death, I am dressing for the Opera. I am going out Ding Dong, but it shall not last . . . George Hanger has sent me a black boy, 11 years old and very honest, but the Duke don't like my having a black, yet I cannot bear the poor wretch being ill us'd. If you lik'd him instead of Michel I will send him to you. He will be a cheap servant, and you will make a Christian of him and a good boy . . .

THE EARL OF BESSBOROUGH, P.C., G.C.M.G.,
Georgiana, p. 78

12. A CONSIDERATE CLERGYMAN

Parson (James) Woodforde (1740–1803) left an invaluable record of his daily life in the second half of the eighteenth century. He held livings in Somerset and Norfolk. He was not, apparently, of a very mystical turn of mind, but he had a genuine wish to help those in need. He was also interested in good food and wine.

(a)

July 4. To some poor ragged Children at the fall gate at Ling [gave] 0.0.6. To 2 naked Children on Colin Green at the fall gate 0.0.6.

> JOHN BERESFORD (ed.), *The Diary of a Country Parson*, Vol. II, pp. 63 and 82

(b)

Aug. 8. [1783] . . . My Servant Boy Jack Warton taken very ill in the Fever that is going about—I gave him some Rhubarb.

Sept. 2. . . . Will very bad all the time he was out to day. Ben also complained this Evening—Jack also bad to-day. Almost all the House ill in the present Disorder and which is called the Whirligigousticon* by the faculty. It is in almost every House in the Village.

> JOHN BERESFORD (ed.), *The Diary of a Country Parson*, Vol. II, pp. 85–91

(c)

Oct. 6. . . . I rode down to Mr. Howletts this morning and christned a Child of his, born last Night, by name William—and it being the first Child that I have christned since the Act† took place

---

* The 'Disorder' in fact appears to have been a bad local outburst of malaria.

† This Act was passed by the Coalition Government of 1783, and entitled, 'An Act for granting to His Majesty a Stamp-duty on the Registry of Burials, Marriage, Births, and Christenings'. A sum of 3*d*. had to be paid in respect of each entry in the register, the Parson being authorized to demand and receive the said sum. It was one of the new taxes to meet the burden of the American War. It was repealed by Pitt in 1794, as it was 'acknowledged to have an injurious operation as regards the morals of the people'.

concerning the Duty to be raised on Christnings Burials and Marriages, and therefore recd. the Duty of 0.0.3.

> JOHN BERESFORD (ed.), *The Diary of a Country Parson*,
> Vol. II, p. 96

(d)

Nov. 10 . . . About 11 o'clock this morning Mr. Press Custance
called on me in a Post Chaise, and I went with him in it to Weston
Church, clerically dressed, and there buried in the Church Mr.
Custances youngest Daughter Mary Anne which was brought to
Church in their Coach and four with Mrs. Alldis the Housekeeper
and the Childs Nurse Hetty Yollop—only in it besides the Corpse.
The Infant was only 16 weeks old. After interring it—I rec^d from
Mr. Press Custance 5.5.0 wrapped up in a clean Piece of writing
Paper. I had also a black silk Hatband and a P^r of white Gloves.

> JOHN BERESFORD (ed.), *The Diary of a Country Parson*,
> Vol. II, p. 213

13. TRAGEDY

HOME NEWS. June 13, 1786. On Saturday morning the
body of a fine young woman was taken out of the Thames at the
end of Strand-lane, where she had drowned herself the preceding
night. She appeared to be about eighteen years of age, and was
known to have been turned out of doors the day before, by one of
those inhuman monsters in the shape of women, who keep brothels
in the neighbourhood of Drury-lane. The poor young victim had
been brought from her parents at the age of eleven years, by the
mistress of the bagnio from which she was dismissed, when her
face grew common, and the charms of extreme youth and novelty
were no longer a temptation to debauched constitutions, and debilitated age. Thus thrown upon the town, pennyless, and heart-
broken, as too many have already done, from the same causes—she
put an end to her existence, in order to get rid of her miseries on
earth.

> THE NEW LADY'S MAGAZINE; or, Polite and Entertain-
> ing Companion for the Fair Sex: Entirely devoted to their Use
> and Amusement, (June, 1786), p. 276

14. INFANT LABOUR

Cotton spinning and weaving increased as the result of greater imports in the mid-eighteenth century. The weavers' cottages became workshops where all members of his family helped with the work. The life of a very young child in the Crompton family is described as follows:

I recollect that soon after I was able to walk I was employed in the cotton manufacture. My mother used to bat the cotton wool on a wire riddle. It was then put into a deep brown mug with a strong ley of soap suds. My mother then tucked up my petticoats about my waist, and put me into the tub to tread upon the cotton at the bottom. When a second riddleful was batted I was lifted out, it was placed in the mug, and I again trod it down. This process was continued until the mug became so full that I could no longer safely stand in it, when a chair was placed besides it, and I held on by the back. When the mug was quite full, the soap suds were poured off, and each separate dollop of wool well squeezed to free it from moisture. They were then placed on the bread rack under the beams of the kitchen-loft to dry. My mother and my grand-mother carded the cotton wool by hand, taking one of the dollops at a time, on the single hand cards. When carded they were put aside in separate parcels ready for spinning.

FRENCH, *Life of Crompton*, pp. 56–7

Conditions were often unsatisfactory. In some cases the cotton was difficult to dry.

Fire at Isaac Hardy's, which burnt 6 lbs. of cotton, 5 pairs of stockings and set the cradle on fire, with a child in it which was much burnt. It happened through the wife improvidently holding the candle under the cotton as it was drying.

ROWBOTHAM, *Diary*, Jan. 14, 1788

15. QUESTIONABLE PROCEEDINGS

William of Wykeham founded 'The College of St. Mary at Winchester' (Winchester College) in 1382. The system was to have a lasting influence on public school education. The college itself was always reserved for the 'scholars', while several hundred 'commoners' were lodged in the adjacent houses. The Warden and Fellows who governed the college experienced great anxiety at the untoward behaviour of the boys in 1793. It was said 'that the contagion of the French Revolution had spread among the lower orders.' They were presumed to be ready to help the rebels. The authorities probably blamed 'the contagion' for the unrest in the school.

The Rebellion of 1793

It appears that the band of the Bucks militia was in the habit of playing in the Cathedral Close on certain days; the Warden gave notice that any boy who should be seen there, would be deprived of his 'leave out' on the Easter Day ensuing. 'If *one* individual is peccant,' wrote the Warden, '*he* shall be severely punished; but if *numbers* are seen, the whole school shall be punished, by being refused leave to dine with their friends' (on Easter Day).

Soon afterwards the Hostarius, Mr. Goddard, encountered in the close one of the Praefects, and he reported the fact to the Warden. The latter punished, not the delinquent only, but the whole school, by forbidding altogether the 'leave out' on Easter Day. He assigned as his reason the well-known line,—

'Quidquid delirant reges, plectuntur Achivi.'

The 'Achivi', not perceiving the applicability of the quotation to them, held a meeting, and the forty seniors bound themselves by an oath to stand by each other. Then they wrote a short Latin letter to the Warden, signed, 'alumni omnes'. It represented the hardship of making all answerable for the fault of one. 'They had,' they said, 'inplicitly obeyed the Warden; but they hoped that, in future, he would act differently.'

To this the boys declare that they received no reply at all for three days; . . . Any way, they sent a second Latin letter, worded respectfully like the former one, and pressing for an answer.

To this the Warden *did* reply, and the terms of his letter are the same in both Reports:— 'If the scholars are so forgetful of their rank and good manners,' he wrote, 'as to insult their Warden by letters of consummate arrogance and extreme petulance, the Warden can give no other answer, than that he shall continue to refuse all indulgence, till the scholars behave more properly'.

This answer was ill-advised. No doubt they [the boys] would have done better to submit; but there were some very determined spirits among them, and they resolved to force the Warden to do them justice. Their first step was to send messages to both the Masters, telling them 'that they would not trouble them to go into school'. Warton was weak enough to comply with the notice sent him. Mr Goddard nevertheless, presented himself in thè school at the usual hour. He found the boys armed with clubs, and in a very rebellious mood; they received him with general hissing and, upon his commanding silence, renewed the uproar more turbulently than before. The juniors began pelting him with marbles, and the Praefects took no steps to put the tumult down. It was useless to persist, and he withdrew.

The Warden now sent for the Praefect of Hall, and afterwards for the whole body of Praefects; but the boys would receive no message from the Warden. As the evening advanced, they began to take more violent measures. They seized the keys of the college, wresting them from the porter. Possessed of the keys, the boys broke into Mr. Goddard's apartments, and blocked up the passage of communication between them and the Warden's lodging with scobs [desks]. They next made an attempt on the Warden's house, and forced their way into it, keeping the Warden himself, the Hostarius, and one of the Fellows, prisoners in the dining-room all night!

In the morning the Warden left his house, followed by many of the boys, armed with clubs, and assailing him with abuse. He was obliged to retire to Dr. Warton's house where he attempted to hold a college meeting; . . . Baffled in this attempt, the Warden sent this message to the boys:— 'As the minds of the scholars are much agitated, and disposed to adopt measures discreditable to the Society, the Warden thinks it advisable to give them leave of absence till April 28th; the scholars are desired to go home immediately.' But the boys declined to avail themselves of the permission.

The Warden and Fellows now resolved to apply to the magistrates for help. The Sheriff, thereupon, accompanied by several magistrates, went down to the college, and tried to persuade the boys to return to their obedience; but the latter had made preparations for resistance. They had victualled the college for a regular siege; they had provided themselves with swords, guns, bludgeons, and had mounted the red cap of liberty and equality—a curious sign of the times. When the magistrates reached the outer gate, they found it strongly barricaded; the court-yard had been unpaved, and the stones carried to the top of the tower; part of the parapet also had been loosened, to hurl on the heads of the assailants, if any attack should be attempted. Being summoned to surrender, they replied that they would burn the college to the ground rather than do so. From the character of some of the ringleaders, it is likely that they would have been as good as their word. It was, perhaps, for this reason that they were left unmolested all that day.

On the third day, the insurgents were induced to leave the matter in the Sheriff's hands, to be arranged between him and the Warden.

But the boys refused to deliver up the keys, or lay down their arms, until they had heard the issue of the negotiations. This was transmitted to them in the following words 'The Warden promises for the future not to punish the community for the sake of an individual, and grant a general amnesty, provided the keys are given up.'

Peace seemed now to be restored. The boys gave up the keys, and went back to their duties; . . . [But] The boys had lost all respect for their Masters; while the latter felt keenly the humiliation they had undergone. Fresh disturbances soon broke out. On the morning of Friday the 5th, the day after that on which the amnesty had been granted, the Hostarius required that four guns, which had been taken out of his house when the boys broke into it, should be restored. The boys at first refused, but Mr Goddard reasoned with them. They thereupon agreed to give them up, on condition of their being sent away immediately to their owners. This was acceded to, and quiet was again renewed.

But the Warden considered that the refusal to deliver the guns in the first instance was a breach of the amnesty on the part of the boys. He summoned them, one by one, to his seat, and told each boy 'seriously to consider whether he meant for the future to obey the rules of the college, and its officers. If they did not *ex animo* intend this, they had better at once consult their friends as to the propriety of an immediate resignation of their scholarships.'

On the following day, the boys replied to the Warden, by a request that a copy of the Statutes might be furnished them; and that the Warden would write down, for their information, exactly what it was that he wished them to comply with.

The Warden replied by producing the copy of the Statutes asked for; but declined to write down any specific requirements.

Once more things might have been smoothly arranged. But in

the week which followed the concession of the amnesty, steps had been taken which were clearly a violation of it. Parents had been written to, urging them either to compel their sons to ask pardon of the authorities, or resign their scholarships. Intimations of these proceedings reached the boys. At length, Dr. Budd, father of one of the senior boys, came to Winchester, in consequence of the Warden's letter, and told his son he must make his submission to the Warden or resign. The boy chose the latter; and the fact was no sooner known, than the whole of Budd's school-fellows drew up another letter, and presented it to the Warden. 'By a promise,' they wrote, 'on which we implicitly relied, a complete amnesty was granted; by which term we have always understood that no mention should be made of, or punishment exacted for, the past. The first has been repeatedly infringed, since that promise. We have been likewise witnesses of the compulsory departure of one who was culpable only in an equal degree with ourselves . . . You cannot be ignorant in what manner we are bound. We are bound to undergo the same punishment that may be inflicted on any individual, on account of the late proceedings. On this account, we are compelled by a solemn oath to quit the college, and we are now determined to resign.'

Setting aside, of course, that their whole conduct in openly refusing obedience to the authorities was *per se* blameable, this was the first false step the boys had taken. Possibly they thought that the Warden would hesitate to incur so grave a scandal and injury to the school, as would be caused by a general departure. But they were mistaken. The resignations were accepted; and when, on the following day, they became sensible of their error, and wished to withdraw them, their request was refused. Five-and-thirty boys were obliged to leave the school.

THE REV. H. C. ADAMS, *Wykehamica. A History of Winchester College*, p. 143

16. VIRTUOUS INDIGNATION

Letter from school boys at Uxbridge to Lady Rockingham
at Hillingdon House.

Bramham, 5 May [1790s]

My Lady,

We have heard with Indignation from some of the Cottagers on Uxbridge Common that some Boy or Boys belonging to our School are suspected of having killed your Ladyship's Swans. You may depend upon it nothing can be more false. Such an act could not have been concealed from all of us—and if any Boy in our Academy could be detected of such wanton Cruelty we would surrender him up to Justice as a Fellow unfit to live in any civilized Society.—Ingratitude is seldom attributed to School Boys and the Sense of your Goodness to us would render any one of our Society contemptible if he injured any Part of your Ladyship's Property.

LADY ROCKINGHAM (ed.), *The Rockingham Papers*, Vol. I, p. 130

17. FEMALE EDUCATION
BABY-BALLS

'To every thing there is a season, and a time for every purpose under heaven,' said the wise man; but he said it before the invention of BABY-BALLS; This modern device is a sort of triple conspiracy against innocence, the health, and the happiness of children. Thus, by factitious amusements, to rob them of a relish for the simple joys, is like blotting out spring from the year. To sacrifice the true and proper enjoyments of sprightly and happy children, is to make them pay a dear price for their artificial pleasures. They step at once from the nursery to the ball-room; and, by a change of habits, as new as it is preposterous, are thinking of dressing themselves, at an age when they used to be dressing their dolls. Instead of bounding with the unrestrained freedom of little wood-nymphs over hill and dale, their cheeks flushed with health, these *gay* little creatures are shut up all the morning, demurely practising the *pas grave*, and transacting the serious business of acquiring a new step for the evening with more cost of time and pains than it would have taken them to acquire twenty new ideas.

The hearts of healthy children abound with a general disposition to mirth and joyfulness, even without a specific object to excite it; like our first parent, in the world's first spring, when all was new, and fresh, and gay about him,

they live, and move,

And feel that they are happier than they know.

Only furnish them with a few simple and harmless materials, and a little, but not too much leisure, and they will manufacture their own pleasures with more skill, and success, and satisfaction, than they will receive from all that your money can purchase.

When we see the growing zeal to crowd the midnight ball with these pretty fairies, we should be almost tempted to fancy it was a kind of pious emulation among the mothers to cure their infants of a fondness for vain and foolish pleasures, by tiring them out by this premature familiarity with them.

> HANNAH MORE, *Strictures on the Modern System of Female Education*, Vol. I, p. 98

18. LOW LIVING

Concern for the poor existed for almost three hundred years before the publication of Sir Frederic Morton Eden's *The State of the Poor* in 1797. But his book was the first of its kind. He was moved to indignation at any curtailment of individual liberty, and had a benevolent but just attitude towards the people whose circumstances he was examining. He advocated self-help as the best remedy for poverty.

STREATLEY.—Expenses and earnings of a labourer's family: The man is 50; he has a wife and seven children, three of whom are out at service. The four youngest, at home, are 5, 7, 12, and 14 years old. The two oldest, who are boys, drive the plough for neighbouring farmers. The two youngest do not work. The wife earns about 1s. 6d. a week throughout the year. The man earns in winter 8s. a week, and at present 12s. a week. For about ten days in the wheat harvest he receives 3s. a day. The earnings of the family amount to about £46. Their yearly expenses are as follows:

	£	s.	d.
Bread	36	8	0
All other food	15	16	4
Candle, soap, salt, fuel, etc.	3	7	4
Home rent	2	5	0
Clothes	6	2	0
Total expenses	63	18	8
Total earnings	46	0	0
Deficiency	17	18	8

The earnings appear to be very high, but the expenses are enormous; it is, however, necessary to observe that the articles consumed are

marked at present prices, which in some instances are a third and upwards higher than a year ago. The house rent is paid by the parish,
and several persons furnish the man with old clothes, and sometimes
shirts; in case of sickness he gets parochial relief. The parish allows
1s. 6d. a week for every child not old enough to work. His yearly
receipt on this account will be £7 16s. This is to be continued as
long as the high price of provisions keeps up. The great consumption of bread is very striking. They eat boiled bacon generally once
a week, and seldom taste fresh meat. Potatoes are seldom cultivated
or used.

   SIR FREDERIC MORTON EDEN, *The State of the Poor*, p.
135

19. CAPITAL PUNISHMENT
ROBERT LADBROKE TROYT

*A boy of Seventeen, executed before Newgate, 28th of November, 1798,
for Forgery, his First Offence*

   Although only seventeen years old, Robert Ladbroke Troyt was
found guilty, at the Old Bailey, of having feloniously forged, a
certain draft, dated the 20th August, for the sum of seventy-five
pounds, payable to Sir William Blackstone, purporting to be the
draft of Messrs Devaynes, Dawes, Noble & Co.

   On his trial this miserable boy was gaily dressed, and appeared
to have no sense of the awful situation in which he stood, behaving
with much unconcern; but at the place of execution he was a
lamentable spectacle. He screamed in horror at the first sight of the
apparatus of death, and during the short time allowed upon the
scaffold for devotion he was in the greatest agony of mind.

   He suffered for his first offence. He had been for a short time clerk
to a gentleman of eminence in the profession of the law, courted the
company of his elders, and tasted the dissipation (which they call
the pleasures) of London. To support such an evil course he committed the fatal deed which so soon put a stop to his career.

   THE COMPLETE NEWGATE CALENDAR, Vol. IV, p.
228

CHAPTER 4
1800–1829

1. INTRODUCTION

The introduction to Pott's *Gazetteer* describes England in 1810. 'In some parts, verdant plains extend far as the eye can reach, watered by streams, and covered with cattle. In others, the vicissitudes of gently rising hills, and bending vales, fertile in corn, waving with wood, and interspersed with meadows, offer the most delightful landscapes of rural opulence.

The *Gazetteer* states that 'commerce is at present almost incredible', but hardly comments on the ill-effects of increasing industrialization. Birmingham is said to be 'one of the healthiest towns in England' in spite of the 'close population, the noxious effluvia of various metallic trades. Manchester had manufactories which are seen rising among the clouds of smoke in almost every direction. The total labour force was 350,000—159,000 men, 90,000 women, and 101,000 children.

Bristol is 'on the whole, handsome and well-built'. 'The African trade, which to the disgrace of this free country was long prosecuted, was ever much less connected with the West Indies at this port than at Liverpool.' This is a discreet reference to the slave trade.

With increasing industrialization, the skies above nineteenth century England grew progressively darker. The era of Allamode and Lutestring gave way to that of Mungo, Shoddy and Fud. Dicraeli's fictional description of factory workers in *Sybil, or the Two Nations* is not as sombre as the truth which follows it.

'Mr. Trafford . . . was the younger son of a family that had for centuries been planted in the land . . .

On the banks of the Mowe he had built a factory, which was one of the marvels of the district . . . Proximity to the employer brings order, because it brings encouragement. In the settlement of Trafford crime was positively unknown. There was not a single person in the village of a reprobate character. The men were well clad, the women had a blooming cheek; drunkenness was unknown.

Marshall, the factory owner in real life, wrote the following reply to question no. 79 in the 1833 government questionnaire:—

'We would observe that it is impossible to form a correct judgment of the extent to which restrictions on the hours of labour of
children in factories are requisite for the protection of their health
and morals; without a careful enquiry into the causes of disease
and immorality . . . that produce many of the evils attributed to too
long hours of work, which if removed would render any great reduction of the present hours of labour undesirable. In our opinion
the health of the workpeople in this and other large towns receives
great injury from the filthy state of many of the streets arising from
want of proper sewerage, draining, and paving, and proper regulations to secure cleanliness and ventilation. This is corroborated
by the increased mortality in towns being almost confined to children under eight years of age. The great number of beer and spirit
shops, and of police generally—the want of adequate means of education and religious instruction and of opportunity of healthy recreation, are all of them evils of the most serious nature, and we
believe that it is the debilitated health and improvident moral habits
produced by these means that in the great majority of cases causes
the usual hours of working to be injurious to the health of children
and workpeople.'

Elihu Burritt, M.A., was an American. In his *Walks in the Black
Country* (1866) he writes with as much enthusiasm as John Macky.
He turns his steps towards the 'skirt of Birmingham . . . Though
the half that it turns to the fire of the Black Country is badly
scorched, crimped and ragged, the other half is a flowing robe embroidered with emerald and gold.'

Unlike the early eighteenth-century travellers, Burritt was as excited by scenes of industry as by evidence of wealth and fine
scenery. 'Further down towards Birmingham, there was a well-
manned battery that poured forth a shower of nuts and bolts; and
Chance's great fortress was all ablaze, with its hot fountains sending
out acres of glass.

The moon rode up with its bland face a little flushed over the
scene, and the whole heavens were suffused with the red illumination, as if in honour of human industry.'

The effects of industrialisation on the countryside are graphic-
ally described as follows:—

'From the Castle Hill of Dudley, Nature is scourged with cat-
o'-nine-tails of red-hot wire, and marred and scarred and fretted
and smoked half to death day and night, even on Sundays. Almost

every square inch of her is reddened, blackened, and distorted by
the terrible tractoration of a hot blister. But all this cutaneous eruption is nothing compared with the internal violence and agonies
she has to endure. The very sky and clouds above are moved to
sympathy with her sufferings and shed black tears in token of their
emotion. When you go over to Hagley you will see what Nature is
where she has the upper-hand. You see her in all the various dresses
she has worn from her birth. On this furzy-breathing hill you see
the simple and homely dress she wore when man first found her
here two thousand years ago or more, and it is all redolent with the
thymy odour that perfumed it then.'

Burritt however, is particularly interesting when observing industrial processes.

'I selected those which have a reputation abroad, especially in the
United States . . . The Brades Iron and Steel company have sunk
seven pairs of coal mines around their works, . . . They also work
and own their own iron ore. Then from the furnace to the forge,
from pig to bar, goes the raw material of their manufactures. A portion is selected with great care for the carbonating kilns. It now
comes out blistered steel . . . but most of it is now broken up into
short pieces for the terrible crucibles of the air furnaces. There are
about twenty of them, all under draught if not blast at once. Each is
charged with its covered pot full of blistered steel with coke to
match. Their lidded mouths dull the roaring sound of the com-
bustion, but the furnace-men show by their looks the intensity of
the heat. The lid is removed from each furnace, and the pot
of molten metal lifted out by a pair of long-handled tongs with
rounded jaws. As the stalwart men, naked to their waists, remove the cover from the pot and pour the fluid into flasks or ingots,
the brightness is almost blinding to one standing at a distance of
several paces.'

Dickens gives a succinct and unforgettable account of a northern
industrial town in *Hard Times*. He called it 'Coketown'. 'It was a
town of red brick, or of brick that would have been red if the smoke
and ashes had allowed it; but as matters stood it was a town of
unnatural red and black . . .'

'It was a town of machinery and tall chimneys, out of which
interminable serpents of smoke trailed themselves for ever and ever,
and never got uncoiled. It had vast piles of buildings full of windows where there was a rattling and a trembling all day long, and

where the pistons of the steam engines worked monotonously up and down, like the head of an elephant in a state of melancholy madness . . . You saw nothing in Coketown but what was severely workful. If the members of a religious persuasion built a chapel there—they made it a pious warehouse of red brick, with sometimes a bell with a bird-cage on the top of it . . . In the hardest-working part of Coketown the chimneys . . . were built in an immense variety of crooked and stunted shapes, as though every house put out a sign of the kind of people who might be expected to be born in it; the multitude of Coketown generically called "the Hands" . . .

'The fairy palaces burst into illumination, before the pale morning showed the monstrous serpents of smoke trailing themselves over Coketown. A clattering of clogs upon the pavement, a rapid ringing of bells, and all the melancholy-mad elephants, polished and oiled up for the day's monotony, were at their heavy exercises again . . .'

Blanchard Gerrold provided the commentary for Gustave Doré's *London*. He described London in 1872. He gave a remarkable account of poverty in London, which was heightened by Doré's illustrations.

'London wears a dismal exterior to the eye of the foreigner, because all London is hard at work. The streets West as well as here in the East, where we are being hustled on our way to the Docks, are filled with people who have errands.

Through shabby, slatternly places, by low and poor houses, amid shiftless riverside loungers, with the shipping-littered Thames on our right; we push on to the eastern dock between Wapping and down Shadwell. Streets of poverty-marked tenements, gaudy public-houses and beer-shops, door-steps packed with lolling, heavy-eyed, half-naked children; low-browed and bare-armed women greasing the walls with their backs, bullies of every kind walking as masters of the pavement—all sprinkled with drunkenness—compose the scene.

[In the parks] the high-bred, delicate, rose-tinted beauty of women and children; the courage and comeliness of the amazons; the calm, solid air of their cavaliers; the perfect horses; the perfect appointments of the liveried attendants; add to the genial air of quiet strength and grace which characterizes the scene.'

The rosy children and their nurses continued to enjoy the London parks. Though factory machinery worked incessantly, and the

'monstrous serpents' of smoke continued to trail over the industrial
cities and towns, a street disturbance occurred in Leeds which
symbolized the beginning of a new epoch for the under-privileged
child. In April 1872, though four hundred children returned to
Marshall's factory after a strike, many recalcitrant ones stayed out
and stoned the factory with great hostility. By 1885 only three
children were employed, and eventually the mill closed down.

2. A FAMILY TOUR

(a)

Their next walk was to Cromford, where are two large cotton
mills, belonging to Sir Richard Arkwright, who, by his ingenuity,
contrived a variety of machines, which have enabled the manufacturer to sell his goods at a much cheaper rate than before . . .
Though the principal part of the work at these mills is performed
by machinery, our travellers had the satisfaction of seeing here a
thousand children employed usefully, and learning an early habit of
industry.

> PRISCILLA WAKEFIELD, *A Family Tour through the
> British Empire; Particularly Adapted to the Amusement and
> Instruction of Youth*, p. 39

(b)

Their next stage was Dunstable, where a number of poor women
offered them baskets of pretty straw-work, ingeniously twisted into
boxes, baskets, hats, bonnets, slippers, and a variety of other small
articles. Most of the poor women and children in this neighbourhood gain a livelihood by making lace or working in straw.

> PRISCILLA WAKEFIELD, *A Family Tour through the
> British Empire*, p. 440

3. CHIMNEY SWEEPS

The sufferings of the sweeps' 'climbing boys' often resulted in deform-
ity, disease (cancer among others), and death. Those who survived often
'came to no good'.

Hanway was one of the earliest reformers to advocate better conditions
for them. The first Bill in 1788 prohibited boys under eight from becom-
ing apprentices. No sweep was to have more than six at one time. The

Lords refused to have sweeps licenced. The Act was almost totally ignored. The Society for Superseding the Necessity of Climbing Boys was formed about 1800. It tried to encourage the use of a version of a brush invented by George Smart. A similar 'device' was not universally used till nearly a hundred years later.

HOME NEWS

London, Dec. 31 [1802]   The dangerous practice of forcing little chimney sweeps to climb up a nich on the outside of St. George's Church, Hanover Square, still continues. A dirty brute, was yesterday employed for near two hours in forcing a child, at the risk of his life, to climb up the place alluded to; sometimes by sending another lad to poke him up, by putting his head underneath him, and at others by pricking him with a pin fastened to the end of a stick. The poor child, in the struggles to keep himself from falling, had rubbed the skin from his knees and elbows, while the perspiration arising from fear and exertion covered his face and breast as if water had been thrown upon him.

THE LADY'S MAGAZINE, or Entertaining Companion for the Fair Sex, Vol. XXXIII, p. 52

4.   BUNDLE-BOY

The naming of foundlings was sometimes difficult. They were often called after famous people. Occasionally they were named derisively, like one Fortune Natus. Others had names designed to recall their misfortune. Such a one was christened *Job Cinere Extractus*. He was found without 'any ragge or cloth' on a heap of ashes, and only lived three days thereafter. *Bundle Boy*, similarly named, had a slightly better start in life, owing to his mother's ingenuity.

HOME NEWS

London, March, 1803.   A few days ago, a woman presented, at a pawn-broker's office, a bundle of clothes as a pledge, demanding at the same time to be informed of the sum which the pawn-broker would lend . . . she was answered that eighteen shillings was the highest sum that could be advanced on the goods; but, as the woman seemed to consider the sum to be inadequate to her wants, she re-packed her bundle with great care, in the presence of the clerk, and withdrew to the door. In about a few seconds she returned, and said she had changed her mind and would accept the sum offered her, laying, at the same time, a bundle on the counter: she, accordingly, received the money, and went away. The clerk took up the bundle to convey it upstairs to the store-room, and had proceeded a part of the way, when he perceived something to move within the bundle; and, upon opening the outside folds of the bundle, his astonishment upon perceiving a fine boy may be easier conceived than expressed. It should be stated that the pawn-broker, having had the child christened, and called Bundle-boy, provided it with proper clothes and a nurse, and has exercized the most attentive humanity to the little orphan.

THE LADY'S MAGAZINE, etc., Vol. XXXIII, p. 164

5. HOME NEWS

London, Dec. 19.   An alarming fire broke out late on Friday night at a green-grocer's shop in the Borough. It unfortunately happened that a careless girl went to put a young child to bed, and in so doing set the curtains on fire: the blaze alarmed her, and, in place of taking the poor infant out she ran down the stairs, leaving the door open; when the outer door was opened, some persons rushed in; when one brought the child out of the bed; but it was unfortunately so dreadfully burnt, particularly about the head and face, that its death took place at seven the next morning.

THE LADY'S MAGAZINE, etc., Vol. XXXIII, p. 669

6. A ROYAL PROTEGÉE

Caroline, then Princess of Wales, was the object of much virulent gossip. Her protégé, William Austin, was one of the targets. The following touching account of his adoption by the Princess appears to bear the stamp of truth.

A Statement of Facts relative to the Child now under the Protection of Her Royal Highness the Princess of Wales; Describing at large, the Circumstances of the Child's being taken from a poor Woman from Deptford; the Particulars of its Birth, &c.; and some Account of the Parents of the Child. [Commission in 1806]

AUSTIN being still out of employ, and his wife hearing that several persons had made application to HER ROYAL HIGH-NESS THE PRINCESS OF WALES to procure a reinstatement

in his Majesty's Dock Yard, she was advised to try on behalf of
her husband . . . His wife accordingly took the petition, and went
with the child (WILLIAM) in her arms, on Saturday the 23rd of
October, 1802, to MONTAGUE HOUSE.

Mr. STIKEMAN appearing, she requested him to present the
petition, stating that the object was to get her husband reinstated . . .
He said, he was 'denied doing such things; having applications of
a similar nature, almost daily.' She urged her distress . . . He then
gave her a SHILLING, took the petition and put it into his pocket,
observed *she had a fine child in her arms, and asked how old it
was*: Mrs. Austin answered, about three months. Mr. STIKE-
MAN replied, *if it had been about a* FORTNIGHT OLD, HE
COULD HAVE GOT IT TAKEN CARE OF FOR HER; she
observed to him that she thought it a better age to be taken from the
mother, than if it were younger; he answered, 'Ah, true.' He then
looked at its legs, saying, 'It's a fine child, give it to me.' He accordingly took the child into the house.

[At a later date] Mrs. Austin made all possible haste, and arrived
at Montague House at about two o'clock . . . Mr. STIKEMAN,
came to her—and desired her to follow him. Mr. STIKEMAN
then shewed her into the *Blue-room*, and told her she was now to
be *introduced* TO HER ROYAL HIGHNESS. *Mrs. Austin waited
for about two hours* . . .

At length, HER ROYAL HIGHNESS came into the room
where Mrs. Austin was, accompanied by two ladies . . . HER
ROYAL HIGHNESS came to her as she stood with the child in
her arms, and touching the child under the chin, said, '*O what a
nice one;—how old is it?*' Mrs. Austin replied, about three months.

One lady then asked her whether she thought she could make up
her mind to part from the child, observing 'what a fortunate woman
she would be to have her child taken under the protection of so
illustrious a personage, and that the child would, in all respects, be
brought up and treated as a young prince; and if he should behave
properly as he grew up, what an excellent thing it would be for
him.' Mrs. Austin replied, that she thought she could part with him
to such a person as her Royal Highness, rather than keep it, and
suffer it to want. The lady then gave her a *pound note*, and desired
her to go into the coffee-room, and get some arrow-root and other
necessaries, for the purpose of weaning the child.

On Monday, at about 11 o'clock, Mrs. Austin left home . . . In

H

her way to Montague House, she met Mr. STIKEMAN.—Observing her cry, he inquired the cause of her grief; she told him they were the mingled tears of joy and grief at parting from her child. He said, '*Make haste up, and make free and ask for anything you want, and the ladies will not think the worse of you by seeing you in trouble at parting from your child!*'

MARY WILSON shewed her into Miss SANDER'S room, which is next to her Royal Highness's sleeping-room . . . Miss SANDER came from her Royal Highness's room, and seeting her much distressed at parting from the infant, she said, '*It is still your option whether to leave it or not with her Royal Highness.*' Mrs. Austin replied, '*she would certainly let her Royal Highness have it, as she knew it would be taken care of.*' Miss SANDER then took the child, saying, 'Take a kiss of your mother, my dear, at parting,' and conveyed it to HER ROYAL HIGHNESS.—Miss SANDER then brought back the clothes which the child wore, when it was brought, even to the very pins.

EDWARDS'S GENUINE EDITION. 'THE BOOK!', p. 116 *et seq.*

7. 'YOUNG COCKNIES'

Robert Blincoe was probably born in 1792. He was placed in St. Pancras workhouse. The amenities provided were enough to preserve life, and he was not overworked. However, he became melancholy. A cotton-factory owner near Nottingham applied for a batch of new apprentices. The children were deliberately misled. They were made to believe 'that they were all, when they arrived at the cotton-mill, to be transformed into Ladies and Gentlemen; that they would be fed on roast beef and plum-pudding, be allowed to ride their masters' horses and have silver watches and plenty of cash in their pockets.'

These falsehoods fired the childrens' imaginations. 'They strutted about like so many dwarfish and silly Kings and Queens in a mock tragedy.' In this exalted state they eagerly agreed to become apprentices. When the waggons carrying the consignment of children arrived at Nottingham they were exhausted. A crowd likened them to lambs led to the slaughter. In many cases local inhabitants were unaware of pauper apprentices working among them until fever broke out which endangered the community as a whole.

At first Blincoe took Lowdam Cotton Mill (about ten miles from Nottingham) for a church. The children entered a large room with a disagreeable oily smell. They had watery porridge and doughy black bread for supper. Discipline was maintained by a large man brandishing a horse-whip. Then some established apprentices came in with matted hair and rank-smelling ragged clothes. They were thin and sallow. Blincoe then went to sleep in a tiered bunk shared with another boy. A bell tolled at five a.m. for breakfast.

Later Blincoe and his associates descended to the lowest depths of human degradation. Either punishments or accidents occurred daily. Some maintain that Robert Blincoe overstated his case. Whether this is so or not, Blincoe's endurance eventually enabled him to make a seminal contribution to industrial reform.

They reached the mill about half past five. Blincoe heard the burring sound before he reached the portals and smelt the fumes of the oil with which the axles of twenty thousand wheels and spindles were bathed.

Blincoe was assigned to a room, over which a man named *Smith* presided. The task first allotted to him was, to pick up the loose cotton. He set to with diligence, although much terrified by the machinery, and not a little affected by the dust and flue with which he was half suffocated. Unused to the stench, he soon felt sick, and by constantly stooping, his back ached. Blincoe, sat down . . . His task-master told him to keep on his legs. He did so, till twelve o'clock, without the least intermission. Blincoe suffered at once by thirst and hunger.

After Blincoe had been employed in the way described, he was *promoted* to the more important employment of a roving winder. Being too short of stature, he was placed on a block; [but] he was not able by any possible exertion, to keep pace with the machinery. He was beaten by the overlooker, and cursed and reviled from morning till night.

About the second year of his servitude, when the whole of the eighty children sent from Pancras Workhouse, had lost their plump and fresh appearance, a most deplorable accident happened in Lowdham Mill. A girl, named Mary Richards, who might be nearly ten years of age, attended a drawing frame, below which, and about a foot from the floor, was a horizontal shaft, by which frames above were turned. It happened, one evening, just as she was taking off her weights, her apron was caught by the shaft. In an instant the poor girl was drawn by an irresistible force and dashed on the floor. She uttered the most heart-rending shrieks! Blincoe ran towards her, an agonized beholder. He saw her whirled round with the shaft—he heard the bones of her arms, legs, thighs, &c, crushed, as the machinery whirled her round, and drew tighter and tighter her body within the works, her blood was scattered over the frame and streamed upon the floor—at last, her mangled body was jammed in so fast, between the shafts and the floor, that the water being low and the wheels off the gear, it stopped the main shaft! When she was extricated, every bone was found broken!—her head dreadfully crushed!—her clothes and mangled flesh were, apparently inextricably mixed together, and she was carried off, as supposed, quite lifeless . . . But neither the spine of her back was broken, nor were her brains injured, and to the amazement of every one, who beheld her mangled and horrible state, by the skill of the surgeon, and the excellence of her constitution, she was saved!—to be sent back to the same mill, to pursue her labours upon crutches, made a cripple for life, without a shilling indemnity from the parish, or the owners of the mill!

. . . It was in the month of November, when this removal took place! On the evening of the second day's journey, the children reached Litton Mill. Its situation, at the bottom of a sequestered glen, remote from any human habitation, marked a place fitted for the foul crimes of frequent occurrence which hurried so many of the friendless victims of insatiate avarice, to an untimely grave.

The lodging-room, the bedding, every thing was inferior to what it was at Lowdham; and the smell, more offensive. Blincoe passed a restless night. Soon after four in the morning, they were summoned to the work, by the ringing of a bell. Blincoe was put to wind rovings.

Blincoe found his companions in a woeful condition—their bodies were literally covered with weals and contusions—their heads full of wounds, and in many cases, infested with vermin!

The apprentices slept about fifty in a room . . . Sometimes the overlookers detained them in the mill the whole dinner-time. On these occasions they had to work the whole day through, generally *sixteen hours, without rest or food!*

On Sunday, bacon-broth and turnips were served out, which they eat with oaten cake, in dirty wooden bowls. There was generally a quantity of broth to spare, which often became fetid before it was cold. Into this hog-wash, a few pails more of water were poured and some meal stirred in, and the disgusting mess was served out for supper, or the next day's breakfast, as circumstances required.

Blincoe declared, that the stench of this broth was often so power-ful as to turn his stomach, and yet, keen hunger forced him to eat it. At other times, when they had rice puddings—the rice being bad and full of maggots, Blincoe not being able to endure such food, used to go to the woods near the factory, and get hips and hipleaves, clover or other vegetable, and filling his bosom, run back to the mill, and eat his trash, instead of the foul rice . . . Excess of toil, of filth, and of hunger, led to the poor children being visited by contagious fevers. This calamity, which often broke, by pre-mature death, the bands of this vile thraldom, prevailed to such an extent, as to stop the works.

It happened one Sunday . . . Thomas Linsey, a fellow 'prentice thought he could like a snack, early in the morning, therefore he took a slice of bacon between two pieces of oat-cake to bed with him, and put it under his head. The next morning about three or four o'clock, as it was a usual practice in the summer time when short of water, for a part of the hands to begin their work sooner, by this contrivance we was able to work our full time or near. Linsey was found dead in bed, and as soon as some of the 'prentices knew of his death, there was a great scuffle who should have the bacon and pat-cake from under his head, some began to search his pockets for his tin, this tin he used to eat his victuals with; some had pieces of broken pots, as no spoons was allowed. There was no coroner's inquest held over Linsey.

Mr. Needham the master stands accused of having been in the habit of knocking down the apprentices with his clenched fists;—beating them with sticks, or flogging them with horse-whips; of seizing them by the ears, lifting them from the ground and forcibly dashing them down on the floor, or pinching them till his nails met! Blincoe declares his oppressors used to seize him by the hair of his head till the crown of his head became bald. John Needham, following the example of his father, lies under the imputation of crimes of the blackest hue . . . To boys, he was a tyrant and an oppressor! To the girls the same, with the additional odium of treat-ing them with an indecency as disgusting as his cruelty was terrific. Those unhappy creatures were at once the victims of his ferocity and his lust.

JOHN BROWN, *A Memoir of Robert Blincoe, an Orphan Boy* (passim).

8. PLEASURE AND PAIN

Thomas Cooper wrote an account of childhood poverty when records
were comparatively rare. He was clearly a gifted child, though hampered
by sickness and adverse circumstances. His father was a Yorkshire
Quaker. He must have been unusually vigorous to have survived so
many vicissitudes.

I was born at Leicester, on the 20th of March, 1805; but my
father was a wanderer by habit; and so I was removed to Exeter
when I was little more than twelve months old. I fell into the Leate,
a small tributary of the Exe, on the day that I was two years old.
After being borne down the stream a considerable way, I was
taken out, and supposed to be dead; but was restored by medical
skill.

A more pleasing remembrance is that of having been taken at
five o'clock on Christmas-day morning to hear the great organ of
St. Peter's Cathedral. I was not then three years old. And I remember, quite as well, how the milkwoman used to give me white
bread thickly covered with cream.

I learned to read almost without instruction; and at three years
old I used to be set on a stool, in Dame Brown's school, to teach
one Master Bodley, who was seven years old, his letters.

My mother became a widow when I was but four years old, and
left Exeter for Lincolnshire.

My earliest recollections of Gainsborough begin with my taking
the small-pox, which I had so severely that I was blind nineteen
days, was worn till the bones came through my skin, at the knees,
hips, and elbows, and was thrice believed to be dead. Measles and
scarlet fever came close upon my weak recovery from the more fell
disease.

As soon as I was strong enough, I was sent to a dame's school,
near at hand, kept by aged Gertrude Aram. Her school-room was
always full; and she was an expert and laborious teacher of the art
of reading and spelling. I soon became her favourite scholar.

I had very little play out of doors, for that year of diseases had
rendered me a very ailing child. So my mother bought me penny
story books, and I used to complete my enjoyment of them by getting them by heart, and repeating them.

On fine Sundays, my mother began to take me into the fields to
gather flowers. And on rainy Sundays, my mother would unwrap

from its careful cover a treasure which my father had bought, Baskerville's quarto Bible . . .

. . . We were not half-way towards Lea, when we were met by Cammidge, a master chimney-sweeper, and his two apprentices bending under huge soot bags. He began to entice my mother into an agreement for me to be his apprentice, and took out two golden guineas from his purse and offered them to her. She looked anxiously at them, but shook her head; and I clung trembling to her apron, and cried, 'Oh, mammy, mammy! do not let the grimy man take me away!' 'No, my dear bairn, he shall not,' she answered; and away we went—leaving the chimney-sweeper in a rage.

THOMAS COOPER, *The Life of Thomas Cooper, Written by Himself.* pp. 4–10

9. FATHERLY CONCERN

Nelson's much admired colleague, Lord Cuthbert Collingwood, was born in 1750. He served in the navy for fifty years; forty-four were spent in active service abroad. His letters to his family show a deep concern for their well-being. His brother said that Cuthbert was 'a pretty and gentle boy'. He entered the navy at the age of eleven. At that time the first lieutenant spoke to him most kindly on finding him home-sick and sad. Cuthbert was so grateful for the encouragement that he offered the lieutenant a large piece of plum-cake baked by his mother.

Letter from Lord Collingwood to J. E. Blackett, Esq.

Ocean. January 1, 1807

I hope you are with my beloved family enjoying yourselves in great comfort; and long may you live uninvaded by the sounds of war . . . Tell the children that [the dog] Bounce is very well and very fat, yet he seems to be not content, and sighs so piteously these long evenings that I am obliged to sing him to sleep, and have sent them the song.

> Sigh no more, Bouncey, sigh no more,
>   Dogs were deceivers never;
> Though ne'er you put one foot on shore,
>   True to your master ever.
> Then sigh not so, but let us go,
>   Where dinners daily ready,
> Converting all the sounds of woe
>   To heigh phiddy diddy.

It is impossible that at this distance I can direct and manage the education of my daughters; but it costs me many an anxious hour. The ornamental part of education, though necessary, is secondary; and I wish to see theirs enlarged by a true knowledge of good and evil, that they may be able to enjoy the one, if it be happily their lot, and submit contentedly to any fortune rather than descend to the other.

I shall have great pleasure in being sponsor to Sir William Blackett's child; and if it be a son, and he will make him a sailor, I desire my little Sarah will begin to teach him his compass, that he know how to steer his course in the world, which very few people do . . .

CORRESPONDENCE AND MEMOIR OF LORD
COLLINGWOOD, p. 261

10. REBELS

In the autumn of 1808 there was another outbreak [at Winchester College]. It appears that it was the custom of the school not to make every Saint's-day a holiday, but to ask the Praefects whether they objected to its being treated as a school-day. The Praefects, with the inveterate Toryism of boy nature, regarded this as an invasion of their privileges. A considerable section of them banded together to order the juniors not to go into school . . . But it soon appeared that only half the Sixth Book had agreed to rebel, and that half chiefly junior Praefects. In a very short time they submitted, and asked pardon, and the Doctor wisely granted a general amnesty, only abstaining from appointing any of the mutineers to the offices in college . . .

THE REV. H. C. ADAMS, *Wykehamica*, p. 166

11. A HORRIBLE MISDEAMEANOUR
THE REV. ABRAHAM ASHWORTH

*Sentenced in 1808 to Three Years' Imprisonment in Lancaster Jail for
ill-treating his Female Pupils*

The Rev. Abraham Ashworth, a clergyman and schoolmaster, at Newton, near Manchester, was brought up to receive the judgment of the court of King's Bench, at Westminster, in 1808, he having been convicted at the last Lancaster Assizes on two indictments: for assaulting Mary Ann Gillibrand and Mary Barlow, his scholars;

and for taking such indecent liberties with their persons as greatly to hurt and injure them.

Mr Justice Grose addressed the defendant to the following effect: 'You have been convicted of an assault upon a child of very tender years; the aggravations of your offence, I am sorry to say, are multi-farious. The object of your brutality was a child committed to your care and instruction, and you are a clergyman and a teacher—a man grey in years, and possessing a large family. Instead of protecting the child from the contamination of the world, you exposed her to your own licentiousness, and sought to corrupt her mind.'

The Court observed that the fear of a greater punishment be-falling him* prevented them from inflicting that of the pillory.

THE COMPLETE NEWGATE CALENDAR, Vol. V, p. 34

12. A LACE SCHOOL

The smaller domestic industries which employed child labour included glove-making, hand knitting, straw plaiting, button-making and lace-making. Children sorted straws at four, plaited a year later, and earned a small wage at six. Three and four year old children were taught to use bobbins and at five were frequently employed in a lace school.

One child was credibly reported to have started work drawing lace at the age of two. At the age of four the child worked twelve hours a day, except for three-quarters of an hour for meals. A Northamptonshire lace school has been described:

Here the hours were from 6 a.m. to 6 p.m. in the summer, and from 8 a.m. to 8 p.m. in the winter. The girls had to stick ten pins a minute. On Saturdays, however, they had a half-holiday, working only to the dinner hour.

They paid 2d. a week (or 3d. in winter) for lights, and in return they received the money realized from the sale of the lace they made, and they could earn about 6d. a day. . . In the evenings eighteen girls worked by one tallow candle, value one penny. . . In the day time as many as thirty girls, and sometimes boys, would work in a room about twelve feet square, with two windows, and in the winter they would have no fire for lack of room.

B. PALLISER, *A History of Lace*, p. 390

* It was apprehended that he would, if pilloried, have been killed there by the enraged populace.

13. AMENDS
PATRICK M'DONALD

A Poor Boy, convicted at the Old Bailey of stealing,
and presented with a Deluge of Shillings

The miserable object of the present case, an emaciated lad of about fourteen, appeared at the bar at the Old Bailey. He was indicted for stealing a jacket, being almost naked, valued at fourteen shillings.

Being asked what he had to say in his defence, he told an affecting tale that he was a cabin-boy in a merchant vessel which arrived six months before, but returned without him; that he found himself destitute; and that cold and hunger alone had compelled him to steal clothes and food.

One of the jury asked him if he had eaten anything that day, to which he answered 'No, sir; nor a bit the day before.' He then burst into tears, which produced such an effect that the sheriff gave him some silver, and the jury, before they gave their verdict, each handed him a shilling.

The judge then ordered that the boy should be taken care of, and observed that he would then procure his pardon.

While this child of poverty and wretchedness was withdrawing, shillings, from all parts of the court and gallery, were thrown to to him, which amounted to a sum sufficient to clothe and nourish him.

THE COMPLETE NEWGATE CALENDAR, Vol. V, p. 87.

14. HOME NEWS

Blackburn, June 1. On Monday morning last this town was thrown into great alarm by seeing a crowd of people assembled on a hill near Grimshaw Park. About twelve o'clock a great concourse, principally boys, paraded the streets for about an hour, armed with long staves. About eleven o'clock the soldiers sallied forth upon them, and after securing about a dozen who appeared the foremost, quickly dispersed the rest.

THE LADY'S MAGAZINE, or Entertaining Companion for THE FAIR SEX; Vol. XXXIII, 1808

15. INFANTILE STRENGTH

In 1808, Vancouver, who recommended apprenticeship for boys, maintained that girls should be treated with greater consideration, and

...that some further regulations should be made to soften the severity of their servitude. Scraping the roads, lanes and yards, turning over mixings and filling dung-pots, is at best a waste of time. What can a female child at the age of ten be expected to perform with mattock or shovel? Or how will she be able to poise, at the end of a dung fork, any reasonable weight, so as to lift it into the dung-pots slung on the horses' backs? Even driving the horses after they are loaded, is by no means an employment proper for such girls, being altogether incompatible with the more domestic duties they ought early to be made acquainted with.

VANCOUVER, *Devonshire*, p. 360

16. OLD SCANDALS

Eton's famous Dr. Keate met a group of his old pupils in Paris soon after Waterloo. They passed the bottle round and raked up old scandals. 'Sumner's flirtation with the fair Martha at Spier's;' 'Lumley's poaching in Windsor Park;' 'Suppers at the Christopher;' and so on. The Doctor expressed a regret that he had not flogged his pupils more.

Evidently the frolic described below was not unique. The masters took their distinguished pupils to a sumptuous hotel. The Hummums was founded in the seventeenth century as a hammam (turkish baths) with hotel accommodation above it.

(a)

[The tutors] Drury and Knapp, were good-natured men enough, but passionately devoted to theatricals. They used to start for London after school, and passed their nights in jovial suppers with Edmund Kean. They terminated these little expeditions by driving back, with very bad headaches in a curricle.

One fine day, these jovial pedagogues took with them two of my chums, John Scott, the son of Lord Eldon, and Lord Sunderland, the late Duke of Marlborough. They arrived in a few minutes at the Hummums, a famous hotel in Covent Garden, where Kean had ordered dinner.

They drank pretty freely; and they sallied out after dinner in search of adventures. They created such a disturbance, that, after several chivalrous encounters with the watchmen, they were taken to Bow Street, and had to be bailed out by the secretary of the Chancellor. This incident created much scandal.

CAPTAIN GRONOW, *Reminiscences and Recollections*, p. 233 Vol. 1

(b) A DISTINGUISHED REGIMENT

My entrance into the Army.—After leaving Eton, I received an Ensign's commission in the First Guards, during the month of December 1812. I joined in February 1813, and cannot but recollect with astonishment how limited and imperfect was the instruction which an officer received at that time; he absolutely entered the army without any military education whatever.

After passing through the hands of the drill sergeant with my friends and mounting guard at St. James's for a few months, we were hurried off, one fine morning, in charge of a splendid detachment of five hundred men to join Lord Wellington in Spain. [Thanks to] Macadam we were able to march twenty miles a day with ease until we reached Portsmouth. There we found transports ready to convey a large reinforcement to Lord Wellington.

CAPTAIN GRONOW, *Reminiscences and Recollections*, p. 1

17. 'LUDDING'

The Luddites' threats to destroy machinery aroused general alarm. This was furthered by their crudely written letters. 'Ludding is going to start here again...', wrote Joseph Ratcliff. 'Ludders this time will Die to a man the Determination to have Blood for Blood the Swear that the Will Shoot thee first old Bellsybub the call the and then shoot the Rest of the Devils after.' Their oath was formidable: 'I do swear in the Presence of Almighty God that I wish to be faithful to the object for which this Oath is taken, Moreover that in Case of Failure in Point of Fidelity by any Person I will pursue to Death and the Verge of Nature.'

West Riding Yorkshire. The information of William Hobson of Lockwood. May 21st, 1814

Who saith that he is an Apprentice of Thomas Riley, that about three weeks after the attack was made by Luddites upon Mr Cartwright's Mill at Rawfolds... his said Master overtook him as he was returning from Huddersfield and said what a shocking thing it was that those two poor lads had been kill'd at Rawfold's fight... and then asked this informant if he could not like to be one of them for they wanted just to make up a dozen to go to Mr Radcliffe's for that purpose 'I believe thou'st a lad of good spirit and thou would make a very good one to go with them—' That this informant replied 'Master let my spirit be as it will I will never go to Murder any Man' upon which his Master said 'Be sure thou never tells any one what I have said to thee for if thou dost thou will be shot for thou knows what's going forward'—

THE LUDDITE PAPERS (at Rudding Park, unpublished), document 135.

18. NAUSEATING MEDICINES

Robert Thornton, M.D. (Cantab.) had few new remedies to offer. An exception was the use of the 'lemon, lime, shaddock and orange' as cures for scurvy. Unfortunately he ascribed this to the citric acid content of the fruit, and not to the ascorbic acid which was the effective agent. He does, however, improve on the early eighteenth century technique of administering nasty potions to children. Instead of 'afriting' them by suddenly appearing from behind a curtain with a whip, and using it, he counsels the addition of honey, sugar, and sliced apples, treacle or molasses to 'horrid medicines'.

(a)

Being requested, says Dr. Fothergill, to visit a poor boy named Thomas Countey in a wretched lodging in Bath, on the sixth day of the fever, [typhus] I found the surface of the body discoloured with purple *petechiae*; attended with great prostration of strength, low tremulous pulse, inquietude, delirium, &c. . . . rather than abandon him to despair, the whole body was directed to be rubbed with olive oil every four hours, and its operation to be aided by warm whey, accompanied by a suitable diet of gruel, and arrowroot, and he took a moderate dose of castor oil. After some time his parched skin became moistened, and at length he broke out into a full perspiration. By continuing this simple plan all the alarming symptoms subsided, the purple spots vanished, and his recovery was speedy beyond my expectation.

ROBERT JOHN THORNTON, M.D., *A Family Herbal* (2nd ed., 1814), p. 17

(b)

SUGAR-CANE

Medical Uses.

Sugar was employed originally to render unpleasant and nau-seating medicines grateful to the sick, especially to children; and for syrups, electuaries, and conserves.

ROBERT JOHN THORNTON, M.D., *A Family Herbal*, p. 49

(c)

WINTER WHEAT

As respects children, bread and milk constitutes their first food, and oftentimes biscuits made without butter, and tops and bottoms, are formed into powder and mixed with the milk. Sometimes children are imprudently attempted to be reared by bread alone, boiled in water, which is called pap, when they become emaciated and rickety. But by all means avoid Dalby's carminative, Godfrey's cordial, syrup of poppies, or other heating drugs for your infant: for these are snares that catch the ignorant, delude, entrap, and, alas, [that] root out myriads scarce before they have seen the light of day.

ROBERT JOHN THORNTON, M.D., *A Family Herbal*, p. 77

(d)

FOETID HELLEBORE. Helleborus Foetidus.

Medical Virtue.

A decoction of about a drachm of the green leaves, or fifteen grains of the dried, is given to children, and repeated three mornings, when it seldom fails expelling the round worms.

ROBERT JOHN THORNTON, M.D., *A Family Herbal*, p. 557

When the celebrations for the Peace of 1814 were over, Thomas Cooper was persuaded to go to sea as a cabin boy. But he returned home after nine days, disgusted with the 'coarse language, the cursing and swearing, and brutality'. He then became an apprentice shoemaker.

19. THE GENERAL PEACE

I have many pleasant remembrances of the time that we lived in the house in front of Sailor's Alley.

These years—from 1811 to 1814—were among the hottest of the war period. And while our town was kept in perpetual ferment by the news of battles, and the street would be lined with people to see old Matthew Goy, the postman, ride in with his hat covered with ribbons, and blowing his horn mightily, as he bore the news of some fresh victory—Ciudad Rodrigo, or Badajoz, or Salamanca, or Toulouse,—Miller and I were pencilling soldiers and horses, or, imaginarily, Wellington and 'Boney'—for we never heard the word 'Napoleon', at that time of day.

The Peace of 1814—'the General Peace', as it was emphatically called,—was celebrated in Gainsborough. There was a general holiday; and there was a grand emblematical procession. A car, drawn by six horses, held figures representing Wellington, Blucher, Platoff, the Czar Alexander, together with the fallen emperor labelled 'Going to Elba'. There were bands of music in the streets, a thanksgiving sermon at church, and feasting parties at the inns, during the day; with a general illumination, bonfires, crackers, and squibs, at night.

The next day, Miller and I laid our young heads together, and enlisted other lads we knew, to accompany us on an adventurous expedition to Lea. Papers were coloured and inscribed, and ribbons procured, and flags formed; and away we went to try our fortunes. I was "Wellington", and was so labelled on the front of my blue cap; and Miller was "Emperor of Russia"; and Mason was "Blucher"; and Jack Barton was "Prince Platoff"; and Joe Cawthrey was "General Salt"; and Tom Aram was "Buonaparte".

We went to Squire Western's, and Farmer Swift's, and Sir Charles Anderson's; stood and sung "Awake, my soul, and with the sun" and "Glory to Thee, my God, this night." and other hymns we had learned at school, gave three cheers, after shouting "Peace and Plenty! God save the King!" and then one of us held his cap for coppers, with a low bow. We were well received. The beloved Sir Charles himself stood and smiled to hear us; and called us "very good boys", as he gave us a real silver half-crown!

THOMAS COOPER, *The Life of Thomas Cooper, by Himself*, pp. 17–24

20. LITTLE EMBRYO

Jane Austen's descriptions of middle-class life are remarkably serene considering the momentous events which occurred between 1775 and 1817. Had her family lived in the north, instead of in the south and south-west, her married friends might have had far more troubles.

(a)

Letter from Jane Austen to Anna Lefroy (Tuesday 29 Nov. 1814)
...I am going this morning to see the little girls in Keppel Street. Cassy was excessively interested about your marrying, when she heard of it, which was not till she was to drink your health on the wedding day. She asked a thousand questions, in her usual way— What he said to you? & what you said to him?—And we were very much amused one day by Mary Jane's asking 'what Month her *Cousin* Benjamin was born in?'—

R. W. CHAPMAN (ed.), *Jane Austen's Letters*, p. 415

(b)

Letter from Jane Austen to Fanny Knight
                    23 Hans Place, Wednesday Nov: 30 1814
...I called in Keppel Street & saw them all—Little Harriot sat in my lap—& seemed as gentle and affectionate as ever, & as pretty, except not being quite well.—Fanny is a fine stout girl, talking incessantly, with an interesting degree of Lisp and Indistinctness. That puss Cassy, did not show more pleasure in seeing me than her sisters, but I expected no better;—she does not shine in the tender feelings.

R. W. CHAPMAN (ed.), *Jane Austen's Letters*, p. 419

(c)

From a letter to Cassandra Austen
                    Chawton, Sunday Sept: 8 1816
...Mrs. F. A. seldom either looks or appears quite well.—Little Embryo is troublesome I suppose...

R. W. CHAPMAN (ed.), *Jane Austen's Letters*, p. 464

21. INSURRECTION AGAIN

Though an unpopular Commoner Tutor was the ostensible cause of

1. The Robinson Family: 'Tommy' and his Siblings

2(a). A Midwife

2(b). Nanny's Picture

Nanny's picture of herself & cousin Tommy

3. Street Sellers: Fine Thread Laces

4. The Departure

5. Rule Britannia

7. Straw Hat Maker

8. Cast Out

9. Brick Makers

10. Street Acrobats

11. Gleaning

12. Children Playing

13. Workhouse Children

15. Doll Makers and Doll Breakers

And Papa and Mamma took them
  home the same day,—
They were glad to go home, and yet
  wanted to stay;
But the train went quite fast, and it
  seemed a nice change
To be back in their own home, where
  nothing was strange;

And always they reckon'd that
  seeing these sights
Was a thing to remember—a week of
  delights;
And, though they may see them all
  many times more,
They'll never enjoy them so much, I
  am sure.

16. Happy Family

the boys' revolt, it is significant that it occurred during another period of social unrest.

Among the Commoner Tutors at this time [1818], there was one who was the special object of the boys' dislike. This Tutor was further suspected of having invited some of the Praefects to dine with him; and the boys having been induced to talk unguardedly of their doings, a report of what they had said was carried to Dr. Gabell. A particular walk, which was a favourite with the Praefects, was interdicted,—the object being, to prevent the practice of shirking into the town and names were called at the bottom of "Hills", instead of, as heretofore, the third stile, thus causing a great many to be reported absent.

Slight as these circumstances were, they were enough to cause a general revolt. It was agreed that the whole of the Commoners, 130 in number, should join their school-fellows in college, and together barricade the latter against the Masters. On Thursday, May 7, about half-past three in the afternoon, the final arrangements were made. The boys armed themselves with sticks, and gaining possession of the keys, rushed tumultuously into college. Arrived there, the insurrection proper commenced. The keys of the college also were seized, and the gates locked behind them. It was unanimously resolved to hold out until the Doctor should restore the old bounds.

The leaders now proceeded to marshal and arrange their forces. Some were appointed to act as sentries at the entrances; others as patrols; others to supervise the commissariat. One of the actors in this strange drama... relates how he sat up all night with his companions, over Middle-gate, wrapped in blankets, drinking beer from the great college jacks, and telling ghost stories.

Breakfast, which the 'cooks' had been preparing, was now served in the college hall. The provisions were potatoes, flour, and bacon; out of these materials [they] had endeavoured to manufacture soup. When the lids of the tureens were taken off, there appeared about two inches of lukewarm fat, under that was a quantity of solid dough, and at the bottom of all a mass of raw potato.

... the Warden himself made his appearance at one of the windows and threw down a sheet of paper. This was found to contain the following words: 'If the scholars in 1793 had intimated to the authorities the subject of their complaints, the trouble and scandal then caused would have been prevented.' ...

I

Probably the receipt of this letter only encouraged the malcontents
to persevere. One of the seniors ordered a washing-stool, an ink-
stand, and a sheet of foolscap to be fetched, and, summoning his
school-fellows round him, gravely inquired of each whether he had
any complaint to make of the Warden. A whole string of *gravamina*
was straightway poured forth, and faithfully transferred to the
paper.

The boys now set themselves to secure the door of the Warden's
house, through which they feared that the soldiers might enter the
court from the Warden's garden. A staple was wrenched from one
of the out-houses, and driven into the centre of the door; a stout
cord was passed through it, and lashed to spars fixed on either door-
jamb. One of the Commoner Tutors was commissioned to inform
the boys that the Riot Act had been read, and the soldiers sent for;
but as the authorities were anxious to prevent injury to the college,
all the boys, if they would surrender the keys, were at liberty to go
home for a fortnight.

Less wise than their predecessors, the boys fell into the trap
prepared for them. They handed over the keys, threw away their
sticks, and rushed joyously through the gate towards High-street,
in order to take advantage of their furlough. They ran down College-
street, and through the Cathedral Close; but as they approached
the narrow stone passage, they encountered a company of soldiers,
headed by an officer. Something of a scuffle followed, and one of the
boys knocked down the officer. But they were not prepared to fight
with their fists against soldiers armed with bayonets. They turned
short round, and ran back through the Close; the red-jackets
followed, making many captures, and handing their prisoners over
to the school authorities.

In this manner they reached College-street, and would have
escaped from the town by the road over Black-bridge, if a second
row of soldiers had not confronted them, drawn across the street just
beyond the college gate. Shut in between two fires, the boys could
do nothing; the College-boys were compelled to pass singly through
the wicket, and were met by the announcement that twenty of their
body were expelled.

Further outrages, indeed, were perpetrated, for which no penalties
could be exacted. The whole of the glass, frames and all, were
smashed in the school-room and Commoner Hall. A considerable
number of the Commoners again escaped, and after a grand dinner

at the 'George', went home to their friends. Some of these were brought back, others left; and things were gradually reduced to something like order.

THE REV. H. C. ADAMS, M.A. *Wykehamica. A History of Winchester College and Commoners*, p. 181

22. PETERLOO

The meeting subsequently known as 'Peterloo' took place on August 9th, 1819. An advertisement on July 31st stated that the purpose of the meeting was 'to take into consideration the most speedy and effectual mode of obtaining Radical Reform in the Commons House of Parliament'. Probably it was merely a holiday outing to the young people and children who took part in it.

An onlooker, Archibald Prentice, saw the crowd going down Mosley Street. He said that though the men were haggard, the general impression was one of gaiety. Most of the crowd consisted of young people in their best clothes. The women wore light-coloured dresses. They walked in an orderly manner and carried flags. When he asked various women if they were afraid, they laughed and wondered what there was to be afraid of. However, when the mounted troop of Manchester Yeomanry in Pickford's Yard were summoned, they came down Nicholas Street at 'a tolerably brisk pace'. A young woman carrying her two-year-old child in her arms stood watching them. Just then one of the Yeomanry who had been detained came past 'at a hand-gallop'. The woman was knocked down and stunned. The child was thrown out of her arms on to its head and was killed. This was the first casualty.

In the account of the trial which follows, a charwoman stated that, after the Yeomanry Cavalry had charged, her house was filled with wounded people, and 'was liker to a slaughter-house than to a Christian's house, with human blood'.

In the King's Bench
between
Thomas Redford, Plaintiff, and Hugh Hornby Birley, Alexander Oliver, Richard Withington, and Edward Meagher, Defendants
for
An Assault on the 16th August, 1819.

William Harrison sworn: examined by Mr Blackburne.

Q. You are, I believe, a cotton spinner and live at Oldham? *A.* Yes.

Q. Did you go with a company of your townsmen from Oldham to Manchester on that day? A. Yes.

Q. Your wife and child went? A. With me along.

Q. Will you tell us what proportion of women were among this 5,000 or 6,000? A. There were as near as I can think, near 1,000 women, young girls, some thirteen years, some ten years old.

Q. Did they march in ranks as soldiers do? A. They did not march as soldiers do, for they had not common sense to do it; such low boys, so little, thirteen or fourteen years of age.

Q. You do not mean to say there was no word of command, till you got to Oldham? A. The banners went before; when the banners stopped we stopped: there were girls dressed in white.

Q. Did you not see children in arms—their mothers' arms? A. Oh! Yes; women with children in their arms plenty, watching.

John Jones.

Q. Did you see the Yeomanry Cavalry come into the field? A. I did.

Q. At what speed did they go down? A. They came as fast as they well could for the crowd. When they got to the hustings they formed round it; when they cleared the hustings, they made a charge on the people.

Q. Did the people try to escape? A. The people fled in all directions, they were riding over men, women, and children. . .

Q. Did you see anything more? A. There came a great mass of people against my door then; the cavalry came up and struck them; the people were groaning and shrieking till an officer came up and said 'Gentlement, forbear, the people cannot get away.'

The Rev. Jeremiah Smith, D.D., sworn.

Q. You the head Master of the Grammar School in Manchester? A. I am.

Q. Did you take any precautions on the morning of that day, as to your doors and windows? A. I dismissed the boys from the school; I collected my own boarders under my own premises, locked both the doors leading to the street, and closed the shutters in front of my house. . .

Q. You say you sent the boys home, what was the reason? A. I feared the most serious consequences from the influx of strangers, and the meeting; many boys absent from school, and did not come

at all. . . During the short time we were in the school several parents
sent for their boys away, after which I dismissed the school. . .

Q. The day scholars are the principal part of your establishment?
A. I have fifteen boarders now. . .

Q. At what time was it you sent the day scholars home? *A.* I think
soon after ten o'clock; we returned into the school from breakfast
at half-past nine, and, as far as I recollect, we did not remain long
together.

Q. There were a great number? *A.* Fifty or sixty. . . Boys of all
ages.

REPORT OF THE PROCEEDINGS ON THE TRIAL OF
THIS CAUSE [see above] AT LANCASTER

23.   WASP-STINGS

Letter 114, from John Keats to George and Georgiana Keats
                                        Sunday Morn, Feby. 1819
. . . The servant has come for the little Browns this morning—
they have been a toothache to me which I shall enjoy the riddance of
—Their little voices are like wasps' stings—'Sometimes I am all
wound with Browns'.

M. B. FORMAN (ed.), *The Letters of John Keats*, p. 317

24.   GIMLET

Letter 137. To Miss Keats, Rd. Abbey's Esqre Walthamstow near London
                                        Winchester August 28th
. . . We are quiet—except a fiddle that now and then goes like a
gimlet through my Ears. Our Landlady's son not being quite a
Proficient . . .

M. B. FORMAN (ed.), *The Letters of John Keats*, p. 408

25.   EGREGIOUS MISTAKES

Dr. Buchan's advice was chiefly based on common sense, like that of
his eighteenth-century predecessor, Dr. Armstrong. However, Dr. Buchan
placed more emphasis on breast feeding, recommended the simplest diet
for infants, and decried the use of constricting bandages, stays, and
'bend leather'.

He also made pertinent remarks on the long-term inutility of sending
children to work at an age when it could but be injurious to their future
development.

(a)

It appears from the annual registers of the dead, that almost one half of the children born in Great Britain die under twelve years of age...

WILLIAM BUCHAN, M.D., *Domestic Medicine*, pp. 1–3

(b)

Nature knows of no use of clothes to an infant, but to keep it warm. All that is neccessary for this purpose is to wrap it in a soft loose covering.

In most parts of Britain the practice of rolling children with so many bandages is now, in some measure, laid aside; but it would still be a difficult task to persuade the generality of mankind, that the shape of an infant does not entirely depend upon the care of the midwife.

Even the bones of an infant are so soft and cartilaginous, that they readily yield to the slightest pressure, and easily assume a bad shape, which can never after be remedied. Hence it is, that so many people appear with high shoulders, crooked spines, and flat breasts, who had the misfortune to be squeezed out of shape by the application of stays and bandages.

WILLIAM BUCHAN, M.D., *Domestic Medicine*, pp. 1–8

(c)

It is strange how people came to think that the first thing given to a child should be drugs. Midwives never fail to give syrups, oils, &c. whether they be necessary or not.

Few things prove more hurtful to infants than the common method of sweetening their food. It entices them to take more than they ought to do, which makes them grow fat and bloated.

All strong liquors are hurtful to children. Some parents teach their children to guzzle ale, and other fermented liquors. Such a practice cannot fail to do mischief. Milk, water, butter milk, or whey, are the most proper for children to drink. If they have any thing stronger, it may be fine small beer, or a little wine mixed with water.

WILLIAM BUCHAN, M.D., *Domestic Medicine*, pp. 9–11

(d)

One very common error of parents, by which they hurt the constitutions of their children, is sending them too young to school. This is often done solely to prevent trouble. Thus the schoolmaster is made the nurse; and the poor child is fixed to a seat seven or eight hours a day, which time ought to be spent in exercise and diversions.

WILLIAM BUCHAN, M.D., *Domestic Medicine*, pp. 14–15

(e)

Many people imagine it a great advantage for children to be early taught to earn their bread. This opinion is certainly right, provided they were so employed as not to hurt their health or growth; but, when these suffer, society, instead of being benefited, is a real loser by their labour. There are few employments, except sedentary ones, by which children can earn a livelihood; and if they be set to these too soon, it ruins their constitutions.

WILLIAM BUCHAN, M.D., *Domestic Medicine*, p. 16

(f)

One of the most common faults of those who nurse for hire, is dozing children with stupefactives. An indolent nurse, who does not give a child sufficient exercise in the open air to make it sleep, and will seldom fail to procure for it a dose of laudanum, diacodum, saffron, or, a dose of spirits. These, though they be certain poison to infants, are every day administered by many who bear the character of good nurses; but if a mother on visiting her child at nurse finds it always asleep, I would advise her to remove it immediately, otherwise it will soon sleep its last.

WILLIAM BUCHAN, M.D., *Domestic Medicine*, pp. 19–20

26. ONEROUS WORK

Servants in husbandry were hired for one year at statute fairs. They were employed wherever a farmer needed extra labour. Pauper children were also apprenticed to farming. There was hardly any work considered too onerous. Mary Puddicombe from Devonshire stated in 1843 that she had worked on a farm with three other girls, and four boys, when she was nine.

I used to be employed when I was apprenticed in driving bullocks to field and fetching them in again; cleaning out their houses, and bedding them up; washing potatoes and boiling them for pigs; milking; in the field leading horses or bullocks to the plough. Then I was employed in mixing lime to spread, digging potatoes, pulling turnips, and anything that came to hand like a boy. I reaped a little, loaded pack horses; went out with the horses for furze. I got up at five or six, except on market mornings twice a week, and then at three. I went to bed at half past nine. I worked more in the fields than in the house.

REPORT ON EMPLOYMENT OF WOMEN AND
CHILDREN IN AGRICULTURE, 1843, xii, p. 109

27. THE SEARCH FOR PROFIT

The business of Marshall & Co. (the flax-spinning factory) was founded in 1788 by John Marshall, who started his career at eighteen working in his father's drapery business. He was phenomenally successful, because he 'subordinated all interests to the search for profit'. He eventually became (in modern currency) a multi-millionaire. Widely esteemed for his philanthropic works, Marshall took a particularly benevolent interest in the well-being of children and young people. In 1822 he persuaded fellow manufacturers to collaborate in establishing a school in Holbeck (Leeds), and in 1825 he started to send children from his mills there for short periods of instruction. Especial care was taken to select the most 'submissive' hands to learn the basic elements of literacy.

After 1815, John Marshall spent the next decade establishing himself among the 'aristocracy' of Cumberland. In 1827 the firm's finances were in a satisfactory state. The costs of manufacturing fell by £8,000, and Marshall's son John saved £1,285 in wages.

1820

The school lately erected by Mister Marshall is being now nearly completed.

With a view of rendering the Institution as useful as possible it is proposed that a day school be opened for the instruction of Children in reading and writing and accounts on the following terms:

	Reading and Writing	per week 2d.
Boys		
	Writing and Accounts at the Rule of 3	per week 3d.
Girls	Reading, Writing Accounts and Sewing	per week 2d.

It is also intended that there shall be an evening school (from 7 to 9 o'clock; at 3ᵈ per week finding candles, or 2ᵈ without light) at the same place which may be very convenient and useful to those young persons who are engaged in the manufactories and other employments during the course of the day.

THE MARSHALL PAPERS (unpublished)

28

ORDER FOR THE MAINTENANCE OF A BASTARD CHILD

WEST-RIDING of YORKSHIRE	THE ORDER OF *the Reverend James Geldart, Doctor of Laws and William Lister Fenton Scott, Esquire*

Two of his Majesty's Justices of the Peace in and for the said Riding, one whereof is of the Quorum, and both residing near unto the Limits of the Parish Church within the Parish of *Bramham*................................... in the said Riding, made the thirtieth .... Day of *September* ...... in the Year of our Lord One Thousand Eight Hundred and Twenty-three .... concerning a *male* .... Bastard Child lately born in the Township of *Bramham* .... in the Parish of *Bramham* .... aforesaid of the Body of *Sarah Barnwell* .... Single-woman.

WHEREAS it hath appeared unto us the said Justices, as well upon the Complaint of the Church wardens and Overseers of the Poor, of the Township of *Bramham* .... in the said Riding as upon Oath of the said *Sarah Barnwell* that on the second *Day of September* .... now last past she was delivered of a *male* .... Bastard Child in the said Township of *Bramham* .... and that the said Bastard Child is now chargeable to the said Township and likely to continue. And further that *John Skelton of Oglethorpe Servant* did beget the said Bastard Child on the Body of the said *Sarah Barnwell*

WE, therefore, upon Examination of the Cause and Circumstances of the Premises, as well upon the Oath of the said *Sarah Barnwell* as otherwise, do hereby adjudge the said *John Skelton* .... to be the reputed Father of the said Bastard Child. And thereupon we do order as well for the better Relief of the said Township of *Bramham* .... as for the Sustentation and Relief of the said Bastard Child, that the said *John Skelton* .... shall and do forthwith upon Notice of this our Order, pay or cause to be paid to the Church-wardens and Overseers of the Poor of the said Township of *Bramham* .... or to some, or one, of them, the Sum of *one Pound nine Shillings* for and towards the lying-in of the said *Sarah Barnwell* .... and the Maintenance of the said Bastard Child, to the Time of making of this our Order. And we do also hereby further order that the said *John Skelton* .... shall likewise pay or cause to be paid to the Churchwardens and Overseers of the Poor of the Township of *Bramham* .... aforesaid for the Time being, or to some, or one, of them, the sum of two Shillings .... weekly and every Week from the present Time for and towards Keeping, Sustentation, and Maintenance of the said Bastard Child, for and during so long time as the said Bastard Child shall be chargeable to the said Township.

AND we do further order that the said *Sarah Barnwell* .... shall also pay or cause to be paid to the said Churchwardens and Overseers of the Poor of the said Township of *Bramham* .... for the Time being, or to some, or one, of them, the Sum of *one Shilling* .... weekly and every Week so long as the said Bastard Child shall be chargeable to the said Township, in Case she shall not nurse and take Care of the said Child herself.

GIVEN under our Hands and Seals, the Day and Year first above-written,

Jas. Geldart
W. L. Fenton Scott

29. ROADMENDING

Gilbert's Act of 1782 had enabled the able-bodied poor to be given relief without entering a workhouse. Inadequate wages were also supplemented. The result was a general lowering of wages, and the widespread abandonment of settled for irregular, seasonal, employment. When the parish provided work for women and children in the winter, it was often road-making, and stone-breaking. James McAdam, giving evidence before the Committee on Labourers' Wages in 1824 said:

I have a great number of instances of men with no less than ten children, and the wife, being wholly employed on the turnpike roads... His sons and himself lift the road, the smaller boys pick the stones, the wife and girls rake the road and keep it in order afterwards... and I have a great number of similar instances.

REPORT ON LABOURERS' WAGES, 1824, vi, p. 42

30. MANSLAUGHTER

GEORGE ALEXANDER WOOD and ALEXANDER WELLESLEY LEITH

Eton College Boys indicted for Manslaughter, 9th of March, 1825, as the Result of a Two-Hours Fierce Fight

The scene of this melancholy event was at Eton College.

On the 9th of March, 1825, George Alexander Wood and Alexander Wellesley Leith, were placed at the bar at the Aylesbury Assizes, charged with killing and slaying the Hon. F. Ashley Cooper, son of the Earl of Shaftesbury.

On Sunday, the 27th of February, about two o'clock, two scholars at Eaton, the Hon. F. A. Cooper and Mr Wood, were in the playground, when some words arose between them. From words they proceeded to blows: they had fought for several minutes when the captain came up and separated them. It was subsequently determined that they should meet on the following afternoon and terminate their differences by a pugilistic contest. The combatants stripped at four o'clock on Monday afternoon and commenced fighting. Mr Cooper was under fifteen years, and his opponent, who was half-a-head taller, was nearly seventeen. Mr Cooper declared that he would never give in. In the eighth, ninth, and tenth rounds he became weak and exhausted, and it was evident that he was not a match for Mr Wood. Some of the 'backers' had brought a quantity of brandy in bottles into the field; and the second of Mr Cooper having, in the eleventh round, poured a portion of it down Mr C.'s throat, he recovered his wind and strength. The young men continued to fight till nearly six o'clock; and when they were in a state of exhaustion they were plied between the rounds with brandy.

They fought about sixty rounds, and at the end of the last round Mr Cooper fell very heavily upon his head, and never spoke afterwards. He was put to bed; but no medical assistance was sent for till four hours had elapsed. Shortly afterwards he expired.

Upon the arraignment of the defendants they pleaded not guilty, and the witnesses for the prosecution did not answer. Mr Justice Gaselee having ordered their recognizances to be estreated, and a verdict of not guilty was returned.

THE COMPLETE NEWGATE CALENDAR, Vol. V, p. 197

31. PLAIN LIVING

In the year 1872 Queen Victoria wrote down with her own hand some reminiscences of her early childhood, the manuscript of which is preserved at Windsor, and which may be quoted here.

"My earliest recollections are connected with Kensington Palace, where I can remember crawling on a yellow carpet—and being told that if I cried and was naughty my 'uncle Sussex' would hear me and punish me. We went to Cumberland Lodge, the King living at the Royal Lodge. When we arrived at the Royal Lodge the King took me by the hand, saying: 'Give me your little paw.'

We lived in a very simple manner; breakfast was at half-past eight, luncheon at half-past one, dinner at seven—to which I came generally (when it was no regular large dinner party)—eating my bread and milk out of a small silver basin. Tea was only allowed as a great treat in later years.

... I was very ill at the time, of dysentery, which illness increased to an alarming degree; many children died of it in the village of Esher. The doctor lost his head, and almost every doctor in London was away. Mr Blagden came down and showed much energy on the occasion. I recovered, and remember well being very cross and screaming dreadfully at having to wear, for a time, flannel next my skin. Up to my 5th year I had been very much indulged by every one, and set pretty well *all* at defiance.

A. C. BENSON and VISCOUNT ESHER (ed.), *The Letters of Queen Victoria*, pp. 10–13

32. GLADSTONE AT ETON

William Ewart Gladstone's decided character ensured that he held aloof from temptation at Eton. It also enabled him to show early signs of leadership, when he checked the sword-slashing activities of rowdy fifth-formers at Salt Hill.

But first one must notice that at the Montem of 1826 he [Gladstone] figured in the procession to Salt Hill disguised as a Greek in white *fustanelle* and embroidered cap. He was one of those who begged for 'salt'—that is, money—in favour of the captain of the school. The 'purse' collected in his favour was one of the largest ever made, and Gladstone contributed not a little to keep most of its contents for Pickering by some energetic action he took in preventing the destruction of flowers in the gardens of the Hotel at Salt Hill. The Fifth Form, who wore scarlet coats, with cocked hats and swords, were wont to draw their swords and lop off the heads of flowers, slash trees and palings, &c., all of which damage had to be paid for by the captain out of his purse. Gladstone appealed to some of his most muscular friends to assist him in checking this wanton destruction; and that year the damages were insignificant compared to what they were sometimes, when they would 'make almost all the salt melt'. As for Gladstone's costume, it was much admired. This was in the year before Navarino, and 'philhellenism' was rampant in public schools.

J. BRINSLEY-RICHARDS, *Seven Years at Eton*, p. 422

33. FINE BOYS

MARINE SOCIETY.—The anniversary dinner of this society (instituted for the Equipment and Instruction of Distressed Boys for the Royal Navy, the East India Company and Merchants' service, and the Fisheries) took place on the 22d March, at the City of London Tavern. The Royal Chairman [The Duke of Clarence] addressed the society repeatedly, and pointed out the peculiar claims for support which a society that supplied the navy with ready-formed seamen, had upon a commercial and maritime country like this. H.R.H. also entered into some details of the benefits conferred by the charity, from which it appeared, that the total number of men and boys provided for by it, from its first commencement down to December 1826, amounted to 75,759. A very fine set of boys belonging to the institution marched round the apartment, bearing the red, white, and blue ensigns, and after giving three hearty cheers, at the sound of the boatswain's whistle, withdrew from the room, leaving a most favourable impression behind them of the effects of the charity from their fine manly and orderly appearance.

THE NAVAL AND MILITARY MAGAZINE, 1827, p. 623

34. A MOTHER AND HER CHILDREN

To the Editor.

Rochester, Sept. 29, 1827

Sir,—On the beach at Gravesend yesterday morning, I saw a gaily dressed young female fondling an infant in her arms, with a fine, lively boy of about three years old running before, who suddenly venturing to interrupt the gravity of a goat, by tickling his beard with a switch, became in danger of over-punishment from the animal. I ran to 'the rescue', and received warm thanks for the achievement. She kissed and scolded her 'dear Lobski', and I inquisitively repeated the appellation. 'Sir,' said she—'it is perfectly ridiculous! his *real Christian* name is Robert.'

—It was brought to my recollection through an incident on the roof of a stage-coach; all of whom, except myself, alighted at Gravesend. One of them, a Londoner, let an expression fall, from whence I suspected he was the husband of Lobski's mother. Being left to pursue the remainder of my journey alone, I perceived a letter. There could not be a doubt that it had escaped from my late fellow-traveller's pocket; It was from his wife and

COPY OF THE LETTER

Gravesend, Thursday aft.

Dear Henry,—We arrived here after a pleasant voyage in one of the Calais steamers. 'Lobski', as usual, quite at home. He really appears to be the flower of Gravesend. He spars with all the sailors who notice him,—nods to the old women—halloes at the boys, and runs off with their hoops—knocks at the windows with his stick—hunts the fowls and pigs, because they run away from him—and admires the goats. As we walk on the beach he looks out for '*anoner* great ship'—kisses the little girls—and torments me. The young ones in the road call him 'Cock Robin'.

He calls to me when he looks at the sea, 'There is my *tub*, Ma.' He was rather frightened, and thought he fell into the water, but not near so much, the guide says, as most children are.

WILLIAM HONE, *The Table Book*, Vol. II, col. 441

35. GROWING CROOKED AT MARSHALL & CO.

Margaret Kendell is 16 yr. old. Came to work with us when 13 yr. old. No. 44 sweeper for 1 year or 1½ year. Line spreader about 1 year. There shewed symptoms of weakness and of growing crooked. Alderson then sent her to Hirst to reel reels for year: went to the infirmary Friday Jan. 6: a patient of D[r] Williamson, admitted an in-patient of Infirmary: no room, will send for her when there is: M[r] Kendell's wife went with her: was asked the hours, and mentioned them correctly 6 to 7.

Sept. 1827. No. 35. 1 year sweeper, had been a spreader 1 month before she left no 35. Left the room when the machinery was removed: went to no 44 Nov. 1828 and spread long line about 1 year: was removed into no 45 about Jan. 1 1831, spread the short line for 160 and 130, began to feel her back weak about May 1831: had our doctor's advice, but put on some cotton bandages which did not appear to do any good: About Aug. or Sept. spoke to Alderson to have her removed: was removed to the reels . . . her back had been worse during that time: no pain: felt weak:—felt better of herself at reels than in the line spreading: did not feel so weak: better appetite: made 6/ or 6/9 at reels, 5/6 at spreading. The reeling was the harder work: . . . her back became worse: about 2 or three weeks ago her father went with her to M[r] Metcalf: said he could not do her any good: recommended her to go to the Infirmary where a machine would be applied to her back:—went to the Infirmary on Friday Jan 6.—was examined by D[r] William, M[r] Smith and about 3 young surgeons—did not take the frock down:— said she was a line spreader: one of them (D[r] W) said he wondered they were not all so: . . . worked from 6 to 7, said that sometimes from 5½ to 7½. M[r] S asked whether she had worked that for 4 months in the year. Ans. only sometimes: sent her to the apoth. shop. had something to take internally and also to apply to her back:— has had no bandage to put on.—has a pain in the left hip when she is sitting.

She never worked regularly at the mill.

THE MARSHALL PAPERS (Unpublished)

CHAPTER 5
1830–1859

1. HIS MAJESTY'S COMMISSIONERS

Between 1830 and 1835 Marshall's took 91 more children under thirteen into employment. That age-group now became 28% of the total working force. Their wages were 3*s*. to 3*s*. 6*d*. a week (about 30/- to 35/- in modern currency). For some time past, John Marshall had been concerned about the very young children of his employees who roamed the 'filthy and unhealthy streets', liable to contract habits of idleness and vice. Therefore he established an infant school in 1832, so that 'the minds of the infant poor' would be set in 'a right temper and disposition'. He also hoped that they would become 'obedient and affectionate towards their masters' and be fitted 'to fulfil the duties of their several stations in after life'.

John Marshall became an affectionate and indulgent father, who was happy to see his own children 'adopt a pleasurable way of life'. They grew up in pleasant surroundings, mixing only with well-bred neighbours. Their interests would formerly have appeared trivial to the 'calculating man of business'. They included hunting, foreign travel and race-horses. Although the youths were sent to the mills at eighteen to learn the family business, they were never imbued with their father's passion for advancement. Nevertheless, he made generous provision for all his children, and gave them in his lifetime £200,000 (in modern currency some £2,000,000).

The Commissioners appointed by His Majesty for enquiring as to the Employment of Children in Factories in the Manufacturing Districts of Great Britain, request from you immediate replies to the following *Queries* with reference to the Persons in your Employment.

Q 1. Name of the Parish or Township, and County, in which the Manufactory, Mill, or Workshop, or Place of Work is situated.
A 1. Township of Holbeck, Parish of Leeds, County of York.
Q 2. Names of the chief descriptions of work carried out thereat.
A 2. Flax spinning:— viz., Heckling, Carding, Preparing, Spinning, Reeling and Drying of Line and Tow Yarns.
Q 10. What is the lowest age at which you employ children?

Have any of them been previously employed at any other trades, and if so, state at what trades?

A 10. None are employed at full time under 11 years of age. A certain number from 9 to 11 years of age are employed in the mill half the day, and required to attend the Mill school the other half of the day. They are paid half wages, no deduction or charge being made for the schooling.

Q 11. Does the nature of your work require the Employment of Children under Twelve Years of Age and why?

A 11. It does not. Children of 11 or 12 years of age are preferred by us to those of 9 or 10. They do more work, and require less superintendence than younger children, provided they have been brought up in habits of order and obedience, otherwise they make worse servants than those who began to work at 9 or 10. [added in other document] . . . but it would be a considerable hardship to the Parents of larger families in poor circumstances if their children could earn nothing before that age.

Q 18. What is the usual number of hours during which Persons UNDER 21 years of age are employed; specifying the ages at which any difference may be made?

A 18. 69 hours per week for all ages.

Q 19. What is the greatest number of hours that your workers, or any of them, have been kept on in any one day during the last year?

A 19. 12 hours 25 minutes.

Q 21. What is the total number of Hours that your works were carried on during the last year?

A 21. From Jan 1 to Dec. 31, inclusive, 3435 Hours.

Q 24. What is the *greatest* number of hours that the same set of Children in your employment have been kept to work during any one day of the last year?

A 24. 12 Hours 28 minutes.

Q 31. What is the objection, if any, where extra hours are required, to have relays, or fresh sets of Children, or persons under twenty-one years of age, by whom those sets which have worked within the ordinary Hours may be relieved?

A 31. The plan of employing occasionally an additional set of children to work extra hours, would be obectionable because the manufacturer could not organize and manage such a system economically unless it were regularly continued. It would be difficult to prevent children, who had worked the ordinary hours in one mill, from working extra hours the same day in another mill. The proposition of night work would also be increased; and the children employed as extra sets of hands would be liable to be frequently thrown out of employment by changes of Trade.

Q 37. State your opinion as to the probable effects of a still further Reduction of Working Hours, and specify the Grounds of such an Opinion.

A 37. We think any great reduction in the working hours below the legal standard now established in the Cotton manufacture of 69 per week, must be attended by a serious reduction of wages, or of profits, or of both. The rate of profit is low in England compared with other countries, and the British manufacturer labours under the disadvantage compared with the foreigner of having to pay his workpeople in proportion to the price of food in England, which is about a third part dearer than in other manufacturing countries with which he has to compete. These limits of working hours and the provision that no children shall be employed in factories under 11 or 12 years of age for more than 6 working hours daily, thus giving sufficient time for that first necessary of life, a good education, and also the requirement of sufficient bodily strength before the commencement of labour, we think are all that specific laws can possibly do for the protection and real benefit of the working people.

Q 57. What are the means taken to enforce discipline on the part of the Children employed in your Works?

A 57. Fines of $1^{d.}$ to $6^{d.}$, for each fault or temporary, or permanent reduction of weekly wages; or finally discharged from the works.

Q 62. Have you forbidden Corporal Punishments, or taken any steps for their Prevention, when you were informed of any instance of their Infliction?

A 62. In all cases when we have known the rule to be infringed the overlooker has been reproved or dismissed.

Q 63. Have any instructions been given by you to your Foreman or to your overlookers, with relation to the Punishment of Children?

A 63. Verbal instructions have been given to all the Foremen or Overlookers, always to punish the Children by fine, reduction of wages, or dismissal, and not in any case to use corporal punishment.

Q 66. What is the difference in skill and general character of those who have been employed in the works, who have been em-

ployed from infancy, as compared with those who have been taken
into employment at later periods?

A 66.   There is on the average a considerable superiority in the
skill and general character of those who have been employed in
the works from infancy, compared with others. It is our almost in-
variable practice to set on no new hands but learners of 11 to 13 years,
who regularly advance as they grow older, and fill the vacancies
that occur amongst the older hands.

THE MARSHALL PAPERS (unpublished)

2. 6d. A WEEK

Large numbers of children were employed in the machine lace-making
industry. Their average weekly wage was 4s. in 1831, working from nine
to fourteen hours daily. Some worked at home, but most were employed
by women who crammed their cottages with up to forty children.
In 1843 a woman testified that she had seen some children working 'who
could scarcely sit on a stool'.

'The masters prefer giving out work to those women who keep
young children, because it can be done at the lowest possible price.'
At some warehouses where witness has gone to seek for work she
has been asked, 'Do you keep hands?' and on answering in the
negative, has been told she would not be employed. 'Children of
very tender age, 6, 7 and 8, can in a short time draw lace almost or
quite as well as grown people, these children do not earn more than
6d., 9d., 1s., or 1s. 3d. a week.'

FACTORY COMMISSION, 1833, p. f 36

3. MARBLES AND TOPS

In some Lancashire cotton mills children below eleven years of age
(4% of the total female labour force) earned an average wage of 2/4¾d.
per week. Those aged eleven to sixteen earned 4/3d., and the sixteen to
twenty-one-year-olds 8/5d. per week. These last formed the largest age-
group—32%. The eleven to sixteen-year-olds, who earned little over half
the wages of the next age-group, comprised 29% of the total labour force.
Only 35% of adult women were employed in these mills.

Employers preferred to employ women whenever possible, as they were
willing to accept lower wages than men. Women and girls were only able
to work on the smaller machines. Doubts had been expressed as to the
ability of the women to keep their assistants (or 'piecers') at work.

Formerly it had been thought necessary to beat the boys many times a day
—but the women had other methods which gave equally good results.

> . . . they used to coax the piecers up . . . They used to ask them if
> they'd mind their work and then they'd give 'em a halfpenny or a
> penny, and then the piecers was pleased, and worked; and if the
> piecers hadn't meat, they used to give 'em meat, and marbles, and
> tops; and at any pastime here gives 'em money; 6d. or 1s.

FACTORY COMMISSION, 1833, xx, p. D1, 79

Both farmers and labourers were in agreement when the former
required the latter's wife and children to work on his farm. Children
were sometimes taken away from school to earn a pittance. Infants taken
with them by their mothers were often prevented from interrupting their
labours by the administration of an opiate such as 'Gregory's' (or
'Godfrey's') cordial. In Sussex it was stated that:

> . . . the custom of a mother of a family carrying her infant with
> her in its cradle into the field rather than lose the opportunity of
> adding to her earnings to the general stock, is becoming very much
> more general now.

2ND REPORT POOR LAW COMMISSION (1835), p. 221

4. 'DOUZE HEURES PAR JOUR'

London silk-weavers became established in Spitalfields at the end of
the seventeenth century. It was primarily a family industry. Even children
in late infancy were able to assist the weavers by 'winding and quilling'.
A larger proportion of women workers were employed towards the end
of the eighteenth century and subsequently. Seven to ten year old girls
helped by performing all tasks, while the boys helped at the loom.
The fact that such work was widely in demand led to the establishment
of a Children's Market at Bethnal Green. On Mondays and Tuesdays it
was possible to hire children from six to eight o'clock in the morning.
A French visitor wrote in amazement:

> Dès leur bas âge, ils sont courbés sur un métier, lançant la
> navette treize à quatorze heures par jour; c'est là le seul exercise que
> prennent ces malheureux, qui respirent rarement un air libre et qui
> ne voient jamais le soleil qu'à travers les fenêtres de leur tristes
> réduits. Dans une visite que je fis a Spitalfields en 1836, apercevant
> une petite fille de onze ans, pâle et mélancholique, qui tissait avec

une activiteé fébrile, je demandais au père: 'Combien d'heures travaile cetteé enfant par jour?' 'Douze heures,' me répondit-il. 'Et vous n'avez pas peur d'excéder ses forces?' 'Ja la nourris bien.'

FAUCHER, *Etudes sur l'Angleterre*, vol. I, pp. 14–15

5. FLOGGING

(a)

Alas! for the next generation, if it had no other hope. Its best hope is, that the spirit of sound instruction will gradually spread through the land, and that its light may at last penetrate even to the chinks and crannies of the monastic walls of Oxford. It is impossible that it can long continue that the felon boys of Newgate and the patrician boys of Eton should be the only flogged boys in the land . . .

THE COMPANION TO THE NEWSPAPER; and Journal of Facts in Politics, Statistics, and Public Economy, 1834 (July) p. 126

(b) 3/10*d*. A WEEK

The small amount of the wages of very young children employed in the factories, Dr. Mitchell justly considers to be anything rather than a matter of regret. 'There will be,' as he remarks, 'the less loss to the parents if they be withdrawn altogether from the factories, and sent to receive education, as they ought to be at that period of life'.

. . . From another table, it appears that of the whole number of persons under eighteen years of age, 10,541 were children under fourteen, of whom 5,941 were males, and 4,600 females. The average net weekly earnings of these children varied from 37.27 pence to 59.24 for each; and the general average was 46.35, or somewhat more than 3*s*. 10*d*.

THE COMPANION TO THE NEWSPAPER; etc., 1834, (December) pp. 242 and 243

(c)

. . . In the 5th resolution, passed at a meeting of deputies from the hand-loom worsted weavers of Bradford, Leeds, and Halifax, held at Bradford in March, 1835, we find among the causes which are considered to have been productive of the present distress, the following:—

. . . 'The unrestricted use (or rather abuse) of continually improving machinery, especially of steam or power-looms, as well as combing machines.' 'The adaptation of machines in every improvement to *children* and *youth* and *women*, to the exclusion of those who ought to labour—the men.'

THE COMPANION TO THE NEWSPAPER, 1835, p. 461

6. SHORTENING LIFE

(a)

MILLINERS, DRESSMAKERS, and STRAWBONNET-MAKERS are often crowded into apartments of disproportionate size, and kept at work for an improper length of time. Their *ordinary* hours are ten or twelve in the day, but they are confined not infrequently from five or six in the morning till twelve at night. The bent posture in which they sit, tends to injure the digestive organs, as well as the circulation and the breathing. Hence girls from the country, fresh-looking and robust, soon become pale and thin. The constant direction of the eyes also to minute work, affects these organs. Sometimes it induces slight aphthalmia, and sometimes at length a much more serious disease, palsy of the optic nerve.

> C. TURNER THACKRAH, *The Effects of the Principal Arts, Trades, and Professions . . . on Health and Longevity . . . and Suggestions for the Removal of Many of the Agents, which produce Disease, and Shorten the Duration of Life,* p. 18

(b)

Boys enter the pits at the age of six or seven, and are employed in opening the trap-doors, driving the horses, propelling the trucks, &c.; and finally, when of sufficient age, they become colliers. Sickness and vomiting sometimes affect persons at their commencing the employ; and many, after a few years' trial, are obliged, by the injury which their health has sustained, and especially by the weakness of their eyes, to leave the mines.

> C. TURNER THACKRAH, *The Effects of the Principal Arts etc. on Health etc.,* p. 28

(c)

Flax Mills

Children and a few overlookers are here the operatives . . . Persons in the dusty departments are generally unhealthy. They are subject to indigestion, morning vomiting, chronic inflammation of the bronchial membrane, inflammation of the lungs, and pulmonary consumption . . .

The majority of operatives in the great flax-mills are young women, girls, and boys.

The process of heckling flax is generally the most injurious to health . . .

5. A. K. aged 23, entered the flax mill at 11 years of age. She was six years employed in the dusty departments; the rest of the time, with the exception of one year, she worked in the reeling room. She is of low stature, and of a sickly appearance; she complains of pain in the right side of the chest, and in the right iliac region, of cough, and of head-ache. Expectorated matter is sometimes tinged with blood. Her general health is bad.

> C. TURNER THACKRAH, *The Effects of the Principal Arts on Health*, pp. 40–42

(d)

The employment of young children in *any* labour is wrong. The term of physical growth ought not to be a term of physical exertion. No man of humanity can reflect without distress on the state of thousands of children, many from six to seven years of age, roused from their beds at an early hour, hurried to the mills, and kept there, with the interval of only 40 minutes, till a late hour at night; kept, moreover, in an atmosphere impure, not only as the air of a town, not only as defective in ventilation, but as loaded also with noxious dust . . . There is scarcely time for meals. The very period of sleep, so necessary for the young, is too often abridged. Nay, children are sometimes worked even *in* the night.

> C. TURNER THACKRAH, *The Effects of the Principal Arts on Health*, p. 45

(c)

CHIMNEY-SWEEPERS necessarily suffer from the soot, with which they are covered. The skin assumes frequently a malignant disease—Cancer scroti. Ophthalmia is produced by the irritation of the soot in the eyes: and the lungs suffer from the substance drawn into the air-tube. Though daily inhaling a large quantity of charcoal, sulphur, and ammonia, they frequently remain for some years free from urgent disorder; like the children in the Flax-mills, who inhale dust for a considerable period, with apparent impunity. But as these ultimately suffer, so also the wretched inspirers of soot, become at length seriously diseased.

The evils of the employ are doubled by intemperance. The sweeps who travel through the country are especially drunken; and lads acquire a craving for liquor from their habit of receiving beer at every house they serve. Many chimney-sweeps die in youth. Surely this shocking and unnatural occupation ought to be abolished!

> C. TURNER THACKRAH, *The Effects of the Principal Arts on Health*, p. 60

(h)

The grand bane of civilized life is *Intemperance* . . .

More shocking is the case, when the evil is found among females; —when the wife is led to imitate her husband. Most shocking, when children, nay infants, are taught to sip with the mother, and thus acquire a taste for the bane of life and health.

> C. TURNER THACKRAH, *The Effects of the Principal Arts on Health*, pp. 113–15

7. A ICKLE BIT OF EGG

The description (given at the request of the Vicar of Taunton) of Charles John Young is as significant as *Little Charlie's Life* itself. It displays an attitude towards childhood which might have seemed alien to Sir Thomas and Lady Robinson. They merely noted down their immediate observations; the anonymous commentator can only interpret Little Charlie's behaviour in biblical and Wordsworthian terms.

(a)

From the PREFACE

I look back some thirty years, and see a pale, serene, grave boy, between four and five years old . . .

. . . The majesty of truth shone on his childish soul from his earliest years. When about three years old, he was standing in the breakfast-room one morning, when his father coming suddenly in, observed a look of shame on his little face. On glancing at the table, the father saw a bit of egg near the pigeon-pie, which gave him a clue.

'Charlie, have you been doing anything since I left the room?'

'Yet (*yes*), papa.'

'What was it, Charlie?'

'I was touching the pie, and going to eat a ickle bit of egg.'

'You would not have done that if I or mamma had been in the room?'

'No, papa.'

'Well, my boy, if I had been here you would not have touched a morsel without leave. Never, therefore, do anything when you are *alone* which you would be ashamed of before your Heavenly Father, for you are always seen by Him.'

Two or three days afterwards, his nurse came to his father, and said, 'Sir, what a very odd idea Master Charlie has got into his head. He was looking over his bird-and-beast book to-day, and he said to me, "Hiny, how very odd it is that God, who has made everything so nicely, and given two eyes to every creature, even to little birds and insects, has kept only *one* for Himself".'

THE REV. W. R. CLARK (ed.), *Little Charlie's Life. By Himself*, p. 7

(b)

Chapter 1st.

I was thinking the other day that I should like to write my Life, for I have read the Lives of others, and I thought I might make something of my own. My name is Charles John Young and I was born at Amport, a pretty little Village in Hampshire 1833.

Chap 10th

As the events of my life passed on, there was one dreadful accident happened to me, perhaps as a punishment for my sins; or to show me that death stands ready at the door to snatch my life away. One night papa had been conjuring a penny, and *I* thought *I* should like to conjure, so I took a round brass thing with a verse out of the bible upon it that I brought in to bed with me. I thought it went down papa's throat, so *I* put it down *my* throat and I was pretty near choked. I called my nurse, who was in the next room, she fetched up papa, and then my nurse brought the basin. Papa beat my back and I was sick! Lo! there was the counter! Papa said Good God! And my nurse fainted! but soon recovered!

Chap 16

Papa and Mama now gave me a great treat by letting me go to Astley's Theatre. It was a children's theatre. I then went into a raised place called a private box. Beneath was an open space called the arena and at one side was a semicircular place full of people called the pit their clamour, noise and bustle, also their horrible cries of Bolap, Bolap, put me quite in a confusion. They were eating oranges and chewing apples. The curtain now drew up. I have but a confused recollection of the play but I remember a shooting of guns, a drawing of swords, a galloping of horses, a tumbling of clowns and a running of clowns after little black boys. When the curtain fell I went home obliged to Papa and Mama for what they had shown me, but not feeling that I had acquired much useful knowledge.

THE REV. W. R. CLARK (ed.), *Little Charlie's Life. By Himself.*

10. PARTING WITH BABY

It occurred to Augustus Hare's widow as just possible that my parents might be induced to give me up to her altogether, to live with her as her own child. In July she wrote her petition, and was almost surprised at the glad acceptance it met with. Mrs. Hare's answer was very brief—'My dear Maria, how every kind of you! Yes, certainly, the baby shall be sent as soon as it is weaned; and, if any one else would like one, would you kindly recollect that we have others.'

AUGUSTUS J. C. HARE, *The Story of My Life*, Vol. I, p. 51

8. BLISS

Letter to Elizabeth Gaskell

Sandlebridge. Thursday Mg [12 May 1836]
. . . Baby is at the very tip-top of bliss. There are chickens, &

little childish pigs, & cows & calves & horses, & *baby horses*, & fish in the pond, & ducks in the lane, & the mill & the smithy, & sheep & baby sheep, & flowers—oh! you would laugh to see her going about, with a great big nosegay in each hand, & wanting to be *bathed* in the golden bushes of wall-flowers—she is absolutely fatter since she came here, & I'm sure stronger . . .

> J. A. V. CHAPPLE and ARTHUR POLLARD (eds.), *The Letters of Mrs Gaskell*, p. 6

9. HAPPY BEINGS

Sir George Head (author of *Forest Scenes and Incidents in the Wilds of North America*) wrote *A Home Tour Through the Manufacturing Districts of England etc.* three years after retiring from the army on half-pay. His remarks are lucid and dispassionate. 'It is with a feeling of veneration that one enters a manufactory . . .' is typical. He had the vision to realize the importance of industry, and was unusually tolerant on the subject of child-labour.

(a)

Pin Manufactory

To make the heads, two little boys are employed. From a piece of elastic wire, such as forms the covering of a fiddlestring, with an ordinary pair of scissors, he snips off, as quick as he can open and shut the scissors, just two threads of the spiral or *helix*, and no more. The elastic wire is prepared by another little boy in the same apartment, who rolls it round a piece of straight brass-wire of the proper dimensions, and about three yards long, by the assistance of a large spinning-wheel.

The pins are headed by little girls with astonishing rapidity. Every pin is taken up between the thumb and finger, and, the head being then strung upon the shaft, it is placed in a small machine, which rivets it at one blow, and disgorges it at another. The little girl sits behind the machine with a basin of pins' heads in her lap, which in that state resembles poppy seeds, and having threaded two shafts, gives the wheel a turn with her foot, when the aforesaid slabs diverge from one another; she then places the two pins in two small horizontal holes made to receive them, and turning the wheel again, the slabs close violently, and rivet the two heads in a moment.

> SIR GEORGE HEAD, *A Home Tour through the Manufacturing Districts of England in the Summer of* 1835, p. 82

(b)

I walked from Dewsbury to the village of Batley Carr, on the river Calder, about a mile distant, where there are several rag-mills, and paid a visit to one of them. The rags were ground, as they term it, in the uppermost apartment of the building, by machines, in outward appearance like Cook's agricultural winnowing-machine, and each attended by three or four boys and girls.

. . . But if the smell of the rag-grinding process can be estimated by the quantity of dust produced, then some little notion may be given by stating, that the boys and girls who attend the mill are not only involved all the time it works in a thick cloud, so as to be hardly visible, but, whenever they emerge, appear covered from head to foot with downy particles that entirely obscure their features and render them in appearance like so many brown moths.

SIR GEORGE HEAD, *A Home Tour through the Manufacturing Districts*, p. 149

(c)

With respect to the general state of the workmen, and especially the children in the factories, I certainly gained, by personal inspection, a happy release from opinions previously entertained; I saw around me wherever I moved, on every side, a crowd of apparently happy beings, working in lofty well-ventilated buildings.

SIR GEORGE HEAD, *A Home Tour through the Manufacturing Districts*, p. 190

(d)

A custom prevails among the seamen of these vessels when traversing the polar seas, to fix, on the first day of May, a garland, aloft, suspended midway on a rope leading from the maintop-gallant mast-head to the foretop mast-head, ornamented with knots of riband, love-tokens of the lads from their lasses.

No sooner does she arrive in the docks than it becomes an object of supreme ambition among the boys of the town, seamen's sons, to compete for the possession of the aforesaid symbol, to which end, they vie with each other in a perilous race up the rigging.

A gallant phalanx, animated by youth and enterprise, sprang from the shore, across the intervening craft, and mounted, in one simultaneous charge, on board the vessel, and still a numerous band continued to scale her sides, and nimbly run aloft by rope and rattlin. Every moment, as the struggle among the competitors increased, the leading spirits rose above the rest, and, finally, one boy alone so far outstripped his fellows, that common consent yielded to him the victory. The boy, about fourteen years old, gained the maintop gallant mast, and descending by the rope, the whole of his body meanwhile, below it, as he clung by his arms and feet, like a fly upon a ceiling, reached the garland, and in the same attitude now drew from his pocket a knife to cut it away. Some time elapsed, and yet he could not execute his purpose. The lad remained in his perilous situation so long, that an intense feeling of anxiety began to manifest. At last he succeeded,—that is to say, he severed the garland, and, with the prize upon his arm, commenced progress upwards, climbing by the rope, when it became immediately evident that his strength, unequal to the exertion, had totally failed, and that he could make no way whatever. But the boy's heart was stout—the garland was the only impediment: this, after a protracted struggle, he placed on one of his feet and kicked to a comrade below. Relieved of the burden, he reached to the maintop-gallant mast-head, gave a few hearty cheers, and then, like lightning, descending on the deck, forthwith received the prize as its lawful owner.

SIR GEORGE HEAD, *A Home Tour through the Manufacturing Districts*, p. 243

(c)

. . . I was on my way to the Saltham pit, to descend which I had obtained permission. On both sides are built small houses for the colliers, where, in proportion to the size of the dwelling, inversely is the stock of little children: these, at all hours, sit, a dozen at a time, like unfledged rooks, on perilous crags of stone, and crawl backwards and forwards from the little alleys which diverge at right angles from the landing-places.

I observed some with red heads, others white heads, but all black faces, alike carelessly clambering up and down, and playing on the verge of precipices awful to behold. One little creature particularly, hardly able to walk, nevertheless made his way up, without any assistance, and alone—a little boy, covered by one single, very short petticoat, and it was curious to observe how cautiously he crawled on all fours, and as he travelled on the back part of his hands and feet, carried his hind quarters high up in the air. 'Do your children never tumble down these steps, and if they do, where in goodness do they stop?' said I to a poor woman. 'O yes, Sir, very frequently,' said she, 'but they hardly ever hurt themselves, somebody always stops them'.

SIR GEORGE HEAD, *A Home Tour through the Manufacturing Districts*, p. 394

(f)

Of these waggons, each bearing a single large basket, one horse draws a dozen, linked together, along the railroad that extends through the middle of the track. The driver of these trains was generally a boy,—sometimes a girl; of the latter sex thus employed, I met three or four during the morning, dressed so nearly in male attire, that it was impossible to say which was which. Owing to the narrow space in the level, there was but barely room for the waggons to go by: not sufficient to allow the driver to keep by the side of his or her waggon, and at the same time pass a foot-passenger going in the opposite direction. Boys and girls both adopted a similar manoeuvre on these occasions; springing nimbly up in the rear of the horse, on the near side, the right shoulder and hip were supported by the animal's hind quarters; the right foot then rested on the bed of the carriage, close to his hocks, while the left was placed upon the chain trace.

SIR GEORGE HEAD, *A Home Tour through the Manufacturing Districts*, p. 400

10. NEW YEAR'S DAY

'Dicky' Doyle was already a talented draughtsman of fifteen when his father John persuaded him to keep a journal. The family of nine was an exceptionally happy and gifted one.

JANUARY

Wednesday. The first of January. Got up late, very bad. Made good resolutions and did not keep them. Went out and got a cold. Did keep it. First thought I would, then thought I would not, was sure I would, was positive I would not, at last was determined I would, write a journal. Began it. This is it and I began it on the first of January, one thousand eight hundred and forty. Hope I may be skinned alive by wild cats if I don't go on with it.

RICHARD DOYLE, *A Journal kept in the Year 1840*, p. 1

11. DICKENS AS FATHER (1)

September 5, 1843, Broadstairs, Kent
. . . Charley [Dickens] is popular with the boatmen. I saw him yesterday through a telescope, miles out at sea, steering an enormous fishing-smack. Katey [Charley's sister, almost four] is supposed to be secretly betrothed, inasmuch as a very young gentleman (so young, that being unable to reach the knocker, he called attention to the door by kicking it) called the other evening, and being gratified in a mysterious request, to speak with the nurse, produced a live crab, which he said he had 'promised her'.

EDGAR JOHNSON (ed.), *Letters from Charles Dickens to Angela Burdett-Coutts* 1841–1865, p. 50

12. GODFREY'S CORDIAL

One of the most appalling features connected with the extreme reduction that has taken place in the wages of lace runners, and the consequent long hours of labour, is, that married women, having no time to attend to their families, or even to suckle their offspring, freely administer opium in some form or other to their infants.

The practice, which is most common, usually is begun when the child is three or four weeks old; but Mr. Brown, the coroner of Nottingham, states that he knows Godfrey's cordial is given on the day of birth . . . The druggist made up in one year 13 cwt. of treacle into Godfrey's cordial—a preparation of opium exclusively consumed by infants. The result of this terrible practice is that a great number of infants perish, either suddenly from an overdose, or, as more commonly happens, slowly, painfully and insidiously.

CHILDREN'S EMPLOYMENT COMMISSION 1843, pp. f.
10–11

13. THE HARDEST WORK

The gang system utilized groups of workers of both sexes from 'open villages', who often had to rent bad, expensive accommodation. These communities grew up as a result of landowners' reluctance to maintain labourers' cottages. The gang system originated in Norfolk about 1826. Great fatigue was caused by the long distances travelled on foot to and from the place of employment, in addition to the long hours of work. Many young children were employed, some from the age of four. They earned about 3d. or 4d. a day. An eleven year old girl's father stated before the 1843 Commission (she had already worked thus for two years):

I'm forced to let my daughter go, else I'm very much against it . . . She has complained of a pain in her side very often, they drive them along—force them along—they make them work very hard. Gathering stones had hurt my girl's back at times. Pulling turnips is the hardest work . . . It blisters their hands so that they can hardly touch anything . . . My girl went five miles yesterday to her work, turniping; she set off between seven and eight; she walked; had a piece of bread before she went; she did not stop work in the middle of the day; ate nothing till she left off; she came home between three and four o'clock. Their walks are worse than their work; she is sometimes so tired she can't eat no victuals when she comes home.

REPORT ON WOMEN AND CHILDREN IN AGRI-CULTURE (1843), xii, p. 276

14. A DAY AT A DERBY SILK MILK

In some of the floors, the machines employed are such as little girls can attend to; in others, elder girls or women are necessary; in some, boys and men form the principal workpeople; but in all silk-mills the larger number of those employed are females.

In one of the long rooms or ranges of the mill a number of young active boys are seen running to and fro with untiring industry, carrying or supporting silken threads in their hands . . . The silk-twisting is, however, effected with great quickness; and the little boys are incessantly engaged in running to and fro, attaching and detaching the remote ends of the silken threads. We were informed that this running amounts sometimes to as much as thirty miles a day.

One very remarkable article of manufacture produced at this establishment is that of silk boot-laces. The *tags* which form the rigid end to each lace are made by two small machines, placed upon low benches, and worked by boys. In the first of these machines, a boy takes in his hand a strip of brass, whose width equals the intended length of the tag; and, placing this in a kind of groove, he brings down a cutting edge to act upon it, which cuts the brass to the required size. The pieces of brass thus prepared are transferred to another bench, where other boys are working on machines which fix the tags to the laces.

THE PENNY MAGAZINE, Vol. XII, April, 1843 (Supplement).

15. LITTLE MONSTERS

(a)

My own experience of Harnish is one of the many instances I have known of how little the character of the head of an establishment affects the members of it. The greater portion of Mr. Kilvert's scholars—his 'little flock of lambs in Christ's fold'—were a set of little monsters. All infantine immoralities were highly popular . . . The first evening I was there, at nine years old, I was compelled to eat Eve's apple right up—indeed, the Tree of the Knowledge of Good and Evil was stripped altogether bare: there was no fruit left to gather.

AUGUSTUS HARE, *The Story of my Life*, Vol. I, p. 168

(b)

From a letter to his mother, Nov. 11, 1843

I will tell you a day at Mr. Kilvert's. I get up at half past six and do lessons for the morning. Then at eight breakfast. Then go out till half-past nine. Then lessons till eleven. Then go out till a quarter-past eleven. Then lessons till 12, go a walk till 2 dinner. Lessons from half-past three, writing, sums, or dictation. From 5 till 6 play. Tea. Lessons from 7 to 8. Bed.

AUGUSTUS HARE, *The Story of my Life*, Vol. I, p. 174

(c)

I may truly say that I never learnt anything useful at Harrow, and had little chance of learning anything. Hours and hours were wasted daily on useless Latin verses with sickening monotony.

I got up a sort of private theatricals on a very primitive scale,

L

turning Grimm's fairy stories into little plays, which were exceedingly popular with the house, but strictly forbidden by the tutor, Mr. Simpkinson or 'Simmy'. One day when we had got up a magnificent scene, in which I, as 'Snowdrop', lay locked in magic sleep in an imaginary cave, watched by dwarfs and fairies, Simmy came in and stood quietly amongst the spectators, and I was suddenly awakened from my trance by the *sauve qui peut* which followed the discovery. Great punishments were the result. Yet, not long after, we could not resist a play on a grander scale—something about the 'Fairy Tilburina' out of the 'Man in the Moon', for which we learnt our parts and had regular dresses made. It was to take place in the fifth form room on the ground floor between the two divisions of the house, and just as Tilburina (Buller) was descending one staircase in full bridal attire, followed by her bridesmaids, of whom I was one, Simmy himself suddenly appeared on the opposite staircase and caught us.

AUGUSTUS HARE, *The Story of my Life*, Vol. I, p. 242

16. A DARK HOLE

G. W. M. Reynolds wrote in 1848 that 'Few persons are fully aware of the horrors endured by a great number of our fellow creatures compelled to work in the coal mines ... receiving in return very indifferent wages for labour which is alike the most unhealthy and the most dangerous'. No modern miner would disagree with this statement in respect of the past. Conditions seem to have deteriorated after the early 1800s. A day-book of the Kirkstall mine in Yorkshire, of that period, does not list any women miners, and the only boy mentioned was the carpenter's son who occasionally accompanied his father.

(a)

We shall begin by stating, that not only are men and boys employed in the mines, but likewise women and girls. Indeed, young girls commence their horrible subterranean career at nine years old, and are employed as *hurriers*. Their avocation consists in propelling small wagons, named *corves*, laden with coal from the seam to the foot of the shaft. In some very thin coal beds they are compelled to go on their hands and knees to draw the corves. These corves weigh a total of eight hundred weight. When loaded, a girl is harnessed with a belt round the waist; a chain coming from the front of the belt, passes between the legs, and is hooked to the corve; —the unfortunate creature then going on 'all-fours', drags the load to the foot of the shaft. Their dress is simply a pair of canvas trousers, supported by the hips, and reaching a little below the knees; the friction of the chain constantly wears holes in the canvas, and leaves excoriated thighs bare. From the waist upwards, they are entirely uncovered; they work amongst the men, who are themselves in a condition of nudity.

*   *   *

A boy commences as early as eight years of age to work in the pits: he is first of all a *trapper*; his duty is to rise between two and three in the morning, descend into the pit, and seat himself behind one of the doors called trap-doors, which are in the barrow-way, for the purpose of forcing the stream of air, from the *down-shaft* to the *up-shaft* of the pit: this door must be opened whenever any person wishes to pass through. His seat is a little dark hole, about the size of a fireplace: he pulls a string to open the door, which shuts of itself when the people have gone by. His solitude is now and then enlivened by a corve coming through the gate; and he derives some consolation from the glimmer of the little candle, of about forty to the pound, which is fixed on it. In this state of sepulchral existence his enemy, *sleep*, gains upon him;—a deputy over-man comes along, and a smart cut of his yard-wand at once punishes the culprit. Black beetles are crawling about him in swarms; and the pits generally abound in mice.

At four o'clock the joyful sound 'Loose! loose!' is heard, and by systematic arrangement sent for many miles round the furthest extremities of the pit. The trapper stops until the last tram is passed, and goes to the foot of the shaft, waiting for an opportunity of getting into the basket and mounting when he can: his wages are ninepence a-day.

At the age of sixteen or seventeen he is promoted to the rank of *driver*.

G. W. M. REYNOLDS, *The Coal Mines of Great Britain*, in Reynold's Miscellany, Vol. I (New Series) p. 456

(b)

Distortion in the spine and pelvis from which colliery women were especially liable to suffer, caused difficulty at childbirth. Many continued to work during pregnancy, and sometimes up to the very day of birth. 'I had a child born in the pit,' said one woman, 'and I brought it up the pit shaft in my skirt'. The evidence of a Lancashire woman who said that four out of the eight children born while she was in the pits were still-born, is one of many given to the same effect, and another witness said: 'A vast of women have dead children and false births, which are worse, as they are not able to work after the latter. I have always been obliged to work below till forced to go up to bear the bairn, and so have all the other women. We return as soon as able, never longer than twelve days; many less. It ruins the women; it makes them old women at forty. Women so soon get weak that they are forced to take the little ones down to relieve them; and even children of six years of age do much to relieve the burthen.'

IVY PINCHBECK, *Women Workers in the Idustrial Revolution*, p. 261

17. MODEL LESSONS

(a)

Work on Infant Education have not hitherto attempted to point out the process by which the faculties of children are to be developed; what the children are to learn is told, but not how the lesson is to be given; . . . What ideas, for instance, does an infant gain, in repeating the names of the books of the Old and New Testaments? How is its knowledge of the Deity increased, by committing to memory a list of attributes it cannot comprehend?

It is hoped that such teaching will speedily be banished from Infant Schools, and in its place substituted instructions calculated to awaken and to develop the best affections of the heart, and to strengthen the faculties of the mind.

ANON. *Model Lessons for Infant School Teachers and Nursery Governesses*, Preface, p. iii.

(b)

Sketch of a Lesson on Scripture Natural History for the
Children of the Model Infant School.

Silver. To illustrate the refiner's work.—Malachi iii. 3.

The children first sang.

A piece of silver ore, and one of bright silver, were then exhibited by the teacher.

Teacher. (Holding up the bright silver.) What is this?

All. Silver.

T. Now tell me what this is (exhibiting the ore).

No answer . . . .

T. And because the bright silver is worth the most money, what is it said to be?

C. Valuable . . .

T. The silver, remember, is in the furnace, and the fire is separating all the impurities from it. The refiner sits down and looks at it, and when the impurities rise to the top, he takes them off. At last the impurities are taken away, and the silver looks so bright that he can see his face in it—he can see his own image. What can he see?

All. His image.

T. Say, "The silver, when purified perfectly, reflects his image."

A little Boy. Teacher, how does he touch it when he wants to do anything with it, and it is so hot?

T. He uses a spoon. He sits there and skims it, until he can see his image in it.

A little Boy. Would he get the silver out of that stone? (Pointing to the ore.)

T. Oh, yes, Jackson; and that is the way in which men get it. It is at first all mixed with impurities; but they break it up into small pieces, and put it into the furnace; and then how is it made pure?

All. By fire.

T. Now tell me, what does Christ do to his people—how does he purify them?

C. He punishes them.

T. How does he punish?

A little Boy. With brimstone and everlasting fire.

T. Yes, but that is everlasting punishment; there are punishments he sends to make them better whilst they are on earth. Do you know one?

C. (After a pause.) Sickness.

T. Yes; he lays them on a sick bed, that they may be led to Jesus. When you have been naughty, and are punished for it, what do you say?

C. "I will be better." "I will be good."

ANON. *Model Lessons for Infant School Teachers*, pp. 168–174

18. ACROBATS

As you pass through one of those low, densely-populated districts of London you will be struck by the swarms of children everywhere collected. They form the great proportion of Mr. Punch's audience, when his scream is heard in the adjacent large thoroughfare.

These children are not altogether the results of over-fecundity of the inhabitants. Their parents live huddled up in dirty single rooms, repelling all attempts to improve their condition and, whenever the rain is not actually pouring down in torrents, they turn their children out to find means of amusement and subsistence, in the streets.

Picture such a bit of [waste] ground, on a fine afternoon, alive with children. Amongst the revellers there is a boy, who for the last five minutes has been hanging by his legs to a bit of temporary railing, with his hair sweeping the ground. On quitting it, he goes to a retired corner of the plot, and, gravely putting his head and hands upon the ground, at a short distance from the wall, turns his heels up in the air, until he touches the house with his feet. This accomplished, he whistles a melody, claps his shoeless soles together, goes through certain telegraphic evolutions with his legs, and then calmly resumes his normal position . . .

This boy is destined to become an Acrobat—at a more advanced period of his life to perform feats of suppleness and agility in the mud of the streets, the saw-dust of the circus, or the turf of a race-course. His life will pass in a marvellous series of positions, and its ordinary level course will be unknown to him. Ladders, with him, will in future only be ascended by twisting in and out the rounds like a serpent; and his fellow-tumblers will be regarded merely as component parts of the living pedestal which is to elevate him, when required, to the level of the first-floor windows.

The young Olympian gradually learns his business. He first of all
runs away from home and joins a troop of these agile wanderers to
whom he serves an apprenticeship. It is his task, whilst sufficiently
light and slender, to be tossed about on the elevated feet of a
'Professor'—to form the top figure of the living column or
pyramid, or to have his heels twisted round his neck, and then to be
thrown about or worn as a turban by the strongest man of the party.
Next, in his hobbledeoy state of transition—when he has grown too
tall for the business just named, his office is to clear the ring with the
large balls at the end of a cord, and to solicit the contributions of the
spectators. And finally, he proves his fibres to be as firmly braced as
those of his companions, and comes out in the ochred cotton tights,
the rusty-spangled braces, and the fillet of blackened silver-cord, as
the perfect Acrobat.

ALBERT SMITH, *Gavarni in London*, Introduction.

19. DICKENS, PHILANTHROPIST

Among the letters Dickens wrote to Miss Burdett Coutts are those
dealing with Urania Cottage, the Home at Shepherd's Bush originally
for 'Fallen Women.' The youngest of them were about fourteen years
old. Dickens maintained that the prostitute had no duty towards society.
'Society has used her ill and turned away from her, and she cannot be
expected to take much heed of its rights or wrongs.' She must be
'tempted to virtue' by kindness; enabled to recover self-respect through
acquiring control, neatness and efficiency at an occupation. 'Her pride,
her emulation, her sense of shame, her heart, her reason, and her interest'
must all be appealed to. Everyone must be given hope that she could
regain a decent position in society, perhaps some day even marry. The
dresses must not be drab prison-like uniforms. There must be recreational
reading, and group singing. Mrs. Chisholm asked Dickens 'if it were
true that the girls at Shepherd's Bush "had pianos" '; 'I shall always
regret,' he wrote, 'that I didn't say yes—each girl a grand downstairs
—and a cottage in her bedroom—besides a small guitar in the wash-
house.'

(a)

November 19, 1852, Tavistock House

It has been necessary to discharge 'Stallion' who turned out to be
of a ferocious temper, and probably would have done some serious
damage to somebody if she had remained.

She had no clothes of her own, and, it being a very wet day, they

gave her an old but decent bonnet and shawl—which she immediately threw away in the Lane. To provide for such a case again,
I told Mrs Morson to buy at a slop-seller's, the commonest and
ugliest and coarsest woman's dress that she could possibly purchase,
and invariably to keep such a thing by her. It occurs to me that they
will be very beneficially astonished when we have occasion to bring
it out.

> EDGAR JOHNSON (ed.), *Letters from Charles Dickens to Angela Burdett-Coutts* 1841–1865, p. 214

Louisa Cooper was one of the best-behaved girls at Urania Cottage.
Eventually she set sail for the Cape of Good Hope, and wrote to Miss
Coutts as follows:

(b)

October 20 1854, Tillington

As I am about to leave England I am most anxious that one of my
last acts should be to thank you my kind Benefactress for all your
goodness to me. I cannot find words to express my gratitude but
with the help of that kind Providence who will never leave me nor
forsake me if I pray to him I will by my future life try to prove it.

> EDGAR JOHNSON (ed.), *Letters from Charles Dickens to Angela Burdett-Coutts* 1841–1865, p. 272.

20. DICKENS AS FATHER (2)

Dickens had troubles at home. He writes:

(a)

April 17, 1851, Devonshire Terrace

Our poor little Dora!—I had just been playing with her, and went
to preside at a Public Dinner to which I was pledged. Before it was
over—she was dead. I had left her well and gay. My servant came
down with the sad news, but they kept it from me until the meeting
was over.

We laid the child in her grave today. And as it is a part of the
goodness and mercy of God that if we could call her back to life,
now, with a wish, we would not do it.

> EDGAR JOHNSON, *Letters from Charles Dickens to Angela Burdett-Coutts*, 1841–1865, p. 183

Later Dickens was full of enthusiasm for his youngest child, Edward. He was to be known as 'the Plornishghenter', 'Mr Plornishmaroonti-goonter', 'the Plornish Maroon', or more usually 'Plorn'.

(b)

May 19, 1853, Tavistock House

I think that must be all a mistake about that Suffolk baby your nephew, because we have in this house the only baby worth mention-ing; and there cannot possibly be another baby anywhere, to come into competition with him. I happen to know this, and would like it to be generally understood.

EDGAR JOHNSON (ed.), *Letters from Charles Dickens to Angela Burdett-Coutts*, 1841–1865, p. 225

21. ILL TREATMENT

Henry Mayew (1812–87) comments that the moral code of the coster-mongers differed drastically from the accepted Christian ethic. Parents were usually glad to delegate the responsibility for their daughters; they had usually paired off with a boy at sixteen. The ceremony of marriage was considered to be a useless expense. The male partners spent all their spare time drinking in tap-rooms. The women were out all day selling their wares. The costermongers completely dominated their womenfolk, who were beaten into submission or cast adrift on the slightest pretext. When children were born, they were left with neighbours at a very early age. The children were left to play all day in the courts and alleys as soon as possible. As soon as the girls were old enough they were deputed to supervise their siblings, or hired out to carry a baby for sixpence a week. At about seven the girls were given a 'shallow-basket' and two shillings for stock money. They hawked seasonal commodities, & all earnings were given to the parents.

STATEMENT OF A PROSTITUTE

A good-looking girl of sixteen gave me the following awful statement:

"I am an orphan. When I was ten I was sent to service as a maid of all-work. When I had been in the place three weeks, my mother died; my father having died twelve years before. I stood my mistress's ill-treatment for about six months, and at last I ran away. I got to Mrs. ——, a low lodging-house. I heard of it from some girls at the Glasshouse (baths and washhouses), where I went for shelter. I went with them to have a halfpenny worth of coffee, and they took me to the lodging-house. I then had three shillings, and stayed about a month, and did nothing wrong, living on the three shillings. [There] I saw nothing but what was bad. I was laughed at, and was told to swear. By degrees I got to be as bad as they were. During this time I used to see boys and girls from ten and twelve years old sleeping together. I can neither read nor write. At the month's end, when I was beat out, I met with a young man of fifteen—I myself was going on to twelve years old—and he persuaded me to take up with him. I stayed with him three months in the same lodging-house, living with him as his wife. At the three months' end he was taken up for picking pockets, and got six months. I was made ill through him; so I broke some windows in St. Paul's-churchyard to get into prison to get cured. I had a month in the Compter, and came out well. I had 2s. 6d. given to me when I came out, and was forced to go into the streets for a living. I continued walking the streets for three years, sometimes making a good deal of money, sometimes none, feasting one day and starving the next. I was never happy all the time, but I could get no character and could not get out of the life. I lodged all this time at a lodging-house in Kent-street. They were all thieves and bad girls. I have known between three and four dozen boys and girls sleep in one room. The beds were horrid, filthy and full of vermin. We lay packed on a full night, a dozen boys and girls squeedged into one bed. I can't go into all the particulars, but whatever could take place in words or acts between boys and girls did take place, and in the midst of the others. Some boys and girls slept without any clothes, and would dance about the room that way.

HENRY MAYHEW, *London Labour and the London Poor*, Vol. I, p. 458 et seq.

22. EARLY LOVE

It is pleasant to record that the courtship of a sensitive young man and an affectionate child of twelve culminated in an exceptionally happy marriage.

(a)

(From the diary of E. F. Benson's father, then aged 23)

1852

Mrs. Sidgewick's little daughter Mary, is this year eleven years old. As I have always been very fond of her and she of me with the love of a little sister, and as I have heard of her fondness for me commented on by many persons . . .

E. F. BENSON, *As We Were. A Victorian Peepshow.* p. 60

(b)

(from the same diary)

1853

. . . and so at last the day came and I spoke to her. Let me try to recall each circumstance: the armchair in which I sat, how she sat as usual on my knee, a little fair girl of twelve with her earnest look, and how I said I wanted to speak to her of something serious, and asked if she thought it would ever come to pass that we should be married. Instantly, without a word, a rush of tears fell down her cheek. I told her it was often in my thoughts, and that I believed that I should never love anyone so much as I should love her if she grew up as it seemed likely. But that I thought her too young to make promises, only I wished to say so much to her, and if she felt the same, she might promise years hence, but not now. She made no attempt to promise, and said nothing silly or childish, but affected me very much by quietly laying the ends of my handkerchief together and tying them into a knot, and quietly putting them into my hand. She repeated the words "Love, children, happiness." "Two of those are mine now," she said.

E. F. BENSON, *As We Were. A Victorian Peepshow.* p. 63

23. PRISONS AND INDUSTRIAL SCHOOLS

Evidence of:– Capt. *W. J. Williams.*

Report of the Cases of Parents or Relatives of Juvenile Male Offenders under Imprisonment in the House of Correction for Middlesex, Tothill Fields, Westminster, visited by Captain *Williams*, Inspector of Prisons, with the view of ascertaining their ability to maintain their Children, whether in Prison or at Industrial Schools.

D—— W——. This man, with a family of seven children, resides at Westminster; they have a single room on the second floor, for which they pay 3s. a week. [They have] scarcely the means to provide food. His eldest son, D—— W——, is now in the Westminster Bridewell for the second time; he is 14. A second son, only 10, has already manifested symptoms of dishonesty, but has not been in prison. The father describes the bad conduct of the sons as owing to the influence of other boys in the neighbourhood, and the love of the plays . . . One evening, when his eldest son was missing, he caught him on the gallery staircase of the Victoria Theatre. He has beat him repeatedly, but it had no effect. The appearance of the room, and his large family, of which four are infants, was most pitiable; there was neither furniture nor bedding; there were several pawn tickets on the mantlepiece, showing but too clearly when the furniture had been disposed of. The father in debt, and the family just above the verge of starvation.

Report from the Select Committee on Criminal and Destitute Children, p. 197

Evidence of:– *William Wolriche Whitmore*, Esq.   8. April 1852

2919. *Chairman*. Have you taken an active part in the establishment and management of the district school of Quatt?—It was originally the workhouse school of Bridgenorth Union.

2942. What discipline is exercised with regard to the children?— Those children who are able to work, are employed about half a day in labour and half a day in education.

2943. What kind of labour?—Entirely in gardening or farming.

2946. Lord *Lovaine*. How many are able to work?—Of boys we have only ten efficient workers, and seven secondary workers. We bring them in as soon as possible; but of course they are not able to dig or do hard work until they have arrived at about 12 years of age.

2948. *Chairman*. What other education is given?—It is chiefly rudimentary; we teach reading, writing, and arithmetic up to the rule of practice, geography, and some little general knowledge . . .

2971. Sir *W. Joliffe*. The food and clothing of the children in the last year amounted per head per week to 2s. 1d., or per annum to 5l. 11s. 7d. The food was 1s. 10d., and the clothing, 3d. . . . The total cost of a child, including establishment charges and food and clothing, last year was 13*l*. 5*s*. 7*d*. per head, being 5*s*. per head per week.

Report from the Select Committee on Criminal and Destitute Children, 1853

24. ALMA MATER

When the exciting variety of the life at Eton is so candidly revealed, it is not surprising that it was always one of the most sought-after educational establishments. Many of its pupils came from the most favoured families in the kingdom, and subsequently left their mark in many different spheres.

(a)

I entered Eton at the beginning of the Football Half, or Michaelmas Term, 1857. I was ten years old . . .

I was much pestered during my first few days by being continually asked—

"Who's your tutor? who's your dame?
What's your form? and what's your name?"

J. BRINSLEY-RICHARDS, *Seven Years at Eton* 1857–1864, p. 6

(b)

When not piecing dactyls and spondees together, we droned through the pages of the Eton Latin grammar . . .

Through the diamond panes of the casement, which stood in deep recesses and were protected by thick wire nettings, very little light filtered into the Lower School. On murky winter days the masses of old oak made it look dark as a church vault, and to juvenile delinquents expecting punishment, most depressing. In the sunniest summer weather it never had the same cheerful appearance as the handsome Upper School, where scarlet curtains, gilt chandeliers, and the marble busts ranged all round the walls, were effectively shown off by two rows of broad lofty windows.

J. BRINSLEY-RICHARDS, *Seven Years at Eton* 1857–1864, p. 16

(c)

Now to my fag-master. While Mr. Hardisty was teaching me to write nonsense, I was learning to make toast and tea, to boil eggs and run occasional errands for the big boy in the Boats, who owned me as his servant, and whom I will name Hall.

Hall had two fags besides myself, and we were always in attendance together . . . One of my co-fags, nicknamed 'Doggie,' was continually being touched up with the toasting-fork for his derelictions of duty . . .

'Pug,' he once cried, 'what do you mean, you young brute, by bringing up my poached eggs with three dead flies on them?'

'Three?' exclaimed Pug, affecting the utmost surprise. 'I thought there were five; what's become of the other two?'

J. BRINSLEY-RICHARDS, *Seven Years at Eton* 1857–1864, p. 25

(d)

But to return to my scrape in the Lower School . . . I had never been chastised since I was in the nursery after the manner in use at Eton. When I first came to the school, and was told how culprits were dealt with, when I was shown the block, and the cupboard under one of the forms, I fancied I was being hoaxed. I never quite believed the stories until I actually saw a boy flogged. It was on a cold rainy morning, when that corner of the Lower School where the block stood looked funereally dark, and the victim doomed to execution was a very white-skinned, curly-headed boy called Neville. As we were all flocking out of school at the end of early lesson, I beheld him standing ruefully alone among some empty forms. A cry arose behind me: 'Hullo! there's going to be a swishing!' and a general rush was made towards the upper end of the school-room.

In the Lower School floggings were public. Several dozens of fellows clambered upon forms and desks to see Neville corrected, and I got a front place. Two fellows deputed to act as 'holders down' stood behind the block, and one of them held a birch of quite alarming size, which he handed to the Lower master as the latter stepped down from his desk.

[The rod] was nearly five feet long, having three feet of handle and nearly two of bush. As Mr. Carter grasped it and poised it in the air, addressing a few words of rebuke to Neville, it appeared a horrible instrument for whipping so small a boy with, Neville was unbracing his nether garments—next moment, when he knelt on the step of the block, and when the Lower master inflicted upon his person six cuts that sounded like the splashings of so many buckets of water, I turned almost faint.

J. BRINSLEY-RICHARDS, *Seven Years at Eton* 1857–1864, p. 70

(e)

... Windsor Fair had just commenced.

This annual fair always caused great excitement in the school. We were strictly forbidden to go to it.

The booths began at the Hundred Steps, and continued to beyond the Town Hall. Their gaudy wards were attractive enough, but we craved the greater excitement of the Acre with its shows, Aunt Sallies, rifle-galleries, and circus of dogs and monkeys. So far as I can recollect we were not desirous of gambling, but when we had been in the Acre half-an-hour we were naturally tempted to do so. All sorts of pastimes offered themselves to our selection. But these amusements, in which you stake money against ginger-bread nuts highly flavoured with cayenne, paled before the fascinations of *roulette*, to which you were invited by cads bawling. 'Now, my little lords, step this way, there's a bootiful snug place just atween those three tents down there. Yer needn't have cause to fear the masters nabbin' you there. We've a big dorg, who'd pin any parson that tried to come arter yer.' Croppie, the Pug, and I made a plunge into one of the *roulette* nooks.

We found about twenty Eton fellows punting away with pence and small silver. Winners were paid at once by a *croupier* with a hooked nose and a greasy leather bag; and the ball went spinning round the roulette-box as fast as stakes were laid upon the coloured squares of a dirty piece of oil-cloth.

Croppie and I quickly lost some money, won it back, and became enthralled by the allurements of the game. We had been playing for several minutes when the cry of 'Master' was raised, and before we could disperse for flight the most unwelcome head of the Rev. J. L. Joynes intruded itself into our *buen retiro*.

J. BRINSLEY-RICHARDS, *Seven Years at Eton* 1857–1864, p. 140

(f)

I was going to say that I was too small to enjoy the house-games, but my master looked so ferocious that I kept silent. All the playing would be done by a dozen of the biggest fellows, and the rest had to trot about doing nothing. I have been pitched headlong with my face in the mud, and backwards beyond the rouge line, with such force that I almost turned a somersault; I have lain in front of goals, with a score of sprawling fellows above, all squeezing the breath out of me. I have had my shins hacked till they were all blue and bleeding, and caused me the most maddening pain. Broken limbs were not frequent (though I think there was a broken leg or collarbone in the school at least once every year), but sprained ankles and partial concussions of the brain, causing sick, nervous headaches, were of daily occurrence.

J. BRINSLEY-RICHARDS, *Seven Years at Eton*, 1857–1864, p. 151

I am not going to try to describe wall-football. The fun consisted in wearing a kind of smock-frock padded at the chest and shoulders, with a cloth bonnet that was tied over the ears; and in stooping against a rough brick wall, and being shoved and grazed during bullies of ten minutes, in the course of which the ball would be jammed tight under somebody's foot. A good run down from calx to calx was a thing of very rare occurrence, and on cold days the 'behinds' and 'corners' who did not form down in the bullies, had to stamp about and blow on their fingers to keep themselves warm.

JAMES BRINLEY-RICHARDS, *Seven Years at Eton*, p. 155

(g)

But the Christopher [Inn] was also much resorted to by boys of the school. When in 1845 Dr. Hawtrey appealed to the Fellows not to renew the lease of the house, he drew a lamentable picture of the evils it had caused. Boys were always slinking into the inn for drink. If caught, they had been to see friends from London, or to inquire about parcels sent down by coach. Often boys got tipsy, and then Shurey's across the road was a convenient place into which to stagger for the friendly emetic of mustard and water. It was so easy

to speed a fag thither for liquor; and presently, the coast being clear
of masters, the youngster would return with his *Princeps* full of beer
or port. The *Princeps* was a receptacle of deceptive appearance made
out of the covers of an early edition of 'Virgil'. It would hide three
bottles, and when carried under the arm looked like a grave folio.

J. BRINSLEY-RICHARDS, *Seven Years at Eton* 1857–1864,
p. 395

M

CHAPTER 6
1860–1889

1. YOUTHFUL ESCAPADES

Though John Sykes wrote 'I never asked to be born, and have some-times wished I never had been . . .', he survived to give an account of childhood and youth in the country. It is particularly interesting for the description he gives of 'the prevailing superstition' that was still the guiding force in many people's lives.

(a)

The Times of Witches and Wizards.

I seem to have been sent into the world when bad times were disappearing and better times approaching.

I first saw the light in a Yorkshire village, by the name of Slawit. Near the spot where I was born the people were great believers in witches and wizards, hobgoblins and ghosts, with all their train of terror.

Frequent discussions were everyday gossip about the powers possessed by some of the neighbours who had an 'evil eye' and who could produce bad luck among others by simply wishing it to occur. Bad omens were plentiful and too serious to go unnoticed.

At a place called Holme crying boggards were plentiful, and witches were numerous.

I never saw a witch—but I was in time to see horse-shoes nailed behind the house doors to keep the witches away, and if in spite of them any of the inmates were troubled with the nightmare the horse-shoes were blamed for allowing the witches to pass in. I well remember hearing much of a witch doctor who lived at Scammonden who was regarded as being able to give safeguards against witches and wizards and who had cures for people hurt by the 'evil eye.'

Personally, I bade defiance to witches and wizards even as a boy, but my nervy temperament was oft the victim to the terror of tales of disembodied spirits appearing in white apparel amongst the tombs in the graveyards.

These spirits, it was reported, had come back for a short time from the other world to avenge some untimely death, and were night-walkers in solitary places, or commissioned to haunt houses until some clergymen could be secured who had the spiritual gift to 'lay them'. The ghostly, chilling stories were always affirmed as 'Gospel truth,' which nobody dare deny until public cemetaries appeared. I can remember to this moment incidents which occurred when I was between three and four years old. My father worked in the third storey of a cotton mill near the canal, and one day whilst speaking to a woman on the canal bank, he took me in his arms and pretended to throw me into her apron.

I remember clinging to his neck, hearing the woman's assurance that I need not be afraid, but at the same time feeling terribly apprehensive lest I might be let slip.

That is all I know of my father, beyond being lifted to look at him as he lay dead in his coffin. A morbid practice obtained in those days of letting children have 'their last look'.

I did not want to look at my father dead, and still remember the chill and terror of that ghastly experience.

JOHN SYKES, *Slawit in the 'Sixties*, pp. 9–13

(b)

Youthful Escapades.

Most childhoods and early years have their narrow escapes from fatal accidents. I had mine. I must have been in my first year. I was tiresome and restive in the cradle.

My elder sister, but a mere child, was in temporary charge, and in order to quieten me took a hot poker out of the fire and put it on my neck.

I believe that for a time I was expected to die, but I survived the fire. I never blamed my sister. We grew up mutually affectionate.

Again, I remember being sent while a mere boy to drown a cat. The creature was tied in a bag and evidently seemed to be aware of my errand and intention.

The place of execution was the edge of a precipice, of about thirty feet above the bend of a deep part of the river Colne.

As I let go my victim, pussy put out a claw and caught the sleeve of my jacket.

By a sudden jerk I only just freed and balanced myself on the land side of the water.

But the sensation of being well nigh drowned I distinctly re-member.

A number of us, lads, were having a jaunt on the hill top on a Saturday morning and came across a huge boulder. It may have weighed a few tons.

It took some dozen of us to move it. But we conceived the idea of seeing it roll down the very steep field in front of us, leading and leaning towards the high road—

But down the hill it had to go, in its passage tearing up by the roots a fifty-year-old tree which luckily broke its force.

At the bottom of the field on a lower level was a public footpath. The thought that someone might be passing filled us with panic all too late until the great rock leapt the footpath and settled in the hollow of a field below.

As soon as we saw that it had stopped we scattered and scampered for dear life.

I never now go over Slaithwaite canal bridge without recalling some of the 'desperate and mad' tricks of youth that obtained in those days, such as 'follow my leader' even if he had led over the coping stones of the canal bridge wall, to fall from which on one side would only land the follower on the bridge, but a fall from the other side would have meant a fall of eight or ten yards and landed us in the bottom of the canal.

JOHN SYKES, *Slawit in the 'Sixties*, pp. 14–16

(c)

Launched on Life's Sea.—My First School.—Old Dame Teacher.

My first school was an old woman's school, a very common village academy in those times, with its rickety forms and its clean sanded stone floors, it was presided over by dames of sixty or seventy years of age; when they could do nothing else they could keep a school.

Our fee was one penny per week. Our dame had her own way of teaching us our A B C, and her own way of controlling us by means of a leather lash tied to a stout walking stick which did a sterner duty if required, while she sat serenely all the while in her old armchair by the fireside.

We frequently tried to get with a comrade near the door and

while the teacher dozed we manoeuvred to slip into the adjoining fields and lanes and into the sunshine.

JOHN SYKES, *Slawit in the Sixties*, pp. 18–21

(d)

The Slaithwaite National Day and Sunday Schools.

It was in my eighth year that I had to go to school in earnest. . . . I was sent to the Church Day School, which under the conditions meant both weekday and Sunday. Our school was then staffed with six or seven male teachers, two or three monitors to instruct us in the three R's, and the schoolmaster's wife to teach sewing and needlework, &c.

Our master was of commanding personality. He was credited with being a stern disciplinarian.

But, there were many excellent points in his teaching.

It was his manner of 'driving it in' that made our schooldays too much a prison life of hard labour.

To leave at thirteen was our hope and outlook.

I remember just one kind word in that five years of bondage.

I was writing at the desk not knowing that he stood behind me, when suddenly I felt his hands stroking the back of my head. I expected a blow, but he remarked, 'You will never be a good writer, my lad. You have not a steady hand, but never mind. They can teach a pig to write, but they cannot teach it to think, and you can think.'

The half-timers were the boys who worked in the mills mornings and afternoons alternately. They worked at Farrar's, Uppermill, or at the Old Corn Mill. Our master never wanted them, but he had to have his share of them. Most of them were 'billy piecers' and their work was to hold a bunch of carded lengths of wool in the left hand and roll them singly with the right hand to another set of lengths moving up the billy sheet and thus making a continuous thread for the 'slubbin.' They often came to school with bleeding fingers.

When the fingers had become inured they were swollen and like strips of raw beef attached to the palms of their hands.

The lads were harshly treated at the mills. If they failed to link a single thread, the man in charge of the machine, who was called the slubber, with a roller of the billy of about five feet in length and one inch in diameter, would hit them on the head. Bleeding heads and bleeding hands were oft their portion, and with this type of fingers they were expected to write. No wonder they sometimes fell asleep in the effort.

The severest form of punishment in our school was termed 'Riding the grey mare.' The doomed subject of it was not placed on another lad's back, but put astride a form and carried shoulder high around the school, followed up, as usual, by the ferrule, causing pain almost beyond mortal endurance.

The very witnessing of such scenes to children of sensitive temperaments was distressing in the extreme; I have seen girls weep and children fret for long after witnessing some of the ordeals.

JOHN SYKES, *Slawit in the Sixties*, pp. 23–29

(e)

Squib-Night

Truly, precautions were needful. The old town went mad . . . Bonfires were lit in the main street—

A 'guy' probably wore a mask, and was covered fantastically in plenty of paper shavings and white or shiny paper, to show up suddenly if a squib was thrown down near one. A certain 'guy' (one of my mother's newspaper boys) came out of the dark street one night into the little dim shop and near the gas-jet, where he could be seen. Then, to my great admiration, suddenly the first boy was gone, and another stood in his place! So, to my astonished eyes, it seemed for a moment or two, until I understood that the boy's back had a different scheme of disguise from the front. A well-equipped 'guy' carried either a switch, or a holder for putting down his squibs far enough away . . . Spluttering and roaring out its stream of sparks, it would chase after any runner, throwing his scampering figure into strong light, and then bursting as if in devilish hatred.

The procession of the Guy Fawkes to the bonfire was dreadful to behold. Consider. For some hours we children had stood at the window in the dark Front Room. There the familiar buildings were but fitfully lit up by the glare of torches, or frequent explosions. Odd figures flitted along for a moment, only to be lost again in the November darkness. In this or that doorway or passage, usually so safe, some fearful miscreant could be seen lurking as if for crime; across the road now, in this darkness and orgy, uncanny men were

stealing quickly by in the gleam of squibs or of bonfires . . . And by
and by, from a distance a different sound took our attention. Hark!
The local Volunteer Band . . . were escorting Guy Fawkes to the
bonfire!

And as it drew nearer the hurly-burly increased, until at last, with
the procession itself, came a perfect uproar of fiendish riot: noise,
flaming torches, screeching squibs, dreadful looking men, and,
horridest of all, a Guy Fawkes, or maybe two of them—ferocious
though motionless figures, wearing masks, black hats, black coats.
They looked like dead men. Their hideous faces, with too much red
about them, gleamed and glowed like a butcher's shop lit by naphtha
flares; and for the rest the straw they were stuffed with, the tar they
were darkened with, made them too inflammably black. A hell of
pitchy blackness hung over the figures of Guy Fawkes.

Overcome with terror, I had crouched down behind the lower
panelling of the window until one could dare look out again.

JOHN SYKES, *Slawit in the Sixties*, pp. 54–58

2. RAGGED SCHOOL

Extract from Mr. Quintin Hogg's Account of how the Regent Street polytechnic was founded

My first experience of religious work of any kind was holding a
Bible class at Eton. . . I left Eton at the end of 1863, and in the
beginning of 1864 tried my prentice hand at London boys . . . I was
painfully struck . . . at the utter absence of any possible means of
innocent recreation, to say nothing of instruction, for the ragged
children . . . My first effort was to get a couple of crossing-sweepers
. . . and offer to teach them to read . . . With an empty beer-bottle for
a candlestick, and a tallow candle for illumination, and a couple
of Bibles as reading-books, what grew into the Polytechnic was
practically started . . .

The following winter the ragged school began in real earnest;
I had a very earnest female teacher in charge . . . and she used to beg
me to open the rooms in the evenings . . . for the purpose of teaching
the elder lads . . . [the experiment was tried, but a riot ensued, and
Mr. Hogg was hastily summoned] . . . On arriving, I found the
whole school in an uproar, the gas fittings had been wrenched off
and used as batons for the boys for striking the police, while the rest
of the boys were pelting them with slates . . . I felt rather alarmed for

the teacher, and rushing into the darkened room, called out for the boys to instantly stop and be quiet. To my amazement, the riot was stopped immediately. In two minutes the police were able to go quietly away, and for the first time in my life I had some kind of instinct or capacity for the management of elder boys.

During all this time the boys had been getting of a very different character and appearance to those who first came. When we first opened the school, no less than five boys came absolutely naked, except for their mothers' shawls which were pinned around them . . . Five separate gangs of thieves attended the school, all of whom were within six months earning their livelihood more or less respectably. Those who showed any desire to get on were passed through the Shoeblack Society and apprenticed to various trades. The young mechanics began to bring their fellow apprentices and other mechanics to the school, so that the truly ragged, unkempt boys of 1864 had been succeeded by the orderly and fairly dressed lads of 1868.

CHARLES BOOTH, *Life and Labour of the People in London*, 3rd Series, Vol. VII, p. 390

3. INFANT PRATTLING
1868

Mildred [aged 3½] speaks of herself wholly in the 3rd person: Susan not coming at her call she supposed, aloud, that Susan did not hear but finding she had said 'Baby said to Baby, 'Pose Minnie not hear Baby call.'—Mary (and all Maries) she calls Mungoach and Jane Munksh.—Being mimicked by Mabel she cried 'Sissie not mock Baby! Baby good mind to cut Sissie.'—*Did be to go* = was going to go—Baby-cuts = little scissors—Church-pockie = alms'-box.

HUMPHREY HOUSE and GRAHAM STOREL (ed.), *The Journals and Papers of Gerard Manley Hopkins*, p. 160

4. MOTLEY LABOUR

(a)

A writer, who visited the different brick-making establishments of the district, estimates that seventy-five per cent. of the persons employed are females; and perhaps two-thirds of these are young girls from nine to twelve years of age. We saw one set of these hands at work at the moulding bench. A middle-aged woman, as we took her to be from some dress indications of her sex, was standing at the bench, butter-stick in hand. With two or three moulds she formed the clay dough into 'loaves' with wonderful celerity. One little girl then took them away and shed them out upon the drying floor. Another girl brought the clay to the bench. This was a heavier task. She was a girl apparently about thirteen. But though there was some colour in her cheeks, it was the flitting flush of exhaustion. She moved in a kind of swaying, sliding way. She first took up a mass of the cold clay, weighing about twenty-five pounds, upon her head, and while balancing it there, she squatted to the heap without bending her body, and took up a mass of equal weight with both hands against her stomach, and with the two burdens walked about a rod and deposited them on the moulding bench. How such a child could ever grow an inch in any direction after being put to this occupation, was another mystery.

Each moulding woman has two, sometimes three, of these girls to serve her. They are generally her own children, but, if not, she employs the children of equally unfortunate mothers. They are called pages, as if waiting upon a queen . . .

A woman with her two or three pages will mould 3,000 bricks in a day by extra exertion; she is paid 2s. 8d. per thousand. Out of this she pays about 2s. per day to the girls that serve her.

As we were leaving, a little boy came up to the bench who was but a little taller than one of its legs. He was seventeen, so that he must have been quite three feet and a half on his bare feet although at first he looked shorter. He probably had found no other time to grow except when a-bed at night or on the Sunday.

ELIHU BURRITT, M.A., *Walks in the Black Country and its Green Border-Land*, p. 205 et seq.

(b)

The nail-maker pays on an average 2s. 6d. a week for his cottage and shop. He must find his own tools, which are rather simple and few in number. As he and his family generally make only one size of nails all their lives, he needs only one heading-tool to each hammer. He utilizes every square foot of space around his forge.

I have seen four girls of about sixteen years of age standing round the same forge at once, each with her rod in the fire.

ELIHU BURRITT, M.A., *Walks in the Black Country and its Green Border-Land*, p. 213

(c)

Towards Bromsgrove I turned into a nailer's shop by the road-side. Here a father and his son were busily at work. The lad was nine years old, standing with bare feet on a stone to raise him breast-high to the anvil. His face was smutty and his long black hair was coarse and unkempt. He could not read. He was a hearty, healthy, merry-eyed boy; still, as he was the first I had seen of his age at the anvil, I wrote my impressions of his condition in an article which had a wide reading in the United States. It excited so much sympathy that, at my suggestion, the American children raised a contribution of about £30 to send him to school, and to pay his father 2s. 6d. a week in lieu of his wages.

ELIHU BURRITT, M.A., *Walks in the Black Country and its Green Border-Land*, p. 308

5. TEETOTALISM

The origins of the various anti-alcohol movements are obscure. Dicky Turner, a working man, is supposed to have coined the term tee-tee-total. Many substitutes were suggested, including nitro-glycerine, ether, and chloroform. The Band of Hope, to encourage children to abstain, was founded in 1847. The *Onward Reciter* was typical of many publications designed for use at temperance meetings.

TO BE SOLD BY AUCTION.

Thomas Jarratt.

Lot One—some stylish clothing, a coat without a tail—
'Twas torn off in the struggle as its owner went to goal;
A hat without a brim, and some boots that have no soles;
With a pair of leather breeches that are full of rents and holes.

Lot Two—some household furniture; that chair against the door,
I'll warrant when you use it, you'll soon be on the floor;
For table turning, I commend this little table brown,
It only needs the lightest touch to turn it upside down!

Lot Three—a rusty porridge pot, a pail and kettle too,
If you are not particular, for riddles they will do;
Then here's a frying pan, well worn, but not with frying meat—
'Twas tied to snarling Rover's tail, and dragged along the street.

Lot Four—some ancient crockery, a dish and platters four,
A spoutless teapot, and a glass whose standing days are o'er;
An army of black bottles, whose perfume tells the tale
That drinking was the only cause that brought about this sale.

Lot Five—a case of treasures, the buyer takes the whole,
A snuff box and tobacco box, an ancient toddy bowl;
A song and jest book, pack of cards, a set of dominoes;
Who'll buy these curiosities, then down the hammer goes?
      Now gentlemen and ladies all take heed to what I say.
      Avoid the drunkard's ruin, and sign the pledge to-day.

WILLIAM DARRAH, *The Onward Reciter*, Vol, I, p. 119

6. BESEECHING SMILES

(a)

Friday, 19 July   [1872]

Katie and the Monk were in the habit of calling over the balusters
'Bigglesy-buggles' to everyone who came up. They were told not to
do so as it was not a nice word for them to use. Soon after Fanny
was reading to them the story of David and Goliath and how
Goliath 'cursed David by his gods'. The Monk asked what this
meant. Fanny said Goliath said some naughty words. 'Do you
think,' asked the Monk in a solemn and awestruck voice, 'do you
think, Aunt Fanny, the giant said "Bigglesy-buggles"?'

WILLIAM PLOMER (ed.), *Kilvert's Diary* 1870–1879, p. 192

(b)

Saturday, 12 July   [1873]

This afternoon I went to see Mrs. Drew and if possible to comfort
her concerning the death of her child. She was filled with sorrow and
remorse because when the child had mouched from school last
Monday and had wandered about all day with scarcely any food she
had whipped him as soon as he came home in the evening and had

sent him supperless to bed, although he had besought her almost in an agony to give him a bit of bread. 'Oh, Mother, oh Mother, do give me one bit of bread.' Her heart smote her bitterly now that it was too late, when she remembered how the child had begged and prayed for food. The next morning soon after rising he fell down in a fit and he died at even. The mother asked me to go upstairs and see the child. He lay in his coffin looking very peaceful and natural with the flowers on his breast and the dark hair curling on his forehead.

WILLIAM PLOMER (ed.), *Kilvert's Diary* 1870–1879, p. 220.

(c)

Friday, 15 January   [1875]

Speaking to the children at the school about the Collect for the 2nd Sunday after the Epiphany and God's peace I asked them what beautiful image and picture of peace we have in the xxiii Psalm. 'The Good Shepherd,' said I, 'leading His sheep to—?' 'to the slaughter', said Frederick Herriman promptly. One day I asked the children to what animal our Saviour is compared in the Bible. Frank Matthews confidently held out his hand. 'To an ass,' he said.

WILLIAM PLOMER (ed.), *Kilvert's Diary* 1870–1879, p. 277

(d)

Saturday, 16 January   [1875]

In the Common Field in front of the cottages I found two little figures in the dusk. One tiny urchin was carefully binding a handkerchief round the face of an urchin even more tiny than himself. It was Fred and Jerry Savine. 'What are you doing to him?' I asked Fred. 'Please, Sir,' said the child solemnly. 'Please, Sir, we'm gwine to play at blindman's buff.' The two little images went solemnly on with their game as if they were in a magnificent playground with a hundred children to play with.

WILLIAM PLOMER (ed.), *Kilvert's Diary* 1870–1879, p. 277

(e)

Tuesday, 13 July   [1875]

As I walked from Shanklin to Sandown along the cliff edge I stopped to watch some children bathing from the beach directly below. One beautiful girl stood entirely naked on the sand, and there as she half sat, half reclined sideways, leaning upon her elbows with her knees bent and her legs and feet partly drawn back and up, she was a model for a sculptor, there was the supple slender waist, the gentle dawn and tender swell of the bosom and the budding breasts, the graceful rounding of the delicately beautiful limbs and above all the soft and exquisite curves of the rosy dimpled bottom and broad white thigh. Her dark hair fell in thick masses on her white shoulders as she threw her head back and looked out to sea.

WILLIAM PLOMER, (ed.), *Kilvert's Diary* 1870–1879, p. 290

7. THE COLD CURE

Mathena Blomefield ('Nessel') was the daughter of a prosperous Norfolk farmer. After an accident, she did not go to school, but learned housewifery and helped on the farm. She was chiefly interested in rearing young animals. Her closest friend was an imaginary companion called 'Palk'.

So upstairs they went. There was a nice fire and a foot-bath of hot water and mustard. Nessel undressed and sat by the fire with her feet in the foot-bath. Over her head was a little white shawl and pinned round her shoulders a red flannel petticoat. Rachel was busy cutting out a piece of brown paper shaped like a bib, only it fitted on back and front. She warmed it before the fire, then lighting the tallow candle dripped tallow over the brown paper until both sides were thickly spotted with grease. Undoing the red petticoat and Nessel's nightie, the tallow plaster was put on over her chest and back, and a piece of flannel pinned over it to keep it in position.

'Now,' said Rachel, 'here is the glass of hot sweet spirits of nitre. I have put in plenty of sugar. You must drink it as hot as you can with the spoon, while I go and get the warming pan to warm the bed.'

How good it felt. Nessel would have enjoyed it only her chest was so tight she could hardly breathe.

'Now,' said Rachel, 'let me rub your nose with tallow grease, and then I think you can go to sleep. I've made you some honey and vinegar with some laudanum in it. It's here on the little table. If you cough you must get it and take some. Here is an acid drop, and when I have cleared up you must go to sleep, but I'll leave the candle lit.'

In the morning the cold was better, but Nessel was not allowed to get up . . . So she had the Dutch dolls and got out a very favourite old doll she had had ever since she was two years old.

Lady Arabella Stewart was her name. It was a china doll with real hair plaited in tiny braids pinned with real tiny hairpins. She was dressed in a fawn plaid skirt and short jacket, with a long white lace jabot round her neck, and high kid boots. A little purple bonnet with strings tied under her chin.

MATHENA BLOMEFIELD, *The Balleymung Pit*, p. 138

8. TUBERCULOSIS

John Whiteley was an exceptionally gifted and precocious youth when he developed tuberculosis. Unfortunately he died not long after his stay in the Ventnor Hospital.

Rambling Remarks and Rough Diary.

1874

Introduction. It was in June 1874 that I first entertained the idea of going to the Royal National Hospital for Consumption at Ventnor, Isle of Wight . . .

Wednesday, Nov. 18th, 1874. I received a ticket to admit me on the 20th of Novr 1874. I had been waiting about 3 months.

Friday, Nov. 20th. Next morning we had breakfast, & then settled the bill, 9/8, took a cab to St. John's Station & booked for Ventnor.

The moment I entered the door of the Hospital, I was introduced to one of the patients, Mr Lloyd & to the nurse. They showed me round & explained various things about the Hospital. The weather was glorious, the flowers sent forth their sweet perfumes, every thing being quite different to dreary old Halifax.

Monday, Dec. 7th. A beautiful morning. Took a walk this morning in the grounds, rather cold. Played at Bagatelle during the afternoon & evening. At night a lot of singers came & sung a few Christmas hymns in front of each block. They sung very well.

Tuesday, Dec. 8th. A cold, wet, windy morning. Sea is very rough. I have seen Dr. Williamson this morning; ordered me a glass of sherry daily & two biscuits, because of the feebleness of my pulse. He asked me if I had no objections to be Librarian. I said no. He gave me keys. Had a game of draughts with Mr Moger, he beat me. Received a bottle of sherry this evening from the nurse, I keep it in the cupboard in the Dining Room. Received a newspaper & book from home. Wrote home. Labelled some books in the Library this afternoon.

Wednesday, Dec. 9th. To-day the 'Transit of Venus' takes place. It is cold, damp and wet. Went to Church this afternoon. Sermon by Curate. Was weighed again this afternoon, and have lost ¼ of a lb. Strange thing, I can't account for it . . .

Wednesday, Dec. 16th. . . . *When I recover* . . . I underline the words 'When I recover', because I have great doubts of recovering from a Consumption! A distinguished physician says 'We don't cure consumption, we dress it.' I think that that is pretty near the truth.

Wednesday, Dec. 23rd. Cold & frosty, but very pleasant in front of the Hospital. Saw Dr Williamson, said I was to take a pill to night for sweating. Played at Bagatelle this morning. Wrote home in the afternoon. Was weighed and had lost 3 lbs. I now weigh 113 lbs. Never so low before. During summer I weighed 123 lbs. The night is rainy & windy; the sea is very stormy.

Thursday, Dec. 24th. A wet day. Labelled some of the Library Books this morning. Read in the afternoon. Very quiet this Xmas eve, nothing particular going on.

Friday, Dec. 25th. Christmas Day. Foggy & damp a drizzling rain at times. Went to Church this morning. The Church was deco-rated. Over the Communion table were the words 'Unto us a child is born' in white letters on a red ground. Along front of the organ was the word 'Hallelujah', white letters on a red ground. The pulpit and lectern were wreathed in evergreens. Sermon by Mr Coleridge. Dinner at 1 p.m. & we all expected seeing roast stag for dinner, but to our great surprise we had roast beef, roast turkey & plum pudding. During the afternoon songs & recitations were given. I read 'Pill Jim's Progress wi' John Bunion'. After tea songs & recitations were given again. We were allowed to stay up one hour longer being Xmas Evening. In the afternoon we had wine, oranges & nuts.

Thursday, Dec. 31st. Ground white with snow and a bitter cold east wind blowing. Played at Bagatelle in the evening. Visited by Mr Coleridge. All patients wishing to see the old year out and the

new in, are requested to go to Block 6 at 9 p.m. I did not go. Went
to bed.

New Years Day. 1875

A thaw has set in to day. Wrote home. Read during the day.
Nothing extra to dinner. Nurses kept an orange for me from last
night's entertainment. Feel very unwell. Pains in the knees. Had a
warm bath after supper, and a horrid one it was too.

Saturday, January 2nd. A beautiful day. Snow has all disappeared.
Walked along front of Hospital all the morning. Very warm.
Wrote a letter for a patient. Copied a recitation this afternoon from
General Reciter. Meditated in the evening.

> Royal National Hospital,
> Ventnor,
> Isle of Wight.
> January 1st/75

Dear Parents,

Winter has set in here as well as at Halifax. The ground is
robed in a white mantle of snow and the weather is bitterly cold.
During the past week we have been our own masters, with Dr
Williamson being away, but he's coming back to morrow and we
shall have to behave ourselves once more.

Yesterday a great man of war ship passed here. A cold east wind is
blowing, and no patient is allowed out of doors. Yesterday and to
day I have been preparing papers to take the Meteorological Observations. I do lots of writing for the Institution.

I am feeling rather better than I did when I wrote last. I hope
father is quite well again. By this time Mr Wood will have got
spliced I suppose. With kind love to you all,

> I remain
> Dear parents,
> Yours Affectionately,
> John Whiteley

JOHN WHITELEY, *Rambling Remarks and Rough Diary*
(unpublished), *passim*.

9. WHIRR AND HUM

A great Temperance Tea was held in 1840 to mark the triumphant
opening of Marshall's new one-storey mill. The façade was built in the

'Egyptian style of Architecture' and was an exact copy of the temple of the Pharaohs at Philae.

However, much had changed by the 1880's. A representative of *The Journal of Domestic Appliances and Sewing Machine Gazette* was not impressed by the famous 'Egyptian' mill and its environs in 1882. He reports that 'the few trees remaining are dressed in a penitential garb of soot, as though mourning their comrades that have succumbed to the axe . . .' Labour troubles had arisen, culminating in a two-months strike in 1872. John Marshall's descendants combined with almost a hundred local manufacturers to break the strike. Stephen Marshall declared his intention to 'meet brute force with brute force'. His determined stand was unavailing. The local population were no longer obedient. The feelings of 'affection towards their masters', with which John Marshall had hoped to imbue 'the infant poor', had changed to bitterness and active hostility. The firm closed down in 1886.

From Raw Flax to Finished Thread

The old fashioned skein threads in pound packets are put up by boys. [They] sit at a long wooden bench, each one having in front of him small wooden pegs fixed upright into the bench. Between them he arranges the skeins in layers and ties them round tightly with another skein; with a little skill with the fingers and by the aid our guide as loudly as though talking to a deaf man, and it is with a wooden stick, he produces a neat and tidy appearance. The knots which tie the skein are arranged by little girls so that they shall be all in one place. The skeins are stretched across a frame and the little girls pull the knots round till they are all of a row. The skeins are next made up into pounds by girls and papered up, each packet having an index number. The labels for the spools, which are already gummed, are stuck on by little girls, and instead of making the tongue perform the damping operation . . . the child damps the label on a narrow brass cylinder, which is made to revolve slowly while the lower half of it is in water . . .

During our progress through the various departments of the mills, excepting the packing and storing rooms, our ears have been subject to a whirr hum and a buzz of machinery; we have had to speak to our guide as loudly as though talking to a deaf man, and it is with a sense of relief we leave this hive of industry for the open air.

SHOE AND LEATHER TRADES' CHRONICLE, August 15, 1882

10. BURIAL CLUB

The subject of the following account, (then) Edith Gladys Fernandes Lewis, is now ninety years old.

I was two years old when my baby brother died. My father was at sea, and his return was delayed. Consequently my mother found it almost impossible to find enough money with which to bury the dead baby. After this harrowing experience she immediately joined a burial club on my behalf, in case the same thing happened again.

MRS. J. H. BIRLEY, M.A., J.P. (Autobiographical fragment).

11. CHEAP AND STRONG

The ladies who first decided to form the *Leeds Ladies Association for the Care and Protection of Young Girls* evidently acted from the best motives. There was clearly a need for some action to be taken on behalf of unfortunate girls.

Friday, June 6. 1884. 10 a.m.

Mrs. B. suggested that when girls came into the Home, sewing and Bible classes should be formed, and that Young Ladies should be asked to come and teach in the afternoons, reading, writing, etc.

June 20.

Miss L. was instructed never to allow the girls to go out for walks by themselves. It was resolved to supply the girls with black dresses for best, if black material could be procured as cheap and strong as coloured . . .

July 18.

Mrs. B. read a letter from Miss H. of Headingley College asking if a situation could be found for an unfortunate girl of 16, already a mother, who had been in her Sabbath-school class and in whose fate she was much interested. The girl was now in London and it was felt very strongly that it would be safer for her not to return to Leeds . . .

Sept. 12.

After prayers the minutes were read, and business commenced by reading the doctor's report of J.G.'s knee. It seemed worse than was at first supposed, and unfortunately had been somewhat mismanaged, and it was resolved to send her to the Infirmary to have it nursed there . . .

The case of H.W. who was in the workhouse along with her baby was considered, and it was thought the time had come to commence a small *Workhouse Magdalene Branch*, which would undertake all work which was not strictly Preventitive.

Dec. 12.

E. D., who had seemed to be doing so well, but had unfortunately been drinking again and had been taken to the lock-up.

Report for 1884

At present we have about twenty girls in Service, many of whom are doing well & paying for their clothing. Of course there are exceptions, & others like the proverbial bad shilling are returned to our hands again & again. Our greatest difficulty lies, as might be expected, in the character of some of the Girls, who, owing in great part to neglect or bad example, are idle, untruthful & quarrelsome in a high degree, & it seems almost impossible to make the slightest impression upon them. This is, however, the very class we want to save.

1886

It was decided that M.E.T. who had been dismissed from her last place for stealing 3^d & a ring, should be handed over to the care of Miss L.

Mrs. C. was requested to write to Mrs. L. strictly forbidding any of her girls to attend Holbeck Feast.

September 1888

R. A. who had been placed in a very comfortable situation was some weeks ago taken away by her Mother to tramp about the country, & all efforts to find her have been fruitless. The Lady with whom she was in service has now taken M. W., the little girl who formerly went singing in the streets, & so far M. is giving satisfaction, & her Mistress is most kindly teaching her in the evenings.

Sept. 20th 1889

E.M. age eight, drunken brutal Mother, brought up Miss G.

E. E. age fifteen, father in prison, brought by Miss G.

E. L. aged 13 & S. H. aged 10—the father of the younger girl is in prison for assault on the elder girl his step-daughter the Mother is in the Infirmary a very clean respectable woman. The Committee decided to accept all three cases.

From the Minutes of the Leeds Ladies' Association for the Care and Protection of Young Girls (unpublished).

12. A DESOLATE ROOM

I remember in one case finding a poor woman lying on a heap of rags. She had just given birth to twins, and there was nobody of any sort to wait upon her. By her side was a crust of bread, and a small lump of lard. 'I fancied a bit o' booter,' the woman remarked apologetically, 'and my mon—he couldna git me iny bootter, so he fitcht me this bit o' lard. It's *rare good*,' said the poor creature . . . However, I was soon busy trying to make her a little more comfortable. The babies I washed in a broken pie-dish, the nearest approach to a tub that I could find. And the gratitude of those large eyes, that gazed upon me from that wan and shrunken face, can never fade from my memory.

ST. JOHN ERVINE, *God's Soldier: General William Booth*, p. 220

13. RAT-TAIL JELLY

Lewis Carroll's absorbing interest in children did not always produce the expected response. At a dinner party he set a puzzle to a little girl, called 'the fox, the goose and the bag of corn', illustrated by an arrangement of biscuits. But she shrieked out, 'I can't do it! I can't do it! Oh Mama! Mama!' and sobbed uncontrollably for several minutes in her mother's lap. However, in the following letters he was wholly successful in amusing little Agnes Hughes.

My dear Agnes,—Three visitors came knocking at my door, begging me to let them in. And when I opened the door, who do you think they were? Why, they were three cats! Wasn't it curious? However, they all looked so cross and disagreeable, that I took up the first thing I could lay my hands on (which happened to be the rolling-pin) and knocked them all down as flat as pancakes! 'If *you* come knocking at *my* door,' I said, '*I* shall come knocking at *your* heads.' That was fair, wasn't it?

Yours affectionately,   Lewis Carroll.

My dear Agnes,—About the cats, you know. Of course I didn't leave them lying flat on the ground like dried flowers: no, I picked them up, and I was as kind as I could be to them. I lent them a portfolio for a bed—they wouldn't have been comfortable in a real bed, you know: they were too thin—but they were quite happy between the sheets of blotting paper—and each of them had a pen-wiper for a pillow. Well, then I went to bed: but first I lent them the three dinner-bells, to ring if they wanted anything in the night.

Well, I told them they might ring [the dinner bells] if they happened to want anything—and, as they rang *all* the bells *all* the night, I suppose they did want something or other, only I was too sleepy to attend to them.

In the morning I gave them some rat-tail jelly and buttered mice for breakfast, and they were as discontented as they could be. They wanted some boiled pelican, but of course I knew it wouldn't be good for them. So all I said was 'Go to Number Two, Finborough Road, and ask for Agnes Hughes, and if it's *really* good for you, she'll give you some.' Then I shook hands with them all, and wished them all goodbye, and drove them up the chimney. They seemed sorry to go, and took the bells and the portfolio with them. I didn't find this out till after they had gone, and then I was sorry, and wished them back again.

How are Arthur, and Amy, and Emily? Do they still go up and down Finborough Road, and teach the cats to be kind to mice? I'm *very* fond of all the cats in Finborough Road.

Give them my love. Who do I mean by 'them'? Never mind.

Your affectionate friend,   Lewis Carroll.

My dear Amy,—You asked me after those three cats. Ah! The dear creatures! they have *never left me*? Isn't it kind of them? And they *are* so kind and thoughtful! Do you know, when I had gone out for a walk the other day, they got *all* my books out of the bookcase, and opened them on the floor, to be ready for me to read. They opened them all at page 50. It was rather unfortunate, though: because they took my bottle of gum, and tried to gum pictures upon the ceiling (which they thought would please me), and by accident they spilt a quantity of it all over the books. So when they were shut up and put by, the leaves all stuck together, and I can never read page 50 again in any of them!

However, they meant it very kindly, so I wasn't angry. I gave them each a spoonful of ink as a treat; but they were ungrateful for that, and made dreadful faces. But, of course, as it was given them as a treat, they had to drink it. One of them has turned black since: it was a white cat to begin with.

Give my love to any children you happen to meet. Also I send two kisses and a half, for you to divide with Agnes, Emily, and Godfrey. Mind you divide them fairly.

Yours affectionately,   C. L. Dodgson.

STUART DODGSON COLLINGWOOD, *A Selection from the Unpublished Writings and Drawings of Lewis Carroll*, p. 214

14. THE LADY IN GREY

(a)

When my parents first went to live at Beavor Lodge they used to be disturbed, night after night, by a strange and uncanny sound as of someone weeping her heart out. At the same time it seemed as though whoever it was who was weeping was also sewing some thick material, for the sound of a needle passing through it was quite distinguishable . . .

On another occasion, but this time at eleven o'clock in the morning, my elder brothers and sister were at their lessons when my mother rang the bell for the parlour-maid. Almost immediately afterwards the door opened and in walked, not the parlour-maid but the lady in grey, holding up her shawl across her face, over the top of which she gazed fixedly at my mother. For a moment she stood behind the children sitting at their lessons, then retreated slowly backwards towards the door and vanished before reaching it.

Although I never saw anything alarming, it was impossible for me not to hear about the grey lady and it was my constant fear, when I went upstairs after dark, that she would suddenly appear and do to me I knew not what.

There was another story that I must have heard when I was

born. One night my parents were awakened by loud screams from the small room adjoining theirs where my sister slept. She must then have been three or four years old. My father went in to see what was the matter. She was sobbing and as she put her arms round his neck she said, 'Oh, daddy, daddy, I do wish nurse wouldn't come up through the floor and look at me with those great eyes and then disappear.'

SIR ARTHUR RICHMOND, *Twenty-Six Years*, 1879–1905, pp. 11–12

(b)

I must have been about two years old when the first clear picture of my childhood was etched indelibly on my mind. Perched on a high chair and held from falling out by a bar across the front, I was doing my best not to swallow the 'pap' which my old nurse was doing her best to induce me to eat. In front of us and behind a tall brass-bound screen a bright fire was roaring up the chimney. On nurse's lap there lay a bowl of that white sticky mixture I did not want to swallow. The space between my gums and my cheeks filled up and would harbour no more. Then the picture fades; the only memory that lives on is one of a pervading and deeply satisfying sense of cosiness. Nurse was cosy; I nestled cosily on her lap; I must have fallen asleep feeling safe and content.

(c)

It may have been the stories of robbers and their adventures of which my head was full that prompted me one day to take down from where it was hanging on the wall of the nursery a broad-headed crescent-shaped dagger which my father had brought back from Egypt. As I sat by the fire taking it out of the scabbard and playing with it, my gaze was drawn to my nurse who was busy ironing. Her right arm fascinated me. What would happen, I wondered, if it were punctured? Would it explode? I got up and, drew the dagger smartly across her upper arm. The result was appalling. She screamed, dropped the iron and gripped her arm as the blood gushed out. Horrified at what I saw I fled headlong and shut myself up in the nearest place of refuge—the W.C. I trembled with terror as I thought that I might have killed her. Gradually the sounds subsided and then began a search for me. Someone thought of the W.C. and called to me to come out. I was too frightened

either to reply or to budge. They would send me to prison; I would
be hung. At last my victim herself came to the door and implored
me to come out, promising that no harm would come to me and she
would forgive me.

> SIR ARTHUR RICHMOND, *Twenty-Six Years*, 1879–1905,
> p. 36

15. MOUNTAINS OF RAGS

Though the following account is fictional in form, A. E. Coppard
assured the author that it was an exact description of his own experiences
as a child in London.

Two or three years after the first Jubilee of Queen Victoria a
small ten-year-old boy might have been seen slouching early every
morning along the Mile End Road towards the streets of White-
chapel. Johnny Flynn was a pale boy of pinched appearance—for
although his black coat was a size too large for him, his black
trousers were a size too small.

The first business in the tailor's workshop was to light the fire.
Then to sweep the room clean of its countless fragments of cloth
and cotton. Heaping these in a wooden box, the boy staggered with
it across the dark passage into a smaller apartment with a window,
looking down into a dank yard where he could see people all day
long going to the privvy. The room contained only a colossal pile
of cloth clippings covering the whole floor, and it was his unending
task to sort these into their various kinds. The pile never lessened.
Sometimes he could scarcely enter the door to get into the room;
and the implacable mountain of rags was watered with the tears
of his childish hungers and despairs.

'You muth get the fresh air into you,' Mr. Alabaster said. 'Itth
good for the lining of the stomach, or I shall have the poleeth on
me. You can go under the railway arch if it rainth.'

Well, the boy would go and walk in the streets. Unless it rained
he avoided the railway arch because someone had done a murder
there, and someone else had painted a white skeleton on the wall; so
he walked about . . . Soon he opened his package of food—wedges
of bread and slips of meat folded in a sheet of newspaper. Scrupu-
lously he sniffed the meat, and not caring for that smell he dropped
the meat into a gutter and chewed the bread with resentment.

Long ere the day was over, the boy regretted his rash disposal of the meat; devastating hunger assailed him and he yearned for any scrap, even a dog's. At such times it was the joy of heaven to him if Mrs. Grainger beckoned at tea-time.

'Johnny, I want you to go and get me a ha'p'orth of tea, a ha'p'orth of sugar and a farthingsworth of milk. There's three-ha'pence—you can have the farthing for yourself.'

Nice old woman! With his farthing he would buy a few broken biscuits; and he would borrow a pinch of her sugar and dip his biscuits in her milk. That did not happen ever day . . .

Kneeling down beside his box among the soft rags, he would dream over the fine doings he had had on Queen Victoria's Jubilee day. That was a day! All the scholars went to school in the morning to pray, to implore God to confound and frustrate certain nameless nations, to receive a china mug with the Queen's face twice on it, a medal with her face again—and a paper bag containing half a sausage pie and a great piece of cake. He ate them all over again and again. Then you marched out to the park with flags, and the park was full—millions of kids. There were clowns and jokers and sports, and you had your mug filled with tea from a steam-roller. And then he forgot everything and fell asleep sprawling among the rags until he was awakened by angry Mr. Alabaster.

'Hi, hi! Thith won't do, you know. I don't pay you for thleeping, it will bankrupt me . . .'

But at the end of the day the kind Mr. Alabaster would some-times give him a penny to ride part of the way home in a tram. With his penny Johnny hurried off to buy a cake or a pie, and thereafter walked cheerfully home . . .

. . . he went leaping and fled to a cookshop in the Mile End Road . . . there you could buy such marvellous cakes . . . Johnny unwrapped the cake and stood gazing at it, seeking the loveliest corner of entry, when a large boy came to him from an alley near by and accosted him.

'Give us a bite, young 'un.'

'Gives nothing.' Master Flynn was positive to the point of heart-lessness.

'I've had nothing to eat all day,' the large boy said mournfully.

Johnny intimated that he was in the same unfortunate case him-self.

'Give us half of it, d'ye hear,' the other demanded in truculent tones, 'or I'll have the lot'.

Johnny shook his head and hiked a shoulder. 'No you won't.'

'Who'd stop me?' growled the bandit.

'Inky,' replied young Flynn. And then, as he lifted the cake to his mouth and prepared to bite a great gap in it, the absolute and everlasting end of the world smote him clump on the ridge of his chin. He heard the rough fellow grunt: 'There's the upper cut for yer'; the cake was snatched from his paralysed grasp. 'And there's another for civility.' Again the end of the world crashed upon his face from the other side . . . and when he looked up, the fellow was gone, and the cake was gone.

A. E. COPPARD, *The Collected Tales*, pp. 114–28, *passim*.

16. SCHOOL MEALS

This letter was presumably written to Herbert Birley as he was chairman of the Manchester Education Committee. It has been lent by his daughter-in-law, Mrs Gladys Birley.

Letter to Herbert Birley

Sutton Oaks,
Macclesfield,
Dec. 24/89

* I refuse all other feeding agencies.

Dear Birley,

In sending you a cheque for 10£ for the Free Meals I wish to say a few words (which I would sooner do in an informal way) about the work, which I have always regarded with mixed feelings. My only inducement to give this money is the confidence that the school Board will take systematic means to detect and bring to justice all men and women who, through idleness or drunken habits, leave their children short of sufficient food—unless this sort of hunting down neglectful parents accompanies the feeding system, it tends to increase the curse under which we labour, viz, reckless marriages and the production of children whom their parents either will not or cannot properly maintain—I do not think the clergy say enough to young people about the evil of very early marriages—They seem to think it a remedy against unchastity, and there I believe they are wrong. Boy husbands are not apt to be faithful—as the records of Bastardy cases in our police courts too often show—One hopes that, by degrees some better ideas of self-restraint and thrift will obtain amongst our working people, but we must be very careful how we offer inducement to recklessness in marriage. I hope you and Mrs Birley and your family are pretty well this Xmas—

With kind regards from us both.

Yours truly

Hubert Philips.

From the Birley family papers (unpublished).

CHAPTER 7
1890-1914

1. TROUBLESOME HAPPENINGS

Compulsory education for children up to 14 years of age had been in force since 1880. From the following notes it is clear that some children slipped through the net, particularly children of unlucky or feckless parents. Some of these children also suffered from some impairment, physical, or mental, or both.

August 5, 1892

P. H. was reported to be in a very serious condition & Miss L. was instructed to ascertain from the child's relations, their wishes with regard to arrangements in case the worst happened.

1894

Mrs. L. W. K. reported the death of a girl in Marshall St. Home, on Tuesday, May 29th, she was 12 years old & had been 3½ years in the Home, she died suddenly & there had been an inquest & the verdict given was 'death from natural causes, from exhaustion after sickness', the funeral had been on Thursday afternoon, the expenses came to £2.7/, which were to be paid out of the expenses for the Home.

Mrs. L. reported that A. M. had returned from the Infirmary, without her foot being amputated, for a month she was to be kept quiet & have the foot rubbed, Mrs. L. W. K. promised to try & get her into the Women's & Children's Hospital for the time.

E. T. aged 14, a nurse-maid, had taken baby in perambulator & boy of five out, & left them outside in Sweet St., while she went into a shop, the perambulator had been pushed & upset & baby killed. It was decided E. must be in the Home for a time & then sent to situation out of Leeds.

December 3rd, 11 a.m. 1894

E. T. had gone to a situation in the Conservative Club at 1/6 a week, no blame had been attached to her at the inquest.

L. J. had got a good place at 3/6 a week, & private help was making up what was necessary for the baby's keep. Mrs. S. stated that she had been to the C.O. Society about the case, & they recommended the workhouse, & it was suggested this must be done, if the girl could not keep her place.

Meeting held January 6th, 1899

Mrs. T. applied for admission for her grand daughter D., aged 10, whose parents were dead. Child was obliged to wear high boot one leg being shorter than the other, the result of an accident. Mrs. L. J. K. was told to write to Mr. M. R., who had operated upon her & ask his opinion of her being able to get about enough to support herself, when grown up, & to admit her if his reply was favourable.

Meeting held May 19th, 1899

Mrs. A. wrote saying she had heard from the Waifs & Strays, who refused to take L. S. on account of her having only one hand.

Mrs. A. had sent 4 cakes & Mrs. B. worn mackintoshes & toys.

From the Minutes of the Leeds Ladies Association for the Care and Protection of Young Girls (unpublished).

2. DEATH, WORK, AND PLAY

Sarah Dyson's diary records the experience of growing up in the north country. It makes an interesting contrast to the accounts of middle-class children to whom 'the country' was primarily a playground. To Sarah it meant participating in a communal way of life which depended in great measure on deriving a subsistence from the land.

In 1883 Mary Emily was born, and died October 23rd 1884 following an accident in the farm-house at Grandma Sutcliffes. Mother had taken her down as usual to see them, and also for a break during the day. Mary Emily was a quick little toddler and there were no fire guards at that time; and she was running around and upset the hot water pan which went over her and she was scalded very badly and died shortly afterwards.

Sam leaves school

Sam a born farmer leaves school at the age of 13 to help with the farm work which he loved so much, and was very well known in the village with having a good milk round. I remember him very well and also the lovely milk-float we had a yellow one. Sam attended Holthead Sunday School and made a special effort to finish his round and walk up to the Sunday school for 10-o'clock and father would finish later.

January 1895

In January 1895 Maggie was born a lovely girl and looked so healthy and at the age of fifteen months she became ill with diphtheria and died after three days illness.

November Pig Killing Time

In November came pig killing time, and soon our ears would be tormented with the screams of the expiring pig, and as children, we watched the performance, and as I look back I think it was cruel; then the pig was washed and cleaned. As children we hung round waiting for the bladder, which when drained we blew up with a clay pipe stem, and then used it for a football.

Dressing up

We loved to dress up when children in Grandmas and mothers things mother had a drawer in her dressing table where she kept her bustles, veils, brouches, bracelets etc. One morning Clara dressed herself up in a long black skirt black cape trimmed with lace and heavy beaded and a black bonnet which was either mothers or Grandmas and went for a walk around the country side.

Baby Houses and Shows

There were many places where we played at baby-house at Hey Farm and we pretended to wash and hang out the clothes and also bake. Clara had a doll house in our bedroom made out of an orange box with two compartments upstairs and downstairs and had lace curtains and toy furniture. Then we had shows in the barn & danced on the large corn bin or kist as they were sometimes called and sometimes our playmates would join us.

Hay-time at Broadfields

We also loved to join in with the haymaking at Grandpa's and ride on the sledge through Ned-Ing, and up into the sunfield and

north field wobbling about on the sledge and sometimes ride down
to the barn, and go onto the haystack and what fun we had dancing
and treading it down to make it solid and firm.

We loved to play in Grandmas parlour and pretend to be grown
ups. Then before we went home Grandma would join us with a
few games, snatch apple etc. and sometimes she would tie a paper
bag over the cats head, then it ran about the room & try to get it
off and I did wish she would take it off but Grandma just laughted.

Leaving School

At that time we could leave school at the age of thirteen and I
was very eager to do so, and I begun to go round with milk with
my father round the Village which I liked very much in the summer, but it was very cold in the winter there were no covered in
vans then but I was always very well wrapped up.

We had two horses, and Punch was a heavy horse and worked
on the farm, Poly was young and frisky I remember going to Water-
side with milk one day coming back Poly began to gallop and one
of the large milk cans fell out on to the road by Brierlys Mill. I
pulled the reins tightly but I could not stop her till we got to the top
of Bridge Street where father was waiting and said he would go
back for it.

Two days holiday

Slaithwaite Feast   or Sanjamis

I remember Slaithwaite feast being held between the Crimble
Viaducts and Spa Mill Terrace. The swings, dobby-horses, switch-
backs, dry-land sailors, and two bazaars, one in Market Place, and
one at the entrance of the show ground, then there was Hodsons
Show which we thought was wonderful, also a brandy snap, and
coca-nut, and ice-cream stall, and a pea saloon . . .

Apprentice to Dressmaking

When I was about 15 I went as an apprentice to dressmaking
with Miss M. Wilkinson, Carr Lane, Slaithwaite for 2 years and
Miss Ada Garside, was also an apprentice and before I left Miss
F. Rothwell, and from our workroom we could see down info the
Spinning Company Shed and it always looked so nice and clean they
called it winding and the girls wore white aprons. At that time

there were three mills. They started work at 6-30 in the morning till 5-30 p.m. After two years as an apprentice we received 8 shillings a week in the busy summer time, and able to do a bit of sewing at home for ourselves. We started work at 8 a.m. till 8 p.m. in the busy time, and half day on Saturday.

Bottoms Wood Sing

1901

When I was about 16 years old the bottoms morning sing was organized by a few gentlemen in Varley Road and conducted by Mr Tom Dyson. What a lovely sight to see the crowds of people dressed in white and different shades and colours which blended so well with the lovely scenery. To the members of our Band of Hope we owe our thanks, and especially to Miss Sowden who has had the tedious work of training the children, for providing an interesting and pleasing entertainment.

The Children's Festival

As usual the scholars met at one o'clock at the school . . . the Vicar gave a brief address, in which he alluded to a most important and wide-spreading evil, cigarette smoking amongst the children . . .

The route of the procession from the Church was up Bank-gate to Mr. A. C. Applebee's, where the children sang heartily the hymn Sweet is the work, my God, my King. The scholars were the recipients of oranges and new pennies. The procession was headed by the Upper Slaithwaite Brass Band and the Sunday School new banner, which floated gaily on the breeze.

Christmas day at Holthead General Sunday School

We always looked forward to our Christmas day party at Sunday School, the tea consisted of hot brown tea cakes well buttered, bread and butter, cheese, home made Christmas cake, seed cake, and hardcakes; both white and brown bread and butter. On the platform was a table with a red victorian table cover and an hamper full of oranges which he gave to the children after reciting etc. and always something good to say after every item and a God bless em. Then came the dialogues, action songs, duets, solo's etc.

SARAH SUTCLIFFE (née DYSON), Unpublished journal.

3. BEST LOVE

(a)

Letters to the Editor of the Girl's Own Paper

J. H.—A young girl of eighteen should not be 'allowed out' at all in the evening after dusk. Certainly she has no business to take walks alone with any man when engaged to another man than he.

The Girl's Own Paper, April 14, 1894, p. 448

(b)

'Beaver Muff' is a silly, romantic girl; she should at once tell her parents. She cannot propose to do anything so wicked and cruel as to marry clandestinely.

The Girl's Own Paper, April 28, 1894, p. 480

(c)

STRICT READER OF THE 'G.O.P.' inquires whether a little 'girl of twelve years old may have a lover', and 'the easiest way to find out whether a boy loves you', and adds, 'I am twelve'. Did this little girl, still wearing a pinafore (if suitably dressed), ever hear of a great damatist called Shakespeare? We answer her in his words, 'Think yourself a baby', and you will then understand how to behave. Your mother is your best and truest lover, for hers is the most unselfish love that exists. A rag-doll is the best love for such a silly little girl as you seem to be.

The Girl's Own Paper, July 28, 1894, p. 688

4. FACTS OF LIFE

David Garnett and his childhood friends were able to grow up in a middle-class paradise. Perhaps the philosophy behind his upbringing was first formulated by Rousseau.

(a)

We moved into Cearne in February 1896, and a full realization of our new grandeur came to me on my fourth birthday. I remember strutting up to the stable in a new long coachman's coat, talking to our new man, Bert Hedgecock, while Nettle, a pretty red bitch, played about us—my dog. Bert was grooming Shagpat—my pony.

DAVID GARNETT, *The Golden Echo*, p. 21

(b)

One morning my uncle came into my bedroom and found me sitting on the chamber pot. He told me that I must not sit on it because it was unmanly and I was a little boy. Girls and women sat on chamber pots. If I could not stand up and hold the pot in front of me for fear of spilling its contents, I had better kneel down in front of it to use it.

DAVID GARNETT, *The Golden Echo*, p. 25

(c)

The Boer War lasted nearly three years . . . My parents were violently opposed to the war . . . When Harold Hobson or I appeared on Limsfield Common, we were pursued by angry cries of 'Kruger!' and sometimes by volleys of stones.

DAVID GARNETT, *The Golden Echo*, p. 59

(d)

When about my eighth birthday I discovered 'the facts of life' by inductive reasoning, it was to Harold that I immediately imparted my theory.

'Let's go and watch those two horses in the next field and see if you are right,' he suggested. But he was sufficiently clear-headed to see that my theory had not been disproved because it had received no supporting evidence after two hours watching a pair of geldings.

DAVID GARNETT, *The Golden Echo*, p. 61   *castrated male horse*

5. CURLY LOCKS

Miss Powers described her childhood experiences with vivid clarity. They were typical of their kind, and she has written an excellent account of a happy family, neither overshadowed by parsimony or penury. But its well-being clearly relied on the hard work and thrift practised by the parents.

(a)

Chapter 5

From the Front Window

At one end of the room, facing the road, was a large window. Our faces were often glued to that window. Being a main London road there were always exciting things going on. Immediately opposite was an entrance to one of the docks. What joy when the big gates opened to let a cart in or out, and enabled us to catch sight of a ship.

When the motor buses first started we enjoyed seeing the horses towing them when they had broken down, and hearing the drivers of horse buses call out mockingly to the less fortunate motor drivers as they left them behind.

The rag factory caused excitement of a very different kind. Three times we were awakened from our sleep by the clanging of fire bells; and on rushing to the window we saw the factory ablaze. We could see the silhouette of the men in their shining helmets; the hoses and jets of water which the firemen were directing on the flames.

The firemen in those days seemed to make much more noise and to-do than their modern counterpart. The horses came clattering over the stony roads, with one fireman clanging the bell the whole way, and the others clinging on to either side of the engine.

MISS F. E. POWERS, *Memories of My Life*, (Unpublished MS.) pp. 9–10

(b)

Some mornings, if we went to the window early enough, we would see the loaded hay and straw carts on their way to the market in Aldgate . . . The carts and wagons were brought from the country, travelling during the night and arriving early in the morning.

MISS F. E. POWERS, *Memories of My Life*, p. 12

(c)

The Christmas trees that decorated the corner each year, with the fairy on the top nearly touching the ceiling, will never be forgotten.

The decorating of the tree was kept a secret from us. Of course, we knew there would be tinsel balls, chains, fairy dolls, glass decorations in bright colours, and bags of sweets.

My mother was a good needlewoman and made something for every girl. One year it was a beautiful doll, with clothes that slipped off and on . . .

You will wonder what the boys had. In those days mother could go to the Caledonian market, a wonderful place for toys. Or there was Houndsditch . . . where you could buy toys much cheaper than in the shops.

> MISS F. E. POWERS, *Memories of My Life*, pp. 20–22

(d)

Before I went to bed my hair had to be curled up in papers . . . I sat and folded papers, preferably soft brown paper, into strips about half an inch wide, and handed them one by one to mother as she wound up little bunches of hair. Oh! how I yelled when odd hairs got caught in the curlers. Some mothers used rag curlers made of strips of old cotton material, and I used to see the children running about in them looking like Topsies.

Saturday night was not a comfortable night! I tossed and turned, trying to find a place in the pillow where the curlers did not dig in. But, oh! how proud I felt when getting dressed in my best, ready to go out on Sunday, with curls instead of straight locks.

> MISS F. E. POWERS, *Memories of My Life*, p. 44

(e)

One scullery game, I remember, was sailing on the large table in the centre of the room. Wet days had to be spent indoors; and when one was still thinking of the lovely time one had at the seaside, what better than to pretend one was still there.

The table was a good, strong, unpolished table, and stood up to the rough treatment. We turned it upside down and fastened an old sheet, from our dressing-up box, from one leg to the opposite corner. Our spades and pails came into this game, of course; the spades being used as oars, in case the sails were not a success, and the pails were very useful to bail out the imaginary water we had shipped!

> MISS F. E. POWERS, *Memories of My Life*, p. 46

6. ENJOYABLE LIFE

John Limbert, a vivacious septuagenarian, recalled his early years as he sat in the miner's cottage where he had been born. It consisted of a steep staircase connecting two small rooms, and a scullery. It had no indoor sanitation. There was a bright coal fire. However, these cottages, so suitable for one or two people, had formerly held families of eight or ten. Another miner (aged 60) remembered that his mother used to deliver babies (in the small overcrowded rooms) for 2s. 6d. by the light of a candle in a jam jar. But John Limbert stressed the loyalty of the villagers to one another, their helpfulness to those in distress, and the fun and good times when someone in the row would start to play an accordion in the street, and everyone would come out and start dancing.

I was nine years old when we came here.

I left school at 12 and was not sorry as the teacher was too strict. The parson used to come in often and if your eyes were not fixed on the teacher all the time, you had to stand in a corner and have three raps of the cane across the palms of your hands. One day we got a very thick long rope and put it all round the school so that the front and back doors couldn't open. The teacher was inside and couldn't get out. We got the cane for that. On mischief night we'd get a button on the end of a string and keep on tapping on the door till some-one came and then run off.

I left school at 12 and worked on a farm seven days a week for 3/6, 7.30 in the morning till 4 or 5. First of all I was shown how to feed the cows with cattle cake and then give the skim milk to the calves and clean out the bullocks. After that I worked in the quarry till I was lamed.

We went to church, some to chapel. But it didn't make a bit of difference. We all got on just the same.

When I was 13 or 14 I went to work at the mine. My father'd been a miner all his life, and died before he retired. I worked on the surface to start with, at the screens.* Then I went down the mine and drove horses. They had proper stables. There were cats there, and plenty of mice. There were oil lamps at the side of the tubs. I worked for 18 men. We all had oil lamps and they tested for gas each morning with an oil lamp turned low. If it went out the air was bad. 25 tubs was a day's work for a man.† Then I did bricklaying.‡

* large sheds where the coal is cleaned by removing lumps of rock etc.
† each tub held one ton.   ‡ the tunnels had to be rebored etc.

After that I did ripping with my father. He wasn't afraid, I said to him 'There's going to be a fall, we're going.' He just laughed and said he wouldn't move, but he did and there was a bad fall. It all came down just where we'd been standing.

We had to cut the timber and put the props up. We *did enjoy* life down the mine. You had to keep fit. We took our snacks with us. When you are cutting the coal with a pick it would fly out and cut your chest. Sometimes they'd want some extra good coal and get us to work in such a narrow place you'd scrape your shoulders. When we were out of work we'd go pea-picking, $\frac{1}{2}d$. for 8 lbs. or $2d$. for 10 lbs., or pick cowslips for cowslip wine.

There were big families in those days—about eight children.

JOHN THOMAS LIMBERT (of Micklefield), (b. 1885), unpublished.

7. HORSES FOR DREAMS

Fortunately the late J. R. Anderson was gifted with powers of total recall. He wrote, at the request of the author, an unusually detailed and clear account of his childhood in Gateshead, Durham, when he was a retired gardener some six decades later.

(a)

My first home was 40 Second Street Gateshead.

The houses were built in flat form. The sitting-room door in our case, was on the immediate left after passing through the glass door, facing you along the passage was the bedroom door, *the only bedroom*, with a window out to the back. To your immediate left when at the bedroom door, was the door to the kitchen... Through the kitchen in the direction of the back door, was a door to what we called the scullery, where all the rougher work was done.

Here stood a heavy cast iron mangle. In the scullery, was also a 'copper', i.e., a square brick fireplace with a metal pan, enclosed in the brickwork, this pan held about 7 or 10 gal. of water.

The chimney was usually connected to the kitchen chimney, all very compact, it was a very compact life, one bedroom for five of us.

In the kitchen was a 'desk bed'. When it was closed it looked like a wardrobe, about 5′ 6″ high. At bed time, the doors were opened, and a gate-like structure was lowered on to two attached feet. The mattress & perhaps all the bed clothes were inside & this was where my brother & I slept for years.

Two pictures on the wall used to fascinate me at one time. They were pictures of horses of the hunting type.

Boys had horses for their dreams then. I spent hours, sat on a board rested on the arms of the arm chair, with another in front of me, my mother used to tie a piece of cord on the back of the chair in front of me & that was the reins so that I could drive in, my childish dreams, the butter and eggs to Morpeth as my grandfather or Uncle Bob used to do. The whole arrangement represented to me a horse & trap.

> J. R. ANDERSON, *Vapourings of an Old Ploughboy: Memoirs of 1892–1914*, p. 1 (unpublished)

(b)

We had our baths in the scullery in a tin bath, the shape of a barge, it had one end a bit higher than the other . . . The bath seemed to be busier on a Frid. after tea than other days. There was plenty of room in the bath for me & my little boat, cut out of a piece of firewood. But the grown ups would spend most of their bathing time stood up.

The boots & shoes were cleaned in the scullery.

The 'back' door out of the kitchen into the yard, seemed to be an impediment to me, when it was open you bumped into it, the scullery was not big enough for the open door.

At the end of the yard was a door in the brick wall, which opened out into the 'Back Lane'. On the left of this door was a door into a little house which had a box-like arrangement about 2 feet 6 inches high. On the top of this bench, was a hole in the middle with a wooden lid, the lid had a handle on it. This box or bench was the seat of the place we call the lavatory to-day. We always called this place 'The Netty'.

The ashes were also tipped down here, I feel sure we had no dust bins.

On a nail in the tidy places was a supply of square cut pieces of newspaper or other paper, in the less tidy a newspaper was just thrown on to the bench.

> J. R. ANDERSON, *Vapourings of an Old Ploughboy*, p. 3

(c)

I have seen boys leaning over the dockside at Newcastle, trying to spear apples with a table fork on a piece of string, the apples were floating in the filthy water between the dock & the boats. They were in great danger of falling in the water 30′ below.

In the Bigg Market in Newcastle, half an hours walk away, you could buy a quarter pound of all sorts of good 'bullets' i.e. sweets for 1 penny. At the sweet shop opposite the school, you got 12 chocolate caramels for ½*d*.

J. R. ANDERSON, *Vapourings of an Old Ploughboy*, p. 6

(d)

I can remember going to school on my first day. It seems to me it was raining that morning. My mother took me to school & she seemed to vanish, after that it is a blank, until just before dinner, I had a box of bricks in front of me on the tiny desk & I was told to put the bricks back in the box, before I went home. I must have been last because I was in an awful state, but they went back in the box at last.

Later on we each took a penny on a Monday that would be school fees. Not long after we seemed to stop taking the penny.

We all seemed to be comfortably dressed, the usual smelly cloak room on a wet day, with the wash basins, that did not seem to be much used.

J. R. ANDERSON, *Vapourings of an Old Ploughboy*, p. 8

(e)

We went to church every Sunday morning, before the grown ups went. We got a little coloured card for every attendance, these cards had pictures of the Good Shepherd & his lambs, & other like subjects. On Sunday afternoons we went to Sunday school at Lady Vernon's school. Later on I was in the choir.

A lot of the boys & girls ran about with bare feet in these parts. I can see the dirty water on a wet day, coming up between their toes, they were inclined to be aggressive & I used to keep moving.

At Easter the church was kept busy. We School children went to church from Lady Vernon School on Good Friday morning. We were all drilled, like a trench raiding party.

A lot of babies died, the undertakers had an unusual cab for these funerals. Under the driver's seat was a glass-sided box & the little coffin was pushed into this box from the side of the cab. Once I went to a little girl's funeral, we walked behind the hearse to Gateshead East Cemetery.

J. R. ANDERSON, *Vapourings of an Old Ploughboy*, p. 10

(f)

At election times schools were used & the children had a day off. We used to go about with a piece of newspaper rolled up hard about the size of a tennis ball to this was tied a piece of string about a yard long, if they thought you were not supporting the right candidate, they swung this 'baster' at you.

We three children used to have a bottle of lemonade sometimes at Sunday dinner time. Another great event was the Sunday of Harvest Thanksgiving, after the morning service we choirboys were given the apples from the offerings.

We played at times with a 'clagger', it was a piece of strong leather with a piece of strong string attached through a hole in the middle. This leather was thoroughly wetted & when pressed on the pavement with your foot, it used to stick by suction, or you could lift up a stone with it.

You could buy a pennorth of potash & sulphur, we mixed it up & then it was used to make some unholy bangs. We used to search for a nut & a loose bolt. The nut was placed on a hard surface, a bit of pot & sul was dropped into the hole, the bolt was then stood up in the hole of the nut & the careful ones stood back while the brave fusilier stepped forward with a big stone & he dropped it on the head of the bolt, it did make noise enough to please us . . .

These various games used to come out every year, no one used to say anything to my knowledge, we would find ourselves playing marbles, then marbles vanished, we would be playing with various shaped tops & whips, or tops & string.

A game we played was 'Kitty cat'. We cut a piece of stick, square in length, we sharpened both ends, it was about 5 inches long. We cut Roman figures I. II. III. IIII. like this on the flat sides. The Kitty cat was laid on the ground & we hit it with a stick on the sharpened end until it rose in the air & when we tried to hit it again while in the air & send it as far as we could.

Another game was 'touch stone' a stone was placed on a pile of stones & we used to try to knock the 'touch stone', top stone, down, the game was to put the touch stone back quickly, it was a game where fingers were hurt.

A queer game was two teams of four or so, one team used to bend down in a row head to tail like a pantomime horse, the front boy with his hands against a wall, the other team used to run in turn to the bending down team & jump astride on to their backs, the first boy had to jump far enough along the bent backs to allow his mates room to jump on. The losers were the team who could not all jump & stay on the bent backs.

We played various games of our own making for days. The pantomime once a year at Christmas. We could not afford to go to the sea for more than a day.

I know now how fortunate I was every school holiday I spent at my grandparents farm, beside that lovely trout stream, on a fine day you could see rows of trout lying on the gravel at the bottom of the pools.

J. R. ANDERSON, *Vapourings of an Old Ploughboy*, p. 14

(g)

Cleaning teeth did not seem of much importance then, I remember tins of pink powder used as tooth cleaning material. But we also gave our teeth a rub with salt & soot, we got a supply of soot by placing a wet finger on the fire back. One thing prominent to me now is toothache, it stopped all play for me at times. There would be dentists, but I don't remember being at a dentist's until in my teens & 30% of my teeth had gone.

A fever case of an infectious & dangerous sort would be taken away in a cab.

My father was a barber. But I have looked through the barber's shop door when it was open & seen a boy perhaps no more than 10 yr of age working as a lather boy, no doubt he worked there all Saturday until an hour later than people would believe possible to day.

We used to have fleas in our beds at times, my mother used to hunt them out. At school I have seen boys necks covered in brown spots caused by either fleas or bug bites.

We moved into the upstairs flat eventually but not before my mother & father had stripped every inch of wallpaper off the walls &

plenty of carbolic acid used in the hot water used for washing. However the place had no insects I heard them say.

J. R. ANDERSON, *Vapourings of an Old Ploughboy*, pp. 15–17

(h)

The boys & girls going to school used to bring their dinner in the form of sandwiches, we also had tin bottles filled with tea or milk, these bottles could be warmed in school on the stove at dinner time.

Piece time, i.e. playtime for a few minutes in the morning & afternoon. Dinner time when the children in the village went home & others ate their food in the yard or anywhere if it was fine.

There would be 40 or 50 of us, for teachers there was the schoolmaster & a lady teacher from 3 miles away.

J. R. ANDERSON, *Vapourings of an Old Ploughboy*, p. 19

(i)

I used to be taken to Isaac Walton's shop in Newcastle as a boy & I believe the price for a 11 yr old boys suit was about 12/6 & the shop man used to slip a pocket knife into my hand with a smile before he started to wrap the suit up in brown paper... The boys always wore a cap ...

J. R. ANDERSON, *Vapourings of an Old Ploughboy*, pp. 22– 25

(j)

I started work on the farm on leaving school at 14. There was no pay, you were clothed & fed, my elders had started work in the same way. We started work on a Mon & worked on until 6 o'clock on a Saturday night. We did not take any notice of any of the Bank holidays.

At the age of sixteen a farmer 5 miles away wanted a boy for the term Nov. to May, I got the job at £7-10 for the term. This farmer thought I should work a little longer as the days got a little longer in the spring. He knew that I felt I was being exploited, he worked among pens of sheep after I had put the horse & cart away & I had to help him. One night his father told him I had done enough for one day. He told his father the time was secondary to his need for my help with the sheep. I knew the sheep could have been attended to in the morning.

J. R. ANDERSON, *Vapourings of an Old Ploughboy*, p. 31

8. THICK SOUP AND CURRANT PUDDING

Charles Booth initiated *The Life and Labour of the People in London* in 1886. His assistants described conditions of direst poverty. Strenuous efforts were made to ameliorate them, by the labours of public, private, religious and philanthropic workers.

Though poverty in general was clearly due to the social and economic pressures of the time, aggravated by misfortune, these observers saw thriftlessness due to alcoholism as '*the* evil'. Clearly deprived children were constantly seen 'running in and out of public-houses carrying great jorums of beer'. Gambling and recourse to pawn-shops were also common.

Atrocious housing conditions, and lack of proper sanitation, ensured the presence of dirt, disease and vermin. However, many of the evils so prevalent in the early years of the survey had shown some improvement by 1900. Children were less obviously ill-treated. Their clothing was better, particularly the girls'. In school there was less hostility, obscenity and truancy. Though the children's general condition was often 'bad enough', there was an increasing desire 'to be better'.

(a)

A free children's dinner in Bethnal Green

I met the superintendent at the mission at 1 o'clock, when the children, of whom there were 233, had just taken their places. With the exception of a few small girls, all were poorly dressed and ill-nourished, but none were bare-footed. One boy I noticed, as they filed out, had a pair of ladies' dress slippers, with high heels and pointed toes; they had to be tied on across the ankle.

CHARLES BOOTH, *Life and Labour of the People in London*, 3rd Series, Vol. II, p. 242

(b)

In a poor Suburb—Sunday night

Inside they were singing Sankey's hymn, 'Safe in the arms of Jesus;' outside, as I stood in the lighted porch, I heard childish voices shouting from the darkness, 'Let's come in, Guv'nor, we won't mike no noise; we'll behive ourselves.' Going towards them, I made out several small, rough-looking children peering through the railings from an adjoining field. I suggested they would be better at home and in bed at this time of night; to which a girl of about eight (and little at that) replied in a saucy precocious style, speaking for herself and a companion, 'Garn, we're ahrt wiv ahr blokes; that's my bloke.' 'Yus,' said the other girl, 'and that's mine' (they pointing to two boys about their own size). At this there was a general shout of laughter; and then came a plaintive plea from the first child, 'give us a penny, will you, Guvnor?'

CHARLES BOOTH, *Life and Labour of the People in London*, 3rd Series, Vol. VI, p. 171

9. LAWFUL COMMANDS

Mr. Walter Castelow grew up on a highly productive small holding. Abundant fresh food, inflexible discipline, and hard work (at school, on the land, and in his father's brewery), were constant factors throughout childhood and early youth. In 1971 he was still working in his chemist's shop at the age of 95.

THIS INDENTURE Witnesseth that Walter Thomas Castelow of Beulah House, Crossgates, in the county of York, by and with the consent of his Father Ben William Castelow doth put himself Apprentice to Eliza Abbott and James John Anning of 145 Woodhouse Lane Leeds to learn their Art and with them after the Manner of an Apprentice to serve from the First day of May One thousand Eight Hundred and Ninetyfour

Unto the full End and Term of Three Years from thence next following to be fully complete and ended During which Term the said Apprentice his Masters faithfully shall serve their secrets keep their lawful commands every where gladly do He shall do no damage to his said Masters nor see to be done of others but to his Power shall tell or forthwith give warning to his said Masters of the same. He shall not waste the Goods of his said Masters nor lend them unlawfully to any He shall not contract Matrimony within the said Term nor play at Cards or Dice Tables or any other unlawful Games whereby his Masters may have any loss with their own goods or others during the said Term without Licence of his said Masters Shall neither buy nor sell He shall not haunt Taverns or Playhouses nor absent himself from his said Masters service day or night unlawfully. But in all things as a faithful Apprentice he shall behave himself towards his said Masters and all theirs during the said Term. And the said Eliza Abbott and James John Anning in lieu of the above services faithfully rendered

their said Apprentice in the Art of a Chemist and Druggist that he can shall teach and instruct or cause to be taught and instructed which he useth by the best means and shall pay to the said Walter Thomas Castelow the sum of six pounds, ten shillings during the first year Nine Pounds Two shillings during the second year and Thirteen pounds during the third year of the said term of Apprenticeship.

And for the true performance of all and every the said Covenants and Agreements either of the said Parties bindeth himself unto the Other by these Presents In Witness wherof the Parties above named to these Indentures interchangeably have put their Hands and Seals

the   day of   and in the   Year of the Reign of our Sovereign Lady   by the Grace of God of the United Kingdom of Great Britain and Ireland Defender of the Faith and in the Year of our Lord One Thousand Eight Hundred and

	Walter Thomas Castelow
	Ben William Castelow
Witness	
Thomas Green	
	Eliza Abbott
	James John Anning

The Amount of the Money or value of
any other matter or thing given or
agreed to be given with the Apprentice
by way of Premium must be truly inserted
in words at length otherwise the
Indenture will be void and double such
amount forfeited.

Godfrey's Cordial (though severely criticized in 1770) was frequently requested by Mr. Castelow's customers before World War II. Though he also sold a *Balsamic Mixture* 'free from any narcotic', many children's prescriptions did contain them.

(a) Godfrey's Cordial

Sedative Liquid of *Opium*	1 drachm
Carraway Oil	4 drops
Spirits of Juniper	4 drops
Tincture of Ginger	
Essence of Aniseed	of each 2 drachms
Liq. Burnt Sugar	
Liq. Licorice Extract	4 drachms
Simple Syrup	to 10 ozs.

(b) Infants' Preservative

Heavy Carbonate of Magnesia	2 drachms
Sugar of Milk	6 drachms
Aniseed Oil	12 drops
Tincture of Asafoetida	30 drops
Ammonium *Bromide*	2 drachms
Water	to 12 ounces

Label: Half to one teaspoonful every one or two hours.

(c)

Mrs. Butler's Baby 28958 July 14. 1897

R	Liq. Ammonium acetate	1 drachm
	Sweet Spirits of Nitre	30 drops
	Chloroform water	1 oz.
	Water	to 2 ozs.

One teaspoonful every four hours.   G.H.R.

10. THE AGRICULTURAL HALL

One hall was the large one you came to first, with the circus ring in the middle, and rows and rows of seats around it and in the galleries above. Behind these seats and the ringside seats below were rows of side shows . . .

There was Tom Thumb and his family, who came out from behind the curtains riding in a carriage drawn by a Shetland pony. I can remember remarking in a very loud voice that they must be squeezed up a lot inside that carriage. My parents quickly moved us away before I made any more remarks.

Then there were the performing fleas. How wonderful it seemed to us that these tiny creatures could have been trained to do their tricks . . .

One show which always fascinated me was the glass-blower's stand. Here they blew glass over a flame and made pretty-shaped glasses, and birds with wonderful tails . . .

Father had to win us a coconut to take home with us, of course, and we had to try and win other prizes.

But now came the Circus. We had our tickets ready for a seat up above. Our artistes always had safety nets under them, and we enjoyed seeing them jump from their swings into these nets and walk along them to the rope ladder down which they climbed into the ring for their final bow.

. . . We had our clowns, the performing dogs and seals, the horses who seemed to understand the rhythm of the music played by the brass band, and the lions performing in cages for us. We did have the added thrill of seeing men standing round the cage with red-hot bars of iron ready in case the lions became obstreperous.

Our sea-lions balanced their balls in the same way, and followed their trainers for the tit-bit of fish in just the same ungainly way.

We had our clowns, too. . . We had a few jolly, white-faced men who made the children laugh and relieved a bit of the tension which some of the turns caused.

We were able to look through the open doors behind the scenes, and see the caravans where the show people lived. They were horse-drawn. . . The caravans were brightly painted, and their brass fittings, of which there were many, beamed with polish. The little curtained windows, with little children often peeping through, looked so cosy. More children sat on the steps. In fact there seemed to be swarms of children, and their pets . . .

MISS F. E. POWERS, *Memories of My Life* (unpublished MS.), p. 90

11. DANGEROUS SURROUNDINGS [LEEDS]

Meeting held March 16th, 1900

Mrs. M. was asked to take L.S. to the Infirmary and inquire whether it would be possible for her to have an artificial hand put on.

Mrs. B.C. promised to help to get it if the Drs. thought it could be done successfully.

Miss L. reported 16 in the Home, all well, three girls were confirmed last week, 2 at St. John's Church & one at the Deaf & Dumb Institute.

K.M., deaf & dumb, was leaving her place the next day, she had not given satisfaction.

Meeting held April 6th, 1900

A.J., 10 years old, mother dead, father insane through drink, recommended to us by Mrs. G., to be admitted.

L.S. had been to the Infirmary, the cost of a hand & arm would be £6, £7, or £8. It was decided Mrs. M. should first find out what was the difference in the arms & hands, also whether L. would be likely to outgrow an artificial arm.

Meeting held April 20th, 1900

L.S. The Infirmary Artificial Limb maker had advised the £6 arm & hand for L.S., as being quite as good as the more expensive one, only not so well finished, & had also said it was unlikely she would grow out of it. It was decided to have the £6 arm & hand as soon as possible, to be paid for out of the funds.

Meeting held June 19th, 1903

Mrs. M. reported she had 19 in the Home. A.M. was now very well in herself & waiting for the false foot.

Meeting held July 17th, 1903

S.J. who had been 7½ years under the care of the Association had died at her place from blood poisoning. She had been six years with Mrs. B., & a very good girl, Mrs. B. had done everything possible for her, providing doctor & nurses. The cost of the funeral was £6. 16/. S. had earned £1 15/ & the Secretary was told to see Mr. A & try to get the money to help with these expenses. Her clothes were to be given to her younger sister, J., who was in the Home.

Meeting held June 17th, 1904

Mrs. F.J.K. stated that the Lady Mayoress had seen Mr. H. about the child E., & he had written saying she was not blind with one

P

eye, but would require certain glasses in a few years time which should make her able to live an ordinary life. He did not think she could be admitted to the Blind School, unless the Guardians would pay for her.

Mrs. F.J.K. stated that J.M., 11 years old, was suffering from lupus in the foot, & could not walk, she had been a few days in the Infirmary & then sent to the Home, but had to attend the Infirmary each day for the X Rays. This was difficult on account of expense of cab fares etc. Mrs. F.J.K. had seen Dr. G. & he had promised to admit her for a short time on the 18th, & it was suggested she might learn to walk with a crutch after.

May 4th, 1906

A.Y., aged 16, had been brought by the Police, wanting training, her mother dead, her father in prison, girl lived at Yeadon & had worked 2 years in a factory & had a good character from there, she had quarreled with her brother on 1st May & had thrown herself into some water & been taken by the Police. Leave was granted for her to stay in the Home.

1908

J.M. was to see Dr. G about her foot, as she wants to go out as sewing-maid.

Meeting held May 1st, 1908

Dr. G. wished J.M. to be under treatment for a short time, & then to go to a Convalescent Home, after which he would say whether she might take a place as Sewing Maid.

Sept. 16th, 1910

Mrs. B. asked for admission for M.M., aged 12, has a mother & step father, a very bad man who had already ruined M.'s elder sister. Now been taken by an Aunt, but was half starved & in danger, recommended by Miss P.

Dec. 6th, 1912

E.S. aged 12, had taken some eye lotion one evening when Miss L. was out, & had been very ill, but had recovered. Her sister was feeble-minded, & although E. seemed bright, there was something not quite natural about her.

Dr. R. on examination, had found signs of tubercular trouble in F.D., & considered she should not be with the other children.

From the Minutes of the Leeds Ladies' Association for the Care and Protection of Young Girls (unpublished).

12. COMPLETE INNOCENCE

Not only did poor children escape the most expensive drastic medical attentions, but were also spared the curious dietary regimen of some boarding schools.

(a)

On my first Sunday I wrote home that I had 'great difficulty in eating the food provided by Mrs. Brownrigg'. The food was excellent and wholesome, but the platter had to be scraped clean. Fat and gristle, hard lumps of porridge, the blackened crust of a rice pudding, they all had to be consumed.

Sago pudding was the one which I faced with most misgiving. Once as I swallowed the last mouthful, nausea overcame me and I vomited into my plate. N.G.B. looked down the table. 'Finish up your pudding, Wuffy.'

ALEC WAUGH, *The Early Years of Alec Waugh*, p. 20

(b)

One of the features of Fernden in my time was a complete sexual innocence. When Mrs. Brownrigg at the end of my second year had her second baby, we learnt something of the facts of maternity, but nothing about paternity. When N.G.B. shortly before I left gave me a talk about the dangers that awaited me at a public school—'how can you ask some pure woman to be your wife, if you have been a filthy little beast at school?—I had no idea what he was talking about.

During my last year we indulged in a form of flagellation, belabouring our bare posteriors on bath nights with knotted boot laces and hair-brushes. This was partly due to a pleasure in inflicting pain, partly due to a desire to show courage under pain.

ALEC WAUGH, *The Early Years of Alec Waugh*, p. 27

13. SWING HIGH

Lady Diana Manners, daughter of the Duke of Rutland, was a peerless young beauty in a brilliant epoch. She epitomised the day-dreams of the fortunate fairy-tale princess. Her numerous admirers paid her homage, and showered her with many exotic tributes of their affection. From early childhood, her mother had successfully managed to adorn her in unusual clothes; when other girls appeared as white swans, Lady Diana appeared as a black one.

(a)

The Woodhouse months became our favourite in the year. The express trains to the North would be stopped especially for us at Rowsley station. We tumbled out, laden with the paraphernalia of art and sport, into two or three flies and a pony cart: they were trotted through the village where the children, pouring *en masse* out of school, would cheer and wave us home . . . Picnics on the moors, fishing for trout, photographing, printing, squeegeeing, casting our own hands and feet in plaster of Paris. There too we had our first gramophone . . . Girls were swung high by the boys and we would sit on moonlit grass reciting Keats's odes and sonnets in turn, and revel rustically on the way home. We would go to empty Haddon Hall most afternoons and, best of all, at full moon for an after-dinner drive in brother John's open screenless racing-car packed with young men and girls—fears and excitements, cries and clappings.

DIANA COOPER, *The Rainbow Comes and Goes*, p. 66

The hostess of Sutton Courtenay, 'dressed mostly in tinsel and leopard-skins and baroque pearls and emeralds', was ahead of her time in her tolerant attitude towards the vagaries of the young.

(b)

But the place of all others for romance . . . was Sutton Courtenay . . . The garden was famous for its imagination and fertility. Flowers literally overflowed everything and drifted off into a wilderness . . .

The chief object of the visit, as Aunt Norah knew, was to drift in a boat all day long with one of the Oxford heroes through the reeds and inlets of the Thames which flowed by the garden—a dinghy

full of poetry books and sweets and parcels and bathing-dresses—
and better still (or worse!) in the moonlight with the best loved.

DIANA COOPER, *The Rainbow Comes and Goes*, p. 72

(c)

It was our first wedding [at] St Margaret's, and the bridesmaids
were Floras from *La Primavera* in blossom-strewn dresses with
rosy wreaths and veils. Sometimes they were blue to be like love-in-
the mist, and the wreaths could be flowers or appropriate myrtle.

DIANA COOPER, *The Rainbow Comes and Goes*, p. 79

(d)

But the summer brought a Coronation and a London at its most
brilliant. Marquees there were—uncompromising red-and-white-
striped tents and discreet fairy lamps twinkling red, white and blue
along the grimy garden paths. Florists were ordered to bring suitable
begonias and smilax to edge the stairs and sprawl over dinner supper
tables.

The young girls were shy, and on the whole deplorably dressed.
They must wear gloves drawn above their elbows, and which of us
could afford a new pair nightly? Shoes were of pink or white satin
and were smudged after the first dance by clumsy boys' boots.

We poor creatures suffered great humiliation, for between dances
we joined a sort of slave or marriage market at the door, and those
unfortunate ones with few friends became cruelly conspicuous wall-
flowers. Those who found such shame unendurable could only
sneak downstairs to the cloakroom, ostensibly to have their dress
mended. The mothers sat all round the room.

The *Bals Blancs*, of which there were three or four a night, were
very trying to me and I would welcome the dawn breaking and the
top-hatted linkman at the door—Mr Piddlecock he was called—
bidding us 'Good Morning' as he packed us into the carriage.

DIANA COOPER, *The Rainbow Comes and Goes*, p. 84

14. TREATS AND PLEASURES

Cecil Beaton grew up during a period when the uninhibited enjoyment
of luxury reached its zenith among the upper classes.

(a)

At Madame Sherwood's dancing school we children wore our patent-leather shoes with their silver buckles and learnt the polka and the hornpipe. The young girls were wrapped in Shetland shawls at children's parties and carried their dancing shoes in a bag, bronze leather pumps with an elastic round them and a little bead on top. Inevitably they were accompanied by their nannies.

CECIL BEATON, *The Glass of Fashion*, p. 11

(b)

It was Aunt Jessie who provided the greatest treats and pleasures for me when I was a child . . . Instead of the yellow soap we had in the nursery, a cake of Pears soap was placed on the side of the wash basin, whose blue and white irises were forever embedded in its china surface. Likewise, how pleasant it was to go to her lavatory, with water lilies decorating the porcelin pan, surrounded by a solid encasement of mahogany and equipped with a gold handle which one pulled up in order to bring about a discreetly gurgling flush of water . . .

Our special occasions I would be allowed to come into her dining-room at the tail end of a luncheon party, just in time to savour the aroma of melon and cigar smoke.

CECIL BEATON, *The Glass of Fashion*, p. 19

15.

Sonia Keppel described the advantages of growing up in a prosperous Edwardian family. Though many poor children might have envied her, they might have been thankful to escape the rigorous attentions of the dental profession.

(a)

WATER BABY

I seemed more in touch with the horse-drawn world. A water-cart, rattled slowly towards me with plumes of water spraying out behind it like a peacock's tail.

At the corner of the square, the cart stopped beside me, and I noticed that it had a ledge across the back of it and a step up beside the back wheel. I climbed up on to the water-cart. And thereafter, I was partially concealed behind a wall of spray.

We forged across Portman Square as though drawn by sea-horses. I felt rather sick but elated, and as wet as a mermaid. So I was sorry when the cart hove-to in Wigmore Street.

To my alarm, a policeman approached the back of it, and lifted me off it, and put me on my feet . . .

The policeman asked my name. I answered 'Baby'. Fortunately, he discovered a label to give me identity: a small gold bangle with a pendant diamond 'S'. Carefully he assessed it and my relative value to it. Then he carried it and me to the police-station in Marylebone Lane.

There, an hour later, Papa found me.

SONIA KEPPEL, *Edwardian Daughter*, p. 17

(b)
POUR ETRE BELLE, IL FAUT SOUFFRIR

At this time, my front teeth were so prominent that I could not shut my mouth, I attended the dentist. With military zeal, into my mouth he built two lines of fortification. Two gold bars, (one top, one bottom), with four protruding hooks on them, were cemented in, completely covering my side teeth and exposing only the front ones. The top pair of hooks was towards the front of my mouth and the bottom ones at the back, and these were attached together by tight elastic bands, renewed every three days. Under the cement it was impossible to clench my teeth and, with new elastic bands in place, it was practically impossible for me to eat. I was told not to brush my teeth and to avoid solid food as much as possible, and only to slacken the elastic bands at night.

SONIA KEPPEL, *Edwardian Daughter*, p. 72

16. SWEET PETTER

A large number of children wrote to Miss Pauline Chase in 1907 and 1908 after seeing her act the part of Peter Pan. Among the names in the published letters are Mona, Marjoree, Basil, Eric, Ada, Mabel, and 'Your loving little Gertie'. Most of them asked to be taught to 'fly'.

Madge writes a P.S., 'If I were a man I would marry you'. Lenaara asks, 'Could you tell me if the words are published, as we are getting up 'Peter Pan' here and are going to act it in the servants hall'. Rex writes 'P.S. I was in the front row of the stalls in an eton suit and a white waist-coat'.

(a)

Dear peter-pan. I liked the play very much. I liked you best of all as peater pan   I am going to see peater pan next year. I am six years old now. I have got a tetty bear and he went to see peater pan. I go to school now. I like on the tree tops best of all the seens. you and vende are the best. I hope you have had a merry Christmas. I would lovee a letter from you if you could spear the time. I have got a little coat like wendes onley it is red. I send you and wende best kisses.

With love from Mary

+   +   +   +   +   +   +

                                                            thimbulls

PAULINE CHASE, *Peter Pan's Postbag*

(b)

St. John's Wood Road.
21st January 1907

My darling Pet sweet petter
I hope the pirateirs are not still at the never-never-land I was allways fond of Faires and tring to fly. Do come and teach me to fly like you did to Wendy and stay with me allways and bring Wendy to. Will you take me to the never-never-never land because I don't want to grow up I'm allways going to swent throuth my legs wehn I ssee a wild amanaul. Wehn I play I detend I am Wendy. Tink was a very good Firy wasent she. I shuld not like to be with pirateirs Like you & Wend were. did not the pirateirs take the Lost boys upruffly. did the red-indians fiat against the pirateirs.
I think you are very poity and so is Wend. did Wend Like na na Wend was very good wasnt she so were you the kite must be very strong to hold Wend must not it. wasnt Lizer a funny Little

thing. I was allways fond of firys. wasnt the pirateirs ship big. did Wend like firys. Send my Love to Wend Tink and all the Lost boys

Love and best kisses from

```
X X X X X X X X X X X X X X
X X X                    X X X
X X X        Joan        X X X
X X X X X X X X X X X X X X
```

P.S. I have a sweet firy doll.

PAULINE CHASE, *Peter Pan's Postbag*, p. 55

(c)

DEaR PETER:

wE HavebeEn cOunting EVeryday till you came fora lOng time (, and weRe so glad to see You again. although we Have seen you heaps of times beforRe and we sometimes play at the nEVER NEVER LAND; but   it is far better to See it real;

We love The SHADOW song so muchandhave got it at home tot sing; and we didso want to Hear you do it again and it didn't come, and please Dear Peter Will you singit again. like you Used to do andoTher people missed itto. and mothers ays we can use dAddys" type-writtere because my writtinhis to big and weare going backto see you againand we we are very glad you are staying for twoweeks and good by

With

l
Love from
US ALL.

PAULINE CHASE, *Peter Pan's Postbag*, p. 63

17. HOUSEMAID'S CUPBOARD

Sonia Keppel described a child's view of the exotic eastern influence of the Russian Ballet on the affluent leisured young in the last 'sweet and carefree' years before August 4th 1914.

In the housemaid's cupboard, the influence of Bakst-in-the-home was early felt by Violet. Heavy lamé curtains shut out the daylight.

The room glowed redly. Persian missals gleamed on the walls, and an ikon faced the sphinx opposite the fireplace. Probably to counteract the homely smells of Sunlight soap and Brasso, now incense hung heavy on the air. The minute Violet's guests arrived, quickly she shut the door on them . . . And I was left outside it.

From relief, quickly my feeling turned to resentment. Especially as, maddeningly, Loïs would not tell me what I missed each evening. Through the doorway, alluring strains of Rimsky-Korsakov's ballet music used to filter, toned down on the gramophone. It did not sound much fun. But I had no means of finding out whether or not it was so.

Hardly worth all the trouble and expense of converting the housemaid's cupboard.

SONIA KEPPEL, *Edwardian Daughter*, pp. 87–90

18. QUEEN OF BEAUTY

Finally, Lady Diana rode in full panoply with Prince Felix Yousopoff, 'an innocent at Oxford, and a mystic of transcendant beauty.' This apparently unimportant event, in retrospect, becomes symbolic of an epoch which was about to end in catastrophe.

> 'Heav'n from all Creatures hides the book of Fate,
> All but the page prescrib'd, their present state.'

The most eligible [young man] of all was Prince Felix Yousoupoff . . . At the many fancy dress balls he wore his eighteenth-century Russian dress of gold and pearls and sables and aigrettes, with embroidered boots and jewelled scimitar. He rode in the procession with me at the revived Eglinton Tournament . . . Letty was part of the musical ride mounted on ordinary-looking horses loaned by the Household Cavalry. These well-bred animals were not dramatic enough for me, so I designed myself a black velvet Holbein dress and hired Richard II's stage horse, Roan Barbary, with mane and tail that swept the ground. Felix wore his Russian robes and mounted himself on a mettlesome snow-white Arab, foaming and flecking and pawing.

DIANA COOPER, *The Rainbow Comes and Goes*, p. 97

INDEX

Anderson, J. R., 202–8
Anne, Queen, 4, 24
apprentices, 35, 209
Armstrong, Dr George, 76–80
Austen, Jane, 116

bastardy, 125
Bath, 1
Bathurst, Lord, 28
Beaton, Cecil, 218
Benson, E. F., 159
Birley, Mrs J. H., M.A., J.P., 182
Birmingham, 2, 95
Blincoe, Robert, 102–5
Blomefield, Mathena, 177–8
Booth, Charles, 208
Booth, Gen. William, 184
Boswell, James, 18, 69, 80
Bristol, 2, 67, 94
Buchan, Dr William, 121–3
Bundle-Boy, 99
Burney, Dr, 81
Burney, Frances, 73–5
Burritt, Elihu, 95, 172–4

Carew, Bamfylde, 13
Caroline, Princess of Wales, 100
Carroll, Lewis, 184–6
Castelow, Walter, 209–10
Chase, Pauline, 219–21
chimney sweeps, 98, 139
Collingwood, Admiral Lord, 107
Companion to the Newspaper, 137–138
Cooper, Lady Diana, 216, 222
Cooper, Thomas, 106, 115
Coppard, A. E., 188–90
Coram, Thomas, 41
Coventry, 2

Crompton (family), 86
Cumberland, Duke of, 34

Daily Courant, 18
Defoe, Daniel, 1, 68
Derby, 30
Devonshire, Duchess of, 82
Dickens, Charles, 96–7, 147, 155–7
Doré, Gustave, 97
Doyle, Richard, 146
Dyson, Sarah, 193–6

Eden, Sir Frederic, 92
Eton (Eaton), 30, 127, 128–9, 161–5

Flying Post, the, 3, 14
Foundling Hospital, 41, 43, 64–6

Garnett, David, 197
Gaskell, Mrs, 142
Gavarni, 154–5
Gerrold, Blanchard, 97
Girl's Own Paper, 197
Gloucester, Duke (Duck) of, 4
Gronow, Captain, 111–2

Hanway, Jonas, 43, 60–5
Hare, Augustus, 142, 149
Head, Sir George, 143–6
Hogg, Quinton, 171
Hone, William, 130
Hopkins, Gerard Manley, 172
Humphreys, Samuel, 35

Johnson, Dr Samuel, 18–19

Keats, John, 121
Keppel, Sonia, 218–9, 221–2
Kilvert, Rev. Francis, 175–7